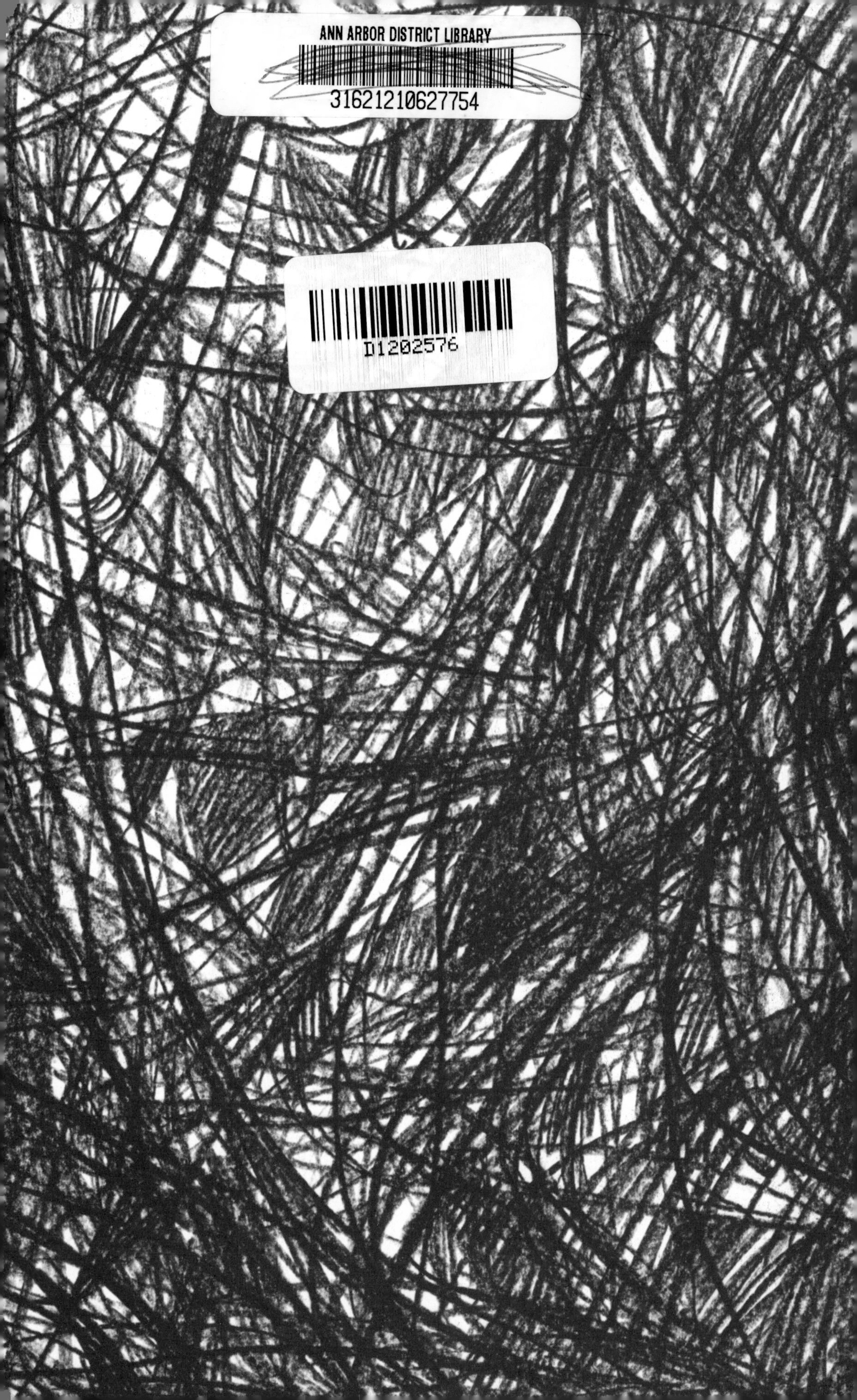

BEAST

First Printing

ISBN: 978-1-60706-147-2

Edited by Claire Gibson & Drew Gill
Book design by Marian Churchland

Published by Image Comics, Inc.
Office of publication:
2134 Allston Way, 2nd Floor
Berkeley, California 94704

International Rights Representative:
Christine Jensen - christine@gfloystudio.com

Printed in South Korea

ast

by
marian
churchland

Introduction
by
Claire Gibson

When Marian began thinking about this story she showed me a sketch of a young woman she had named Colette. There were fragments of ideas that came first, of course, like the old story of the *Beauty and the Beast*, and the Renaissance art we saw together in Florence one summer. How good David Bowie looks in a suit. It all had an effect, but that first sketch of Colette came before the earliest drafts of the script, before the character had a history or the story had bones. When I try to remember how *Beast* started, I remember Marian putting that name to a face on a piece of paper.

The house where Colette first sees Beast is the kind of house that Marian and I never noticed as children. There seemed to be one on every street, tall and handsome, overlarge by today's standards, falling gradually into disrepair when we were small and being torn down while we attended the high school where we met. These houses are prized now in Vancouver, carefully renovated or split up into apartments, and it was an apartment like this where Marian began *Beast*.

By the time Marian had pages to show me, I recognized the house in a different way. Much of the interior is based on my parent's home. Marian would come over and take pictures of the back porch or the staircase. It still surprises me to see Colette walk into a mysterious house in a neighborhood

Dedicated to my mum and dad,
Leslie and Mark Churchland

Be

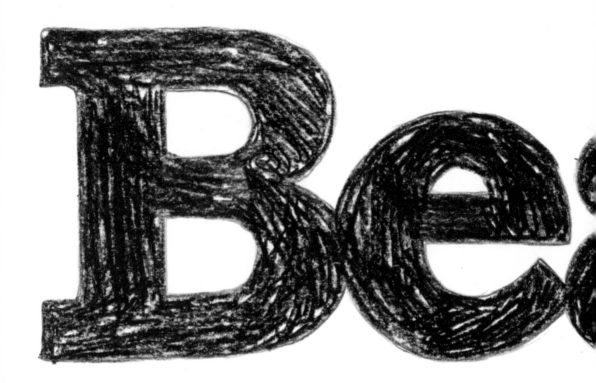

I almost know, but not quite, and suddenly be in my kitchen.

And there are other likenesses. Colette reminds me of Marian. They are comforted by the same things, like Indian food delivered in brown paper bags, mugs of tea, a hot bath, or a muffin. Marian was virtually living on muffins when she drew the bulk of this comic, and she too favours Raphael. Not the artist, but the other one. The real one.

But *Beast* isn't built purely on familiar or comfortable territory. The predicament that grows from Colette's connection with her muse isn't easily resolved. How much is she willing to risk for art? What securities will be sacrificed? There aren't any hard and fast answers here, no characters that are all bad or only good, which makes for a rich and nuanced story that reminds me very much of actual people, of real life. *Beast* knits itself together around its big questions with an easy grace that still surprises me. What I did expect was how beautiful the art would be. It's deeply gratifying to me that more people will be exposed to Marian's talent through this book. Here it is, I can say. Look. Did I mention I know her? She's been doing this all along.

In this story, Colette finds her stepping off point. All hesitation must, sooner or later, be left behind. When Marian began *Beast*, the idea of drawing comics for a living was still foreign to her. She wasn't sure she could do it. I find a gratifying symmetry in that. The shadow in the suit, it turns out, is an attendant of ideas made tangible, a gateway to work undone. Here at last the features of the incorporeal may be carved in stone.

More impressive still, this is the first graphic novel by my closest friend, Marian Churchland. I can't recomment it to you more highly than that.

Claire Gibson

Vancouver, B.C.

July 9th, 2009

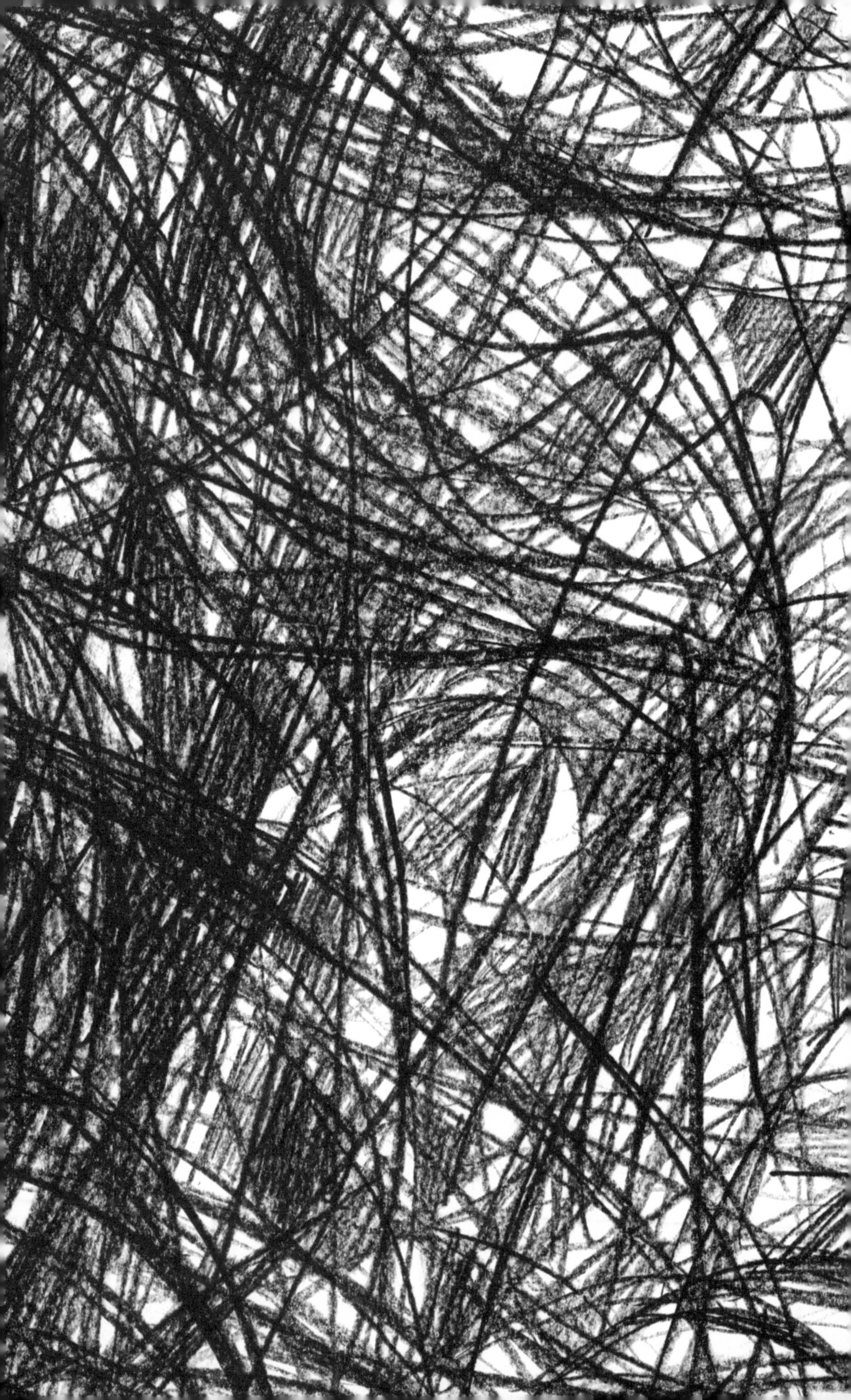

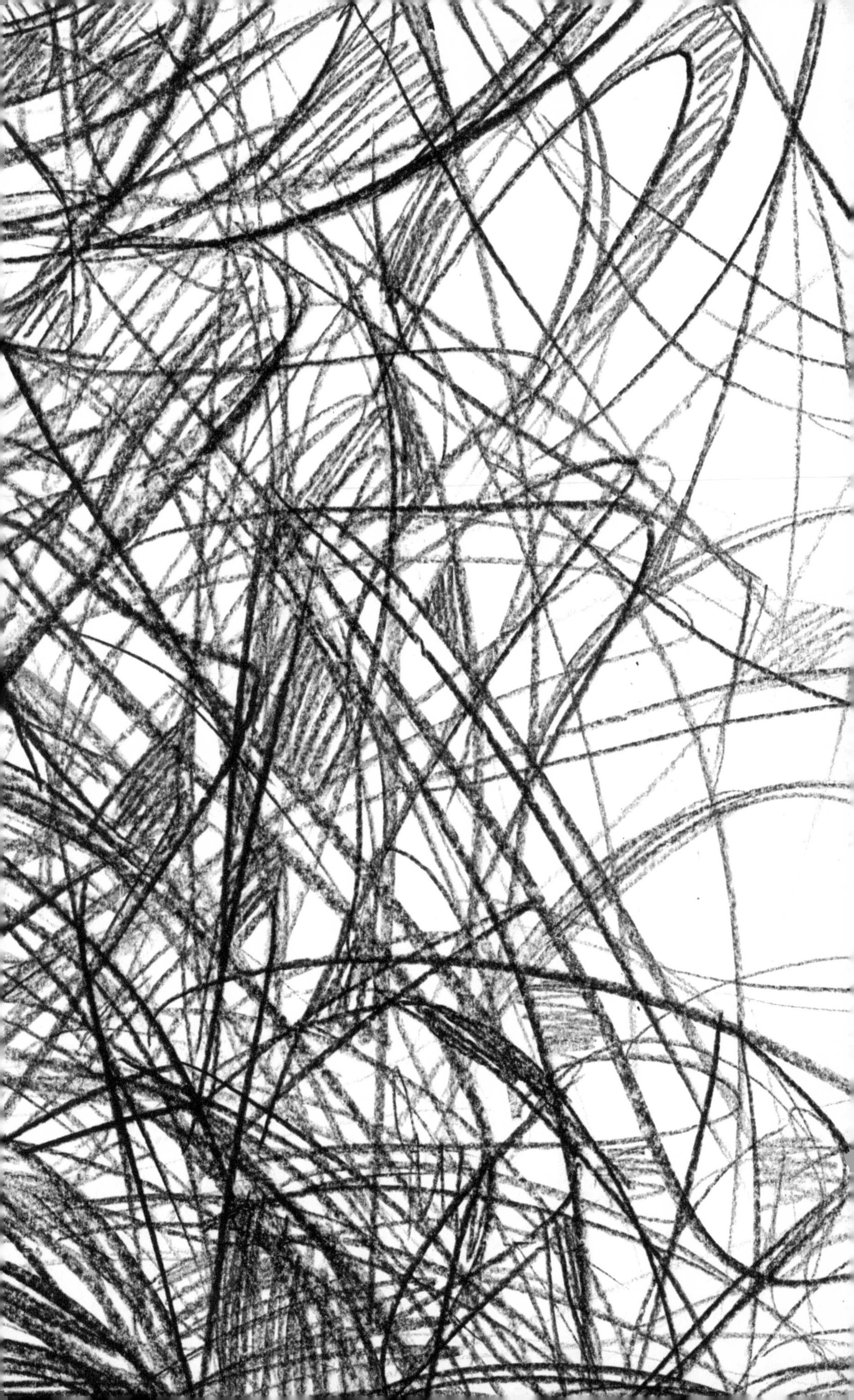

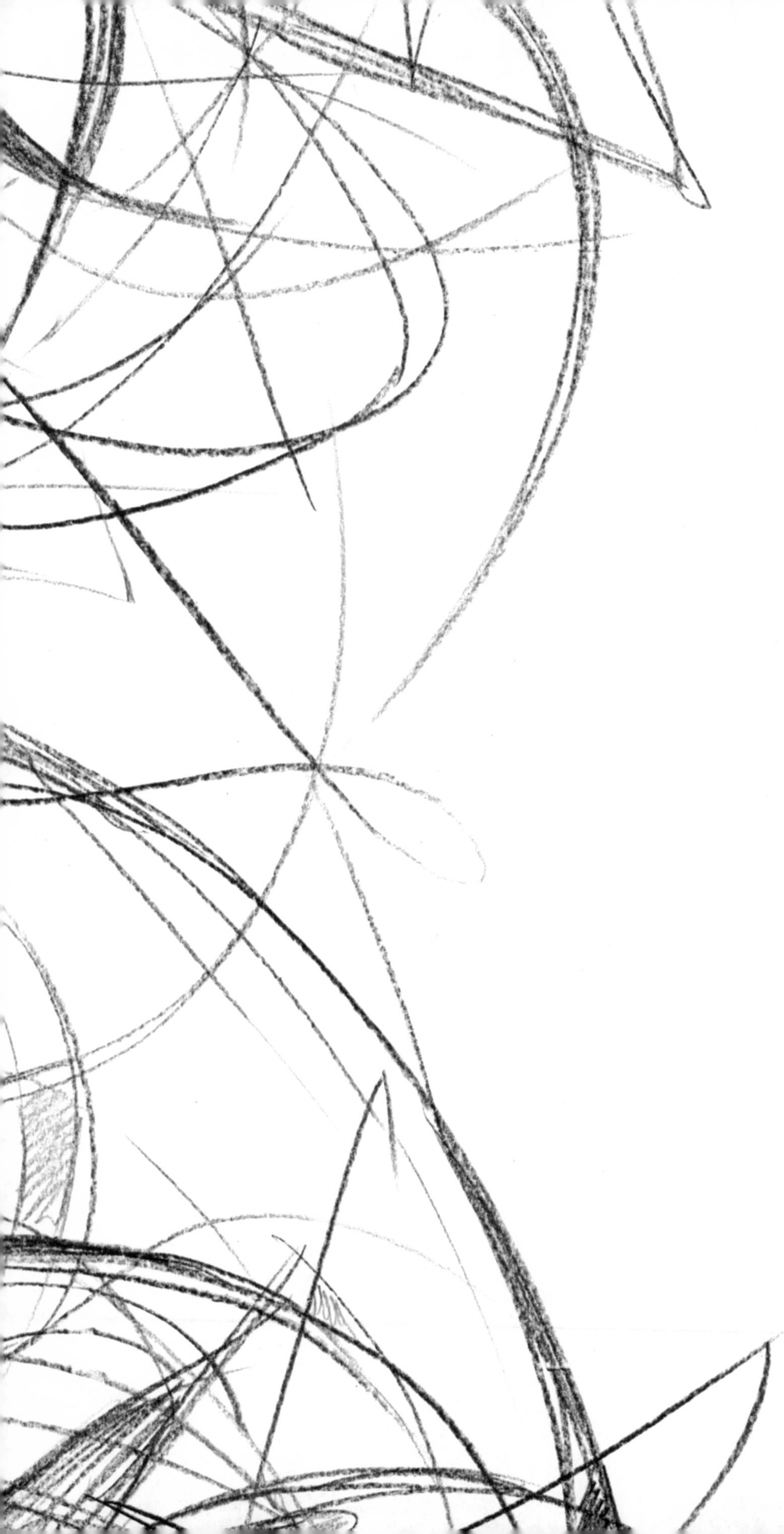

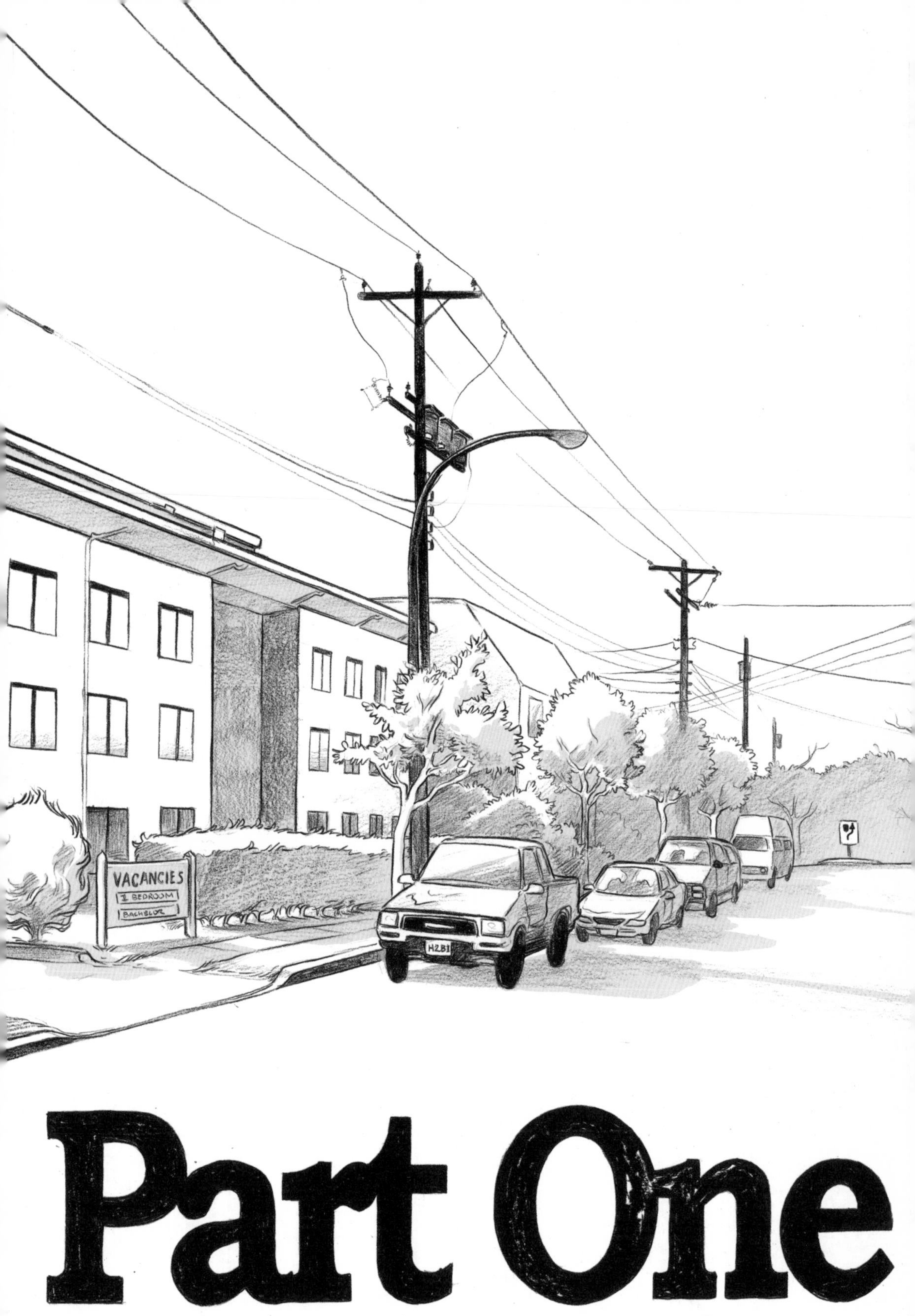
VACANCIES
1 BEDROOM
BACHELOR
H2B1

Part One

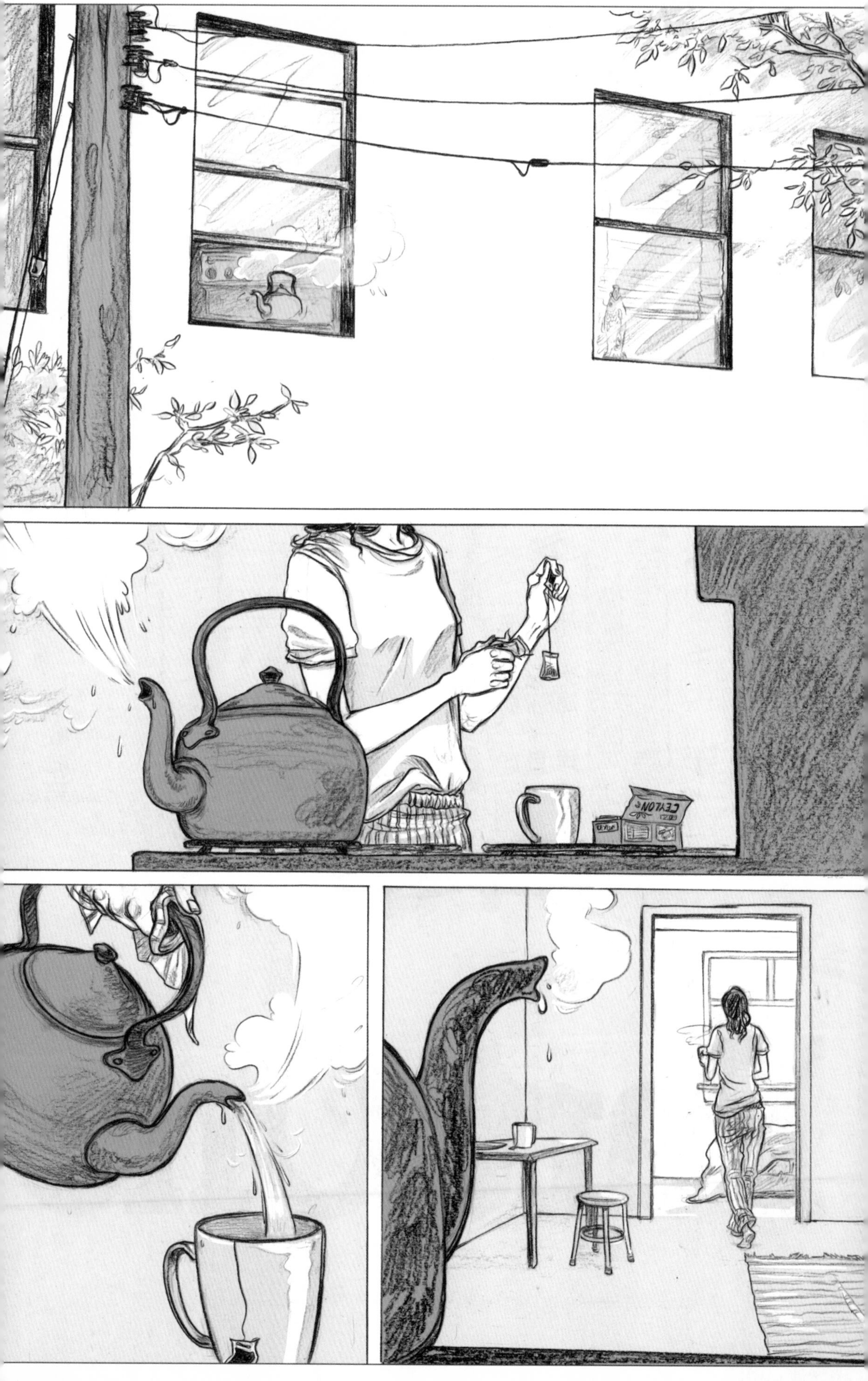
CEYLON

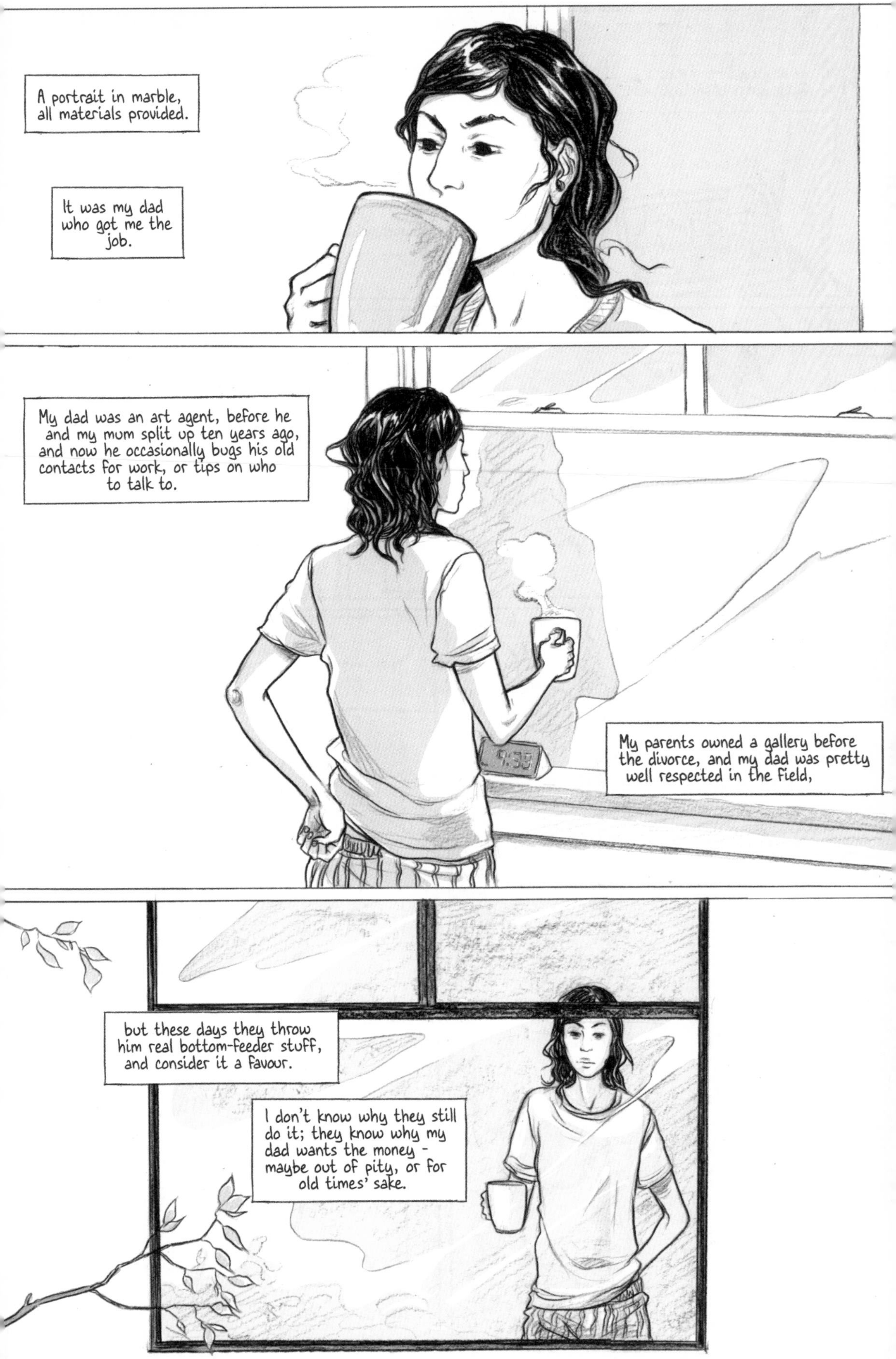
A portrait in marble, all materials provided.
It was my dad who got me the job.
My dad was an art agent, before he and my mum split up ten years ago, and now he occasionally bugs his old contacts for work, or tips on who to talk to.
My parents owned a gallery before the divorce, and my dad was pretty well respected in the field,
but these days they throw him real bottom-feeder stuff, and consider it a favour.
I don't know why they still do it; they know why my dad wants the money - maybe out of pity, or for old times' sake.

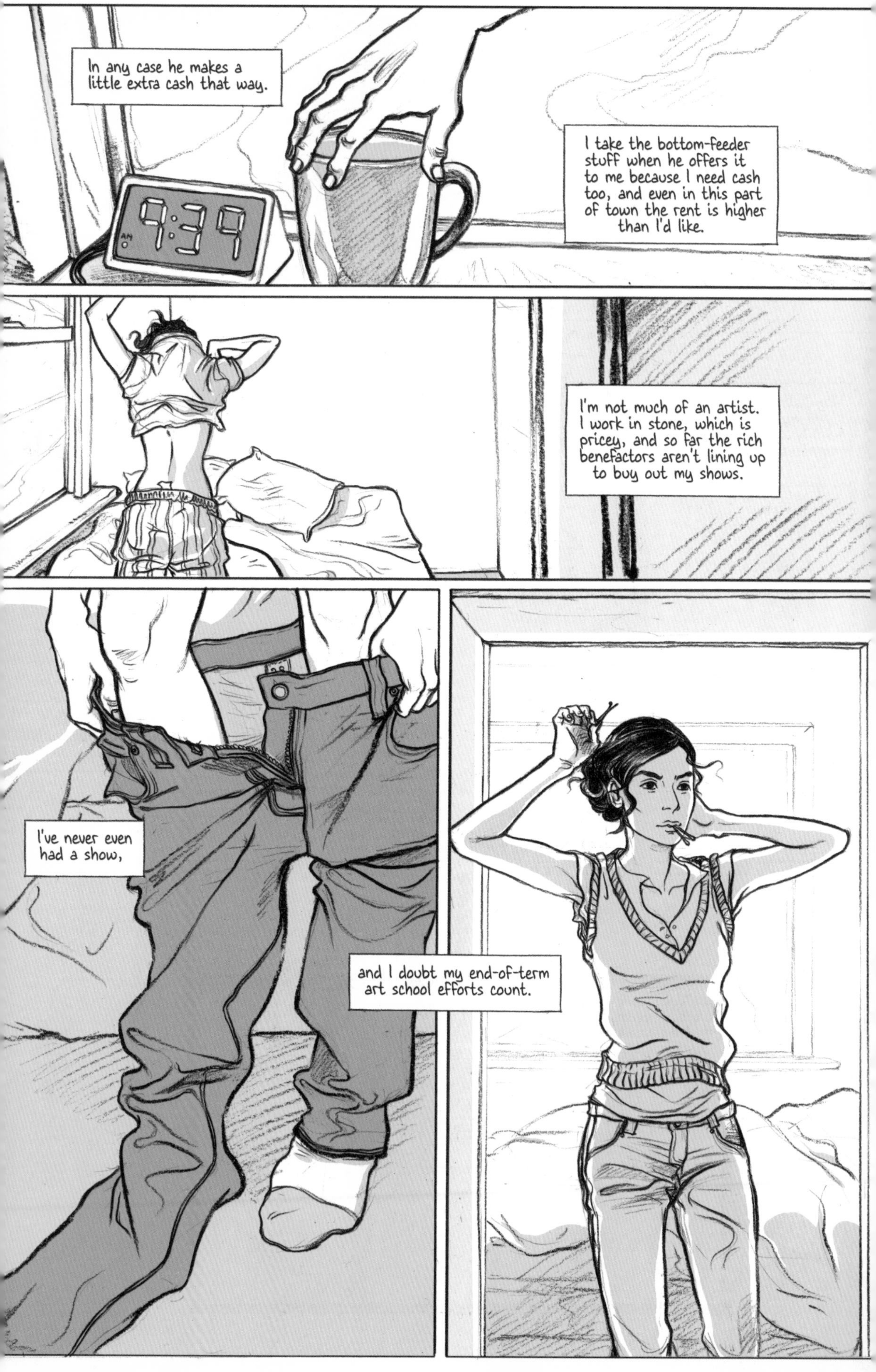
In any case he makes a little extra cash that way.
I take the bottom-feeder stuff when he offers it to me because I need cash too, and even in this part of town the rent is higher than I'd like.
9:39
AM
I'm not much of an artist. I work in stone, which is pricey, and so far the rich benefactors aren't lining up to buy out my shows.
I've never even had a show,
and I doubt my end-of-term art school efforts count.

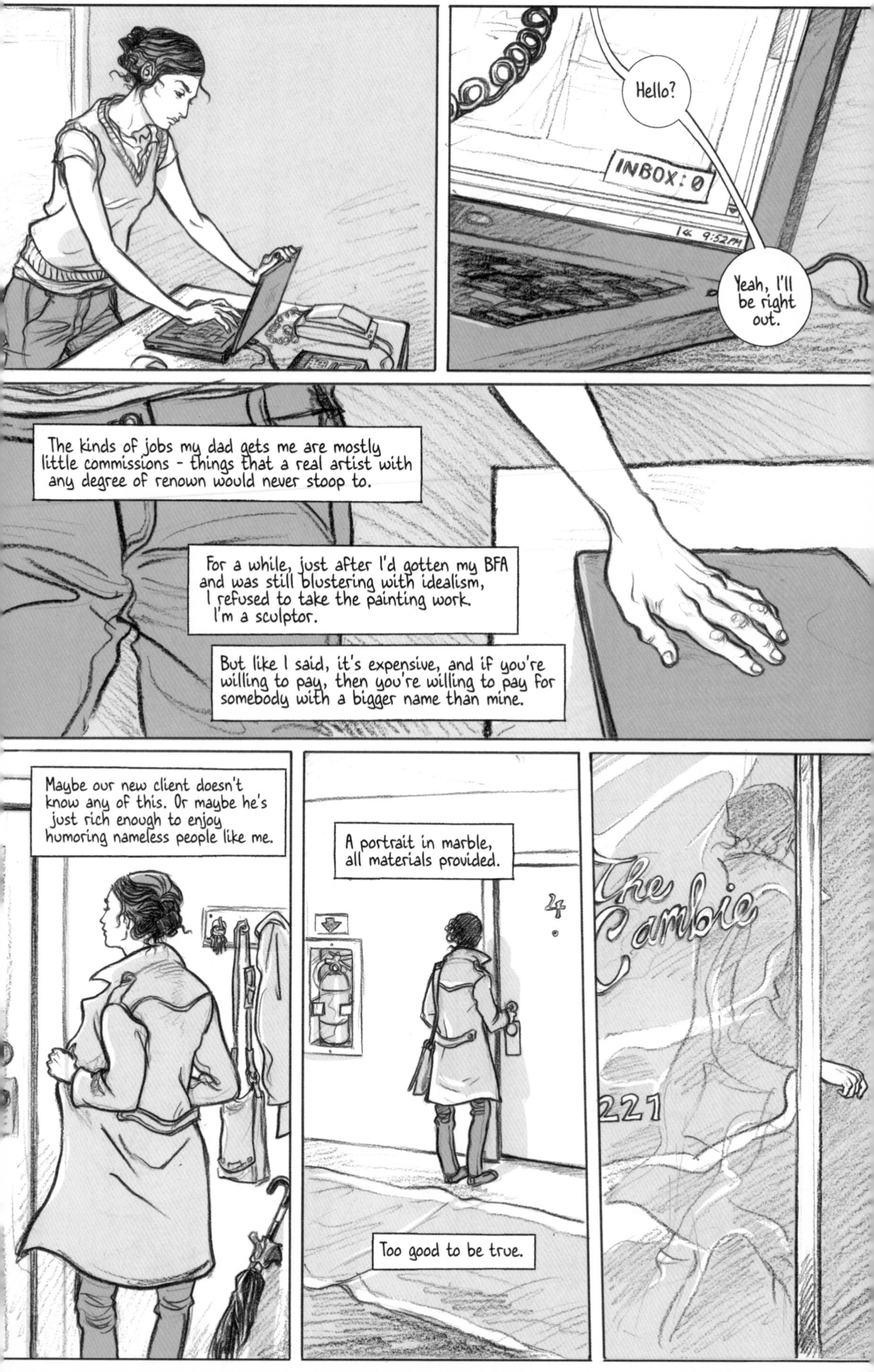
Hello?
INBOX: 0
9:52PM
Yeah, I'll be right out.
The kinds of jobs my dad gets me are mostly little commissions - things that a real artist with any degree of renown would never stoop to.
For a while, just after I'd gotten my BFA and was still blustering with idealism, I refused to take the painting work. I'm a sculptor.
But like I said, it's expensive, and if you're willing to pay, then you're willing to pay for somebody with a bigger name than mine.
Maybe our new client doesn't know any of this. Or maybe he's just rich enough to enjoy humoring nameless people like me.
A portrait in marble, all materials provided.
Too good to be true.
The Cambie
221

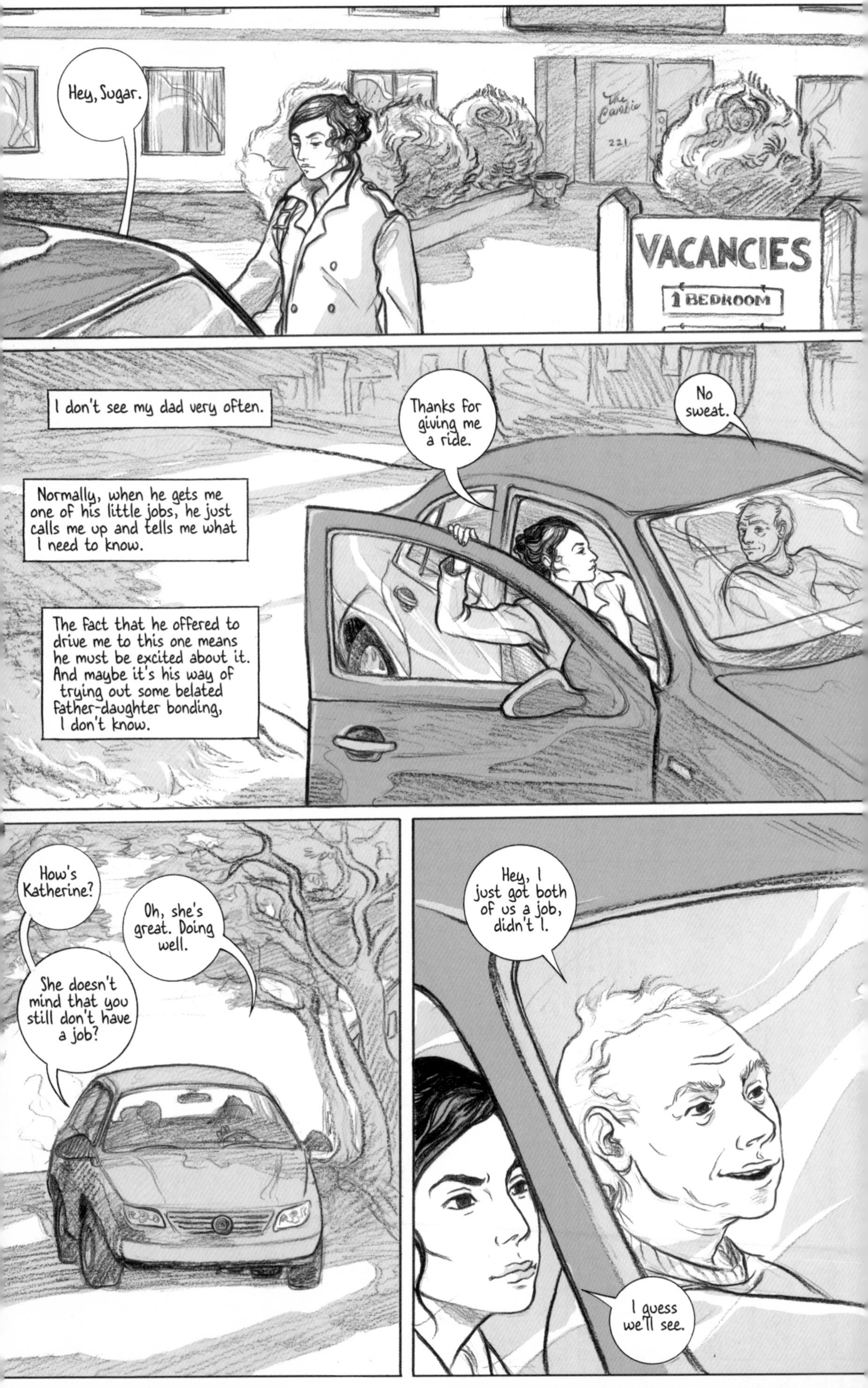
Hey, Sugar.
VACANCIES
1 BEDROOM
I don't see my dad very often.
Normally, when he gets me one of his little jobs, he just calls me up and tells me what I need to know.
The fact that he offered to drive me to this one means he must be excited about it. And maybe it's his way of trying out some belated father-daughter bonding, I don't know.
Thanks for giving me a ride.
No sweat.
How's Katherine?
Oh, she's great. Doing well.
She doesn't mind that you still don't have a job?
Hey, I just got both of us a job, didn't I.
I guess we'll see.

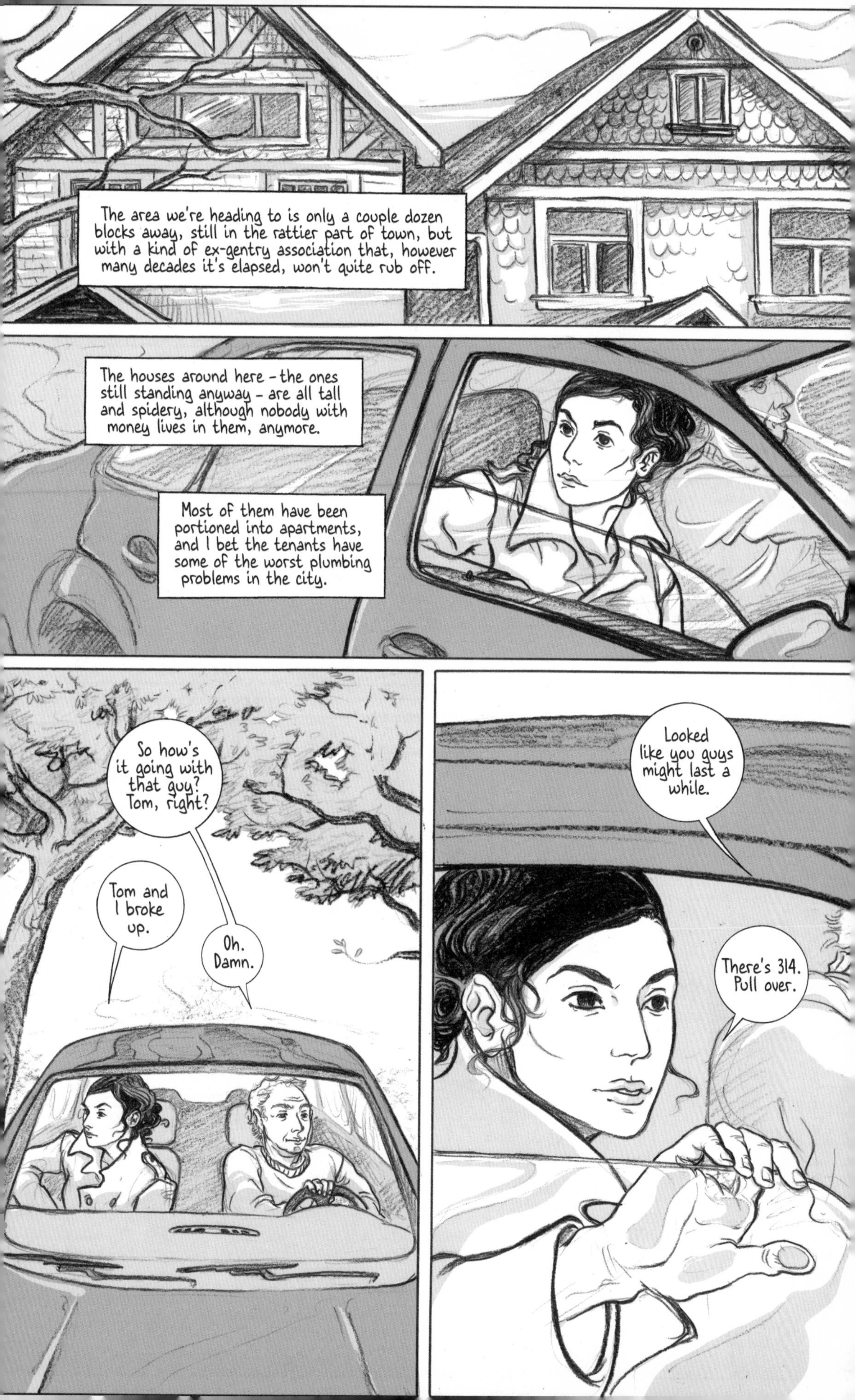

The area we're heading to is only a couple dozen blocks away, still in the rattier part of town, but with a kind of ex-gentry association that, however many decades it's elapsed, won't quite rub off.
The houses around here – the ones still standing anyway – are all tall and spidery, although nobody with money lives in them, anymore.
Most of them have been portioned into apartments, and I bet the tenants have some of the worst plumbing problems in the city.
So how's it going with that guy? Tom, right?
Tom and I broke up.
Oh. Damn.
Looked like you guys might last a while.
There's 314. Pull over.

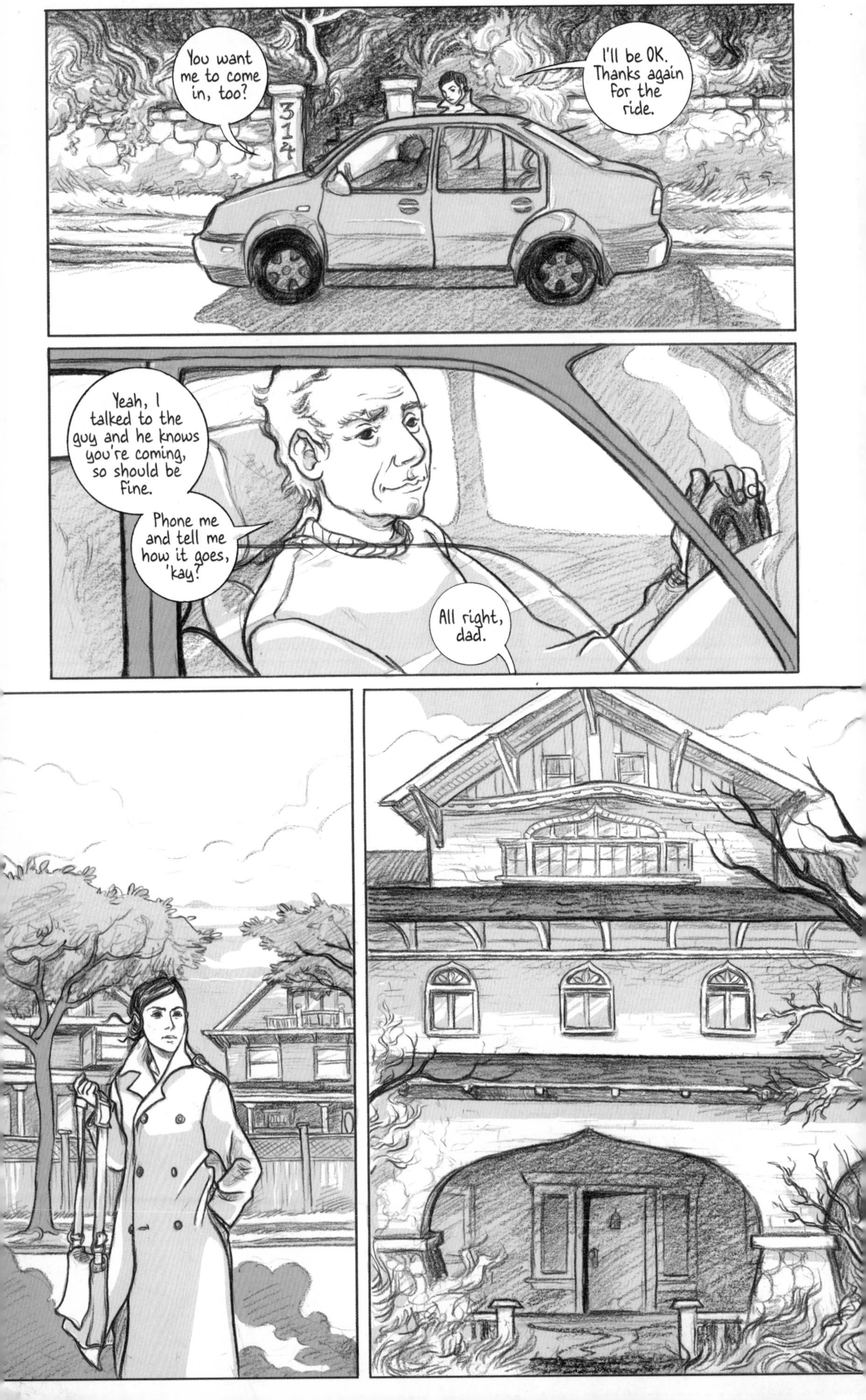
You want me to come in, too?
I'll be OK. Thanks again for the ride.
314
Yeah, I talked to the guy and he knows you're coming, so should be fine.
Phone me and tell me how it goes, 'kay?
All right, dad.

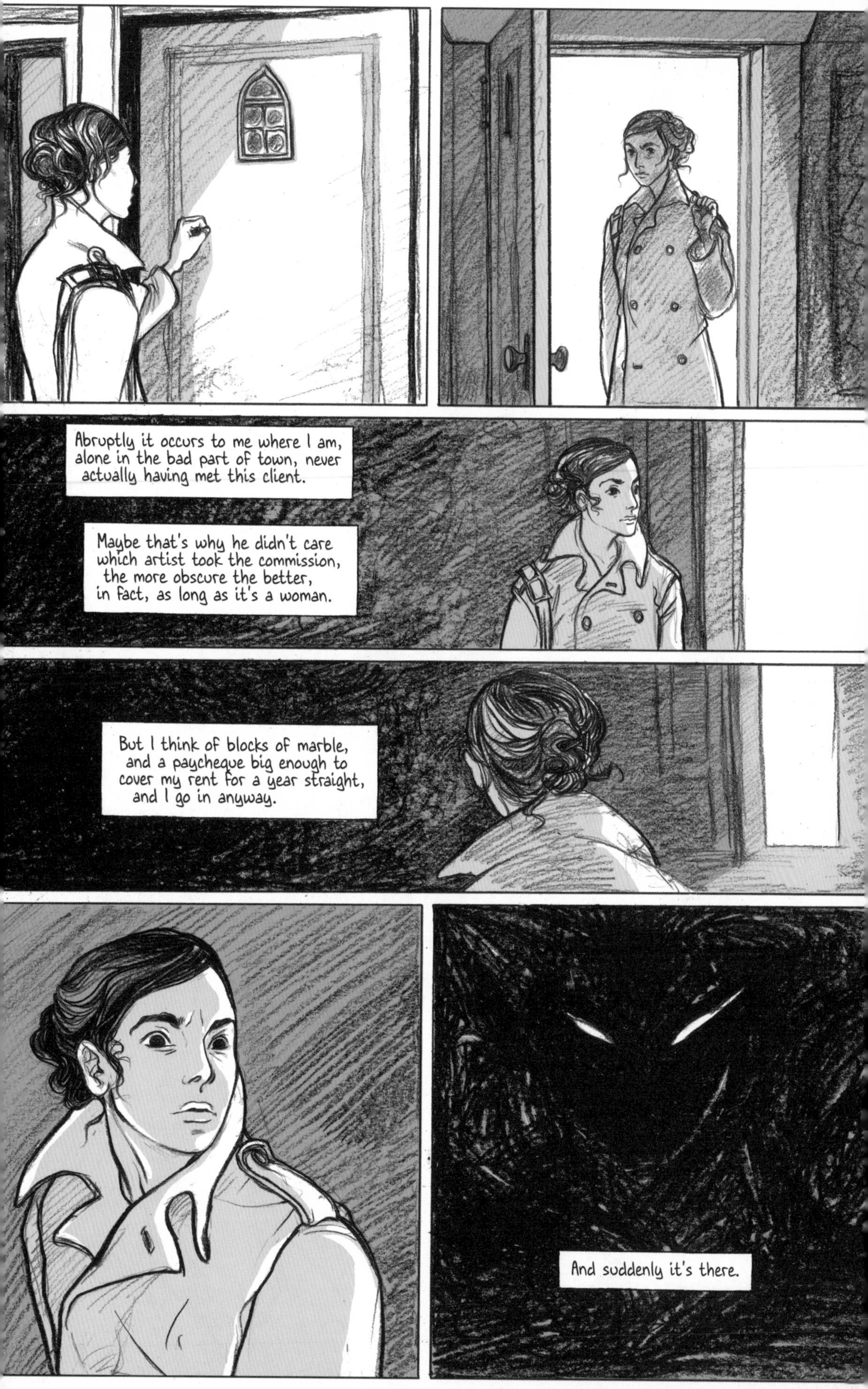
Abruptly it occurs to me where I am, alone in the bad part of town, never actually having met this client.
Maybe that's why he didn't care which artist took the commission, the more obscure the better, in fact, as long as it's a woman.
But I think of blocks of marble, and a paycheque big enough to cover my rent for a year straight, and I go in anyway.
And suddenly it's there.

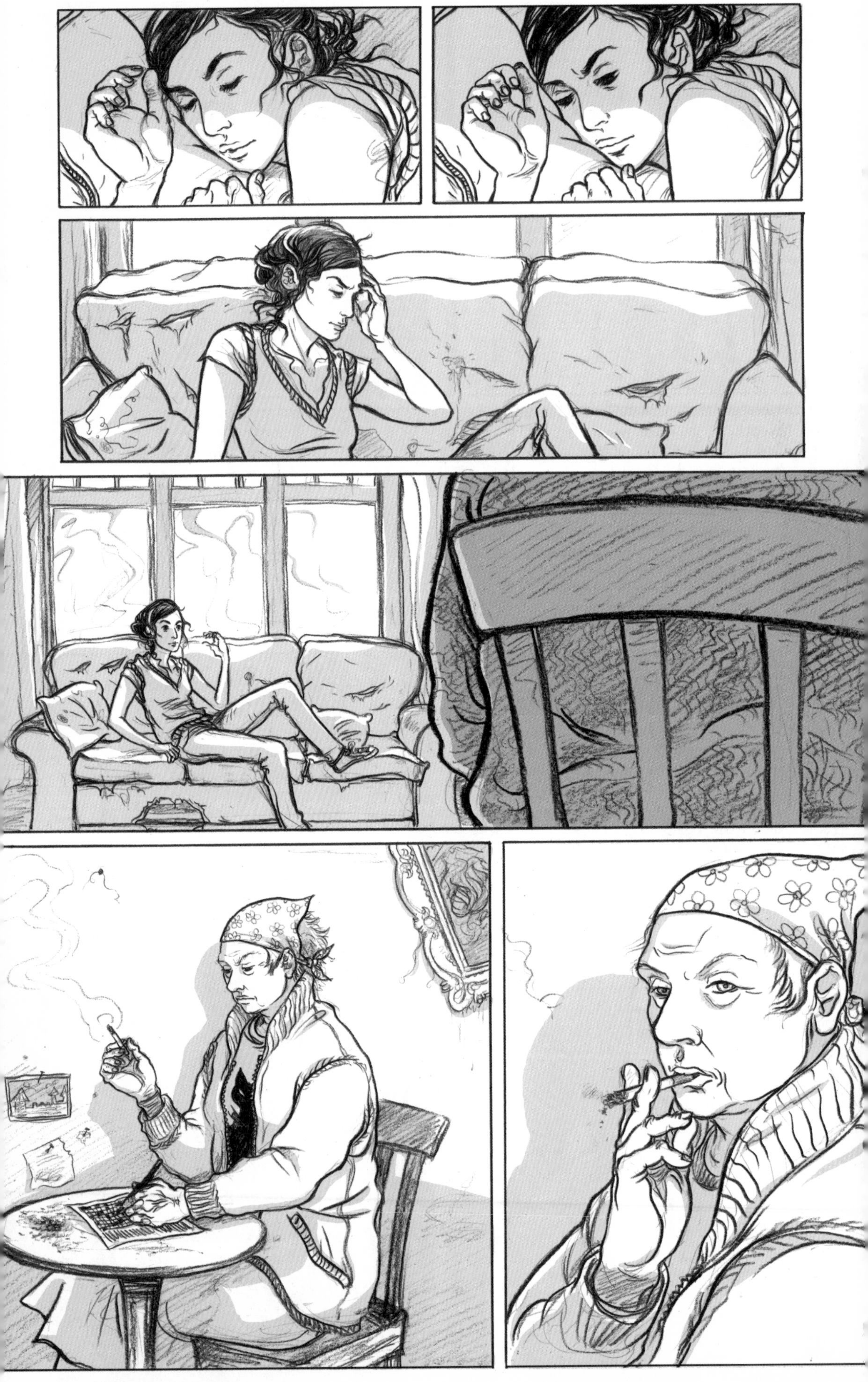

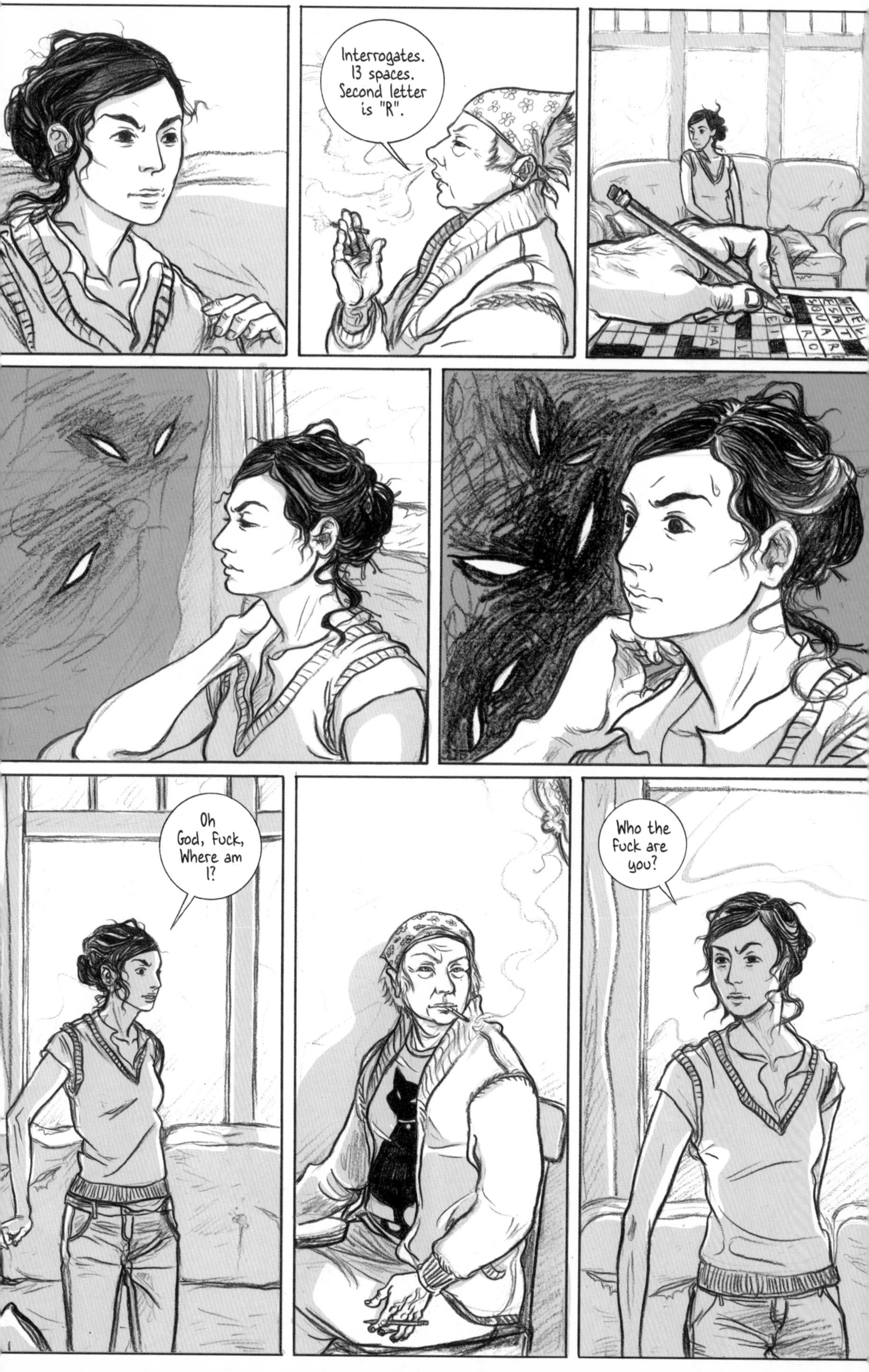
Interrogates. 13 spaces. Second letter is "R".
Oh God, fuck, Where am I?
Who the fuck are you?

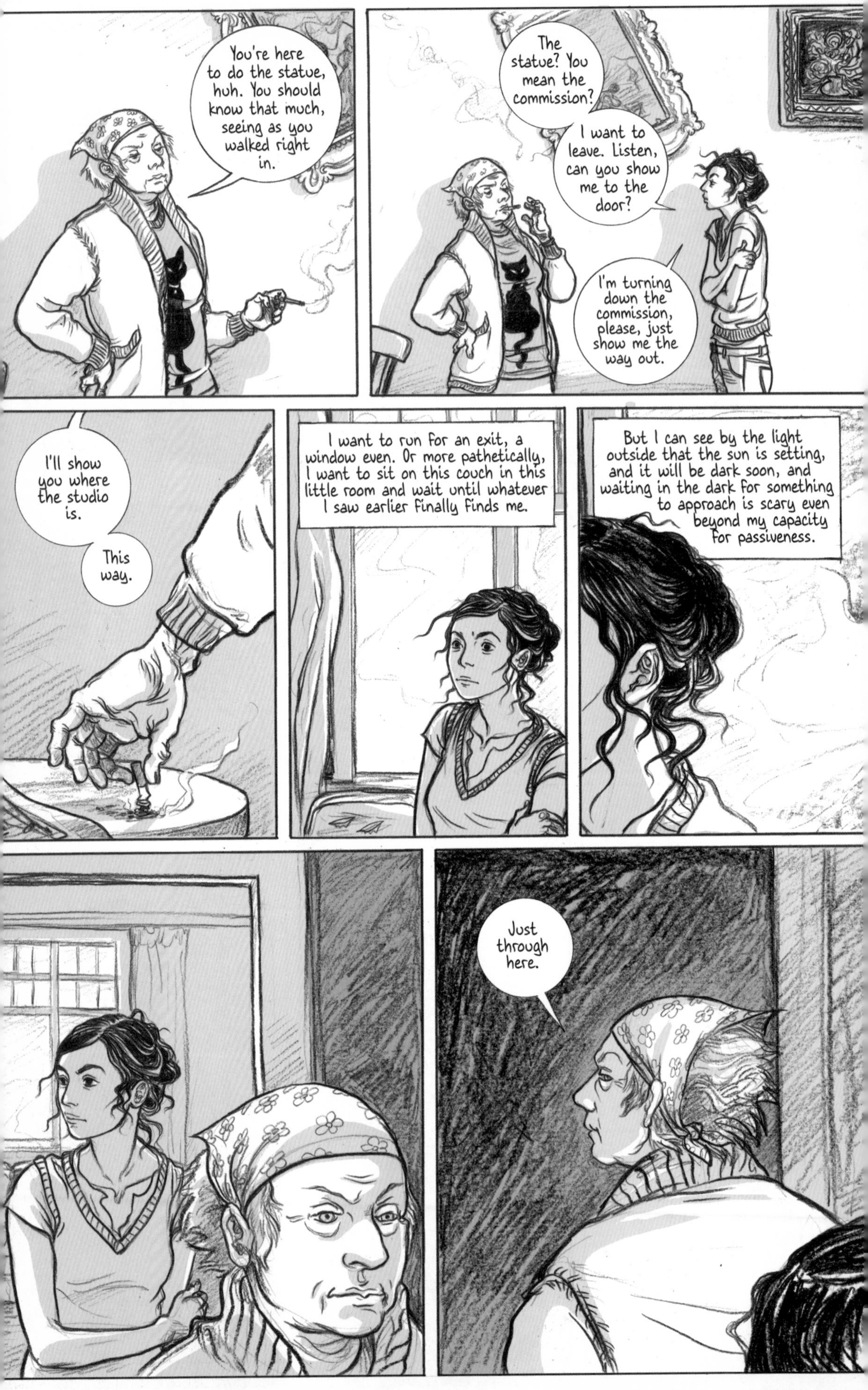
You're here to do the statue, huh. You should know that much, seeing as you walked right in.
The statue? You mean the commission?
I want to leave. Listen, can you show me to the door?
I'm turning down the commission, please, just show me the way out.
I'll show you where the studio is.
This way.
I want to run for an exit, a window even. Or more pathetically, I want to sit on this couch in this little room and wait until whatever I saw earlier finally finds me.
But I can see by the light outside that the sun is setting, and it will be dark soon, and waiting in the dark for something to approach is scary even beyond my capacity for passiveness.
Just through here.

When she says studio, apparently, she means big empty room. The block of marble is there, though, as promised, right in the centre:

the first thing I see when I walk in, pale and enormous. Latent, somehow.

Waiting.

It takes me another moment to notice that the shadow underneath it is stirring,

arranging itself,

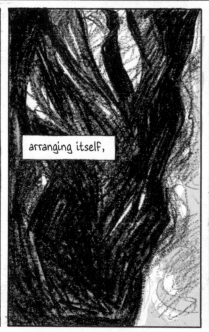

Stepping out into the light, now.

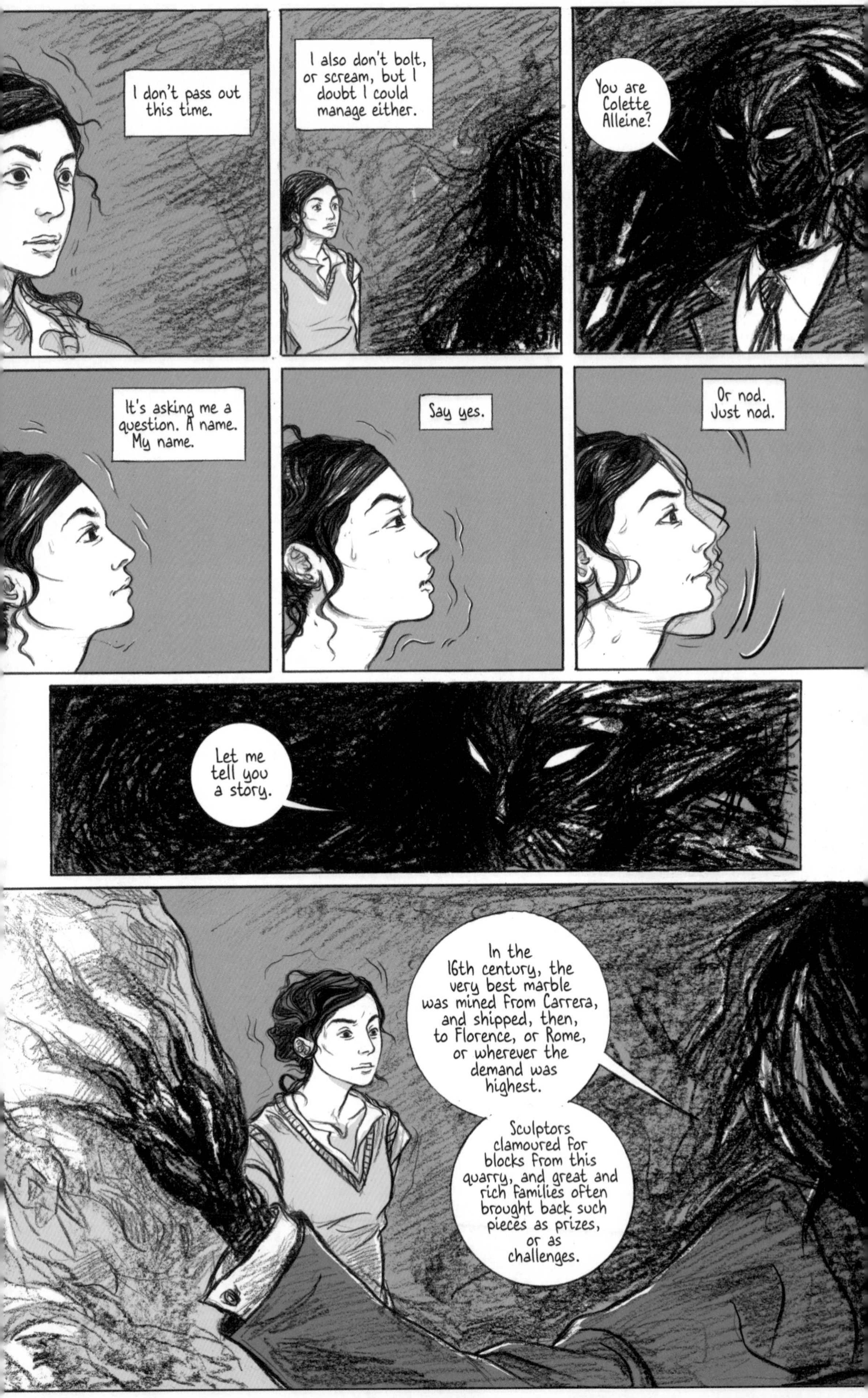

I don't pass out this time.
I also don't bolt, or scream, but I doubt I could manage either.
You are Colette Alleine?
It's asking me a question. A name. My name.
Say yes.
Or nod. Just nod.
Let me tell you a story.
In the 16th century, the very best marble was mined from Carrera, and shipped, then, to Florence, or Rome, or wherever the demand was highest.
Sculptors clamoured for blocks from this quarry, and great and rich families often brought back such pieces as prizes, or as challenges.

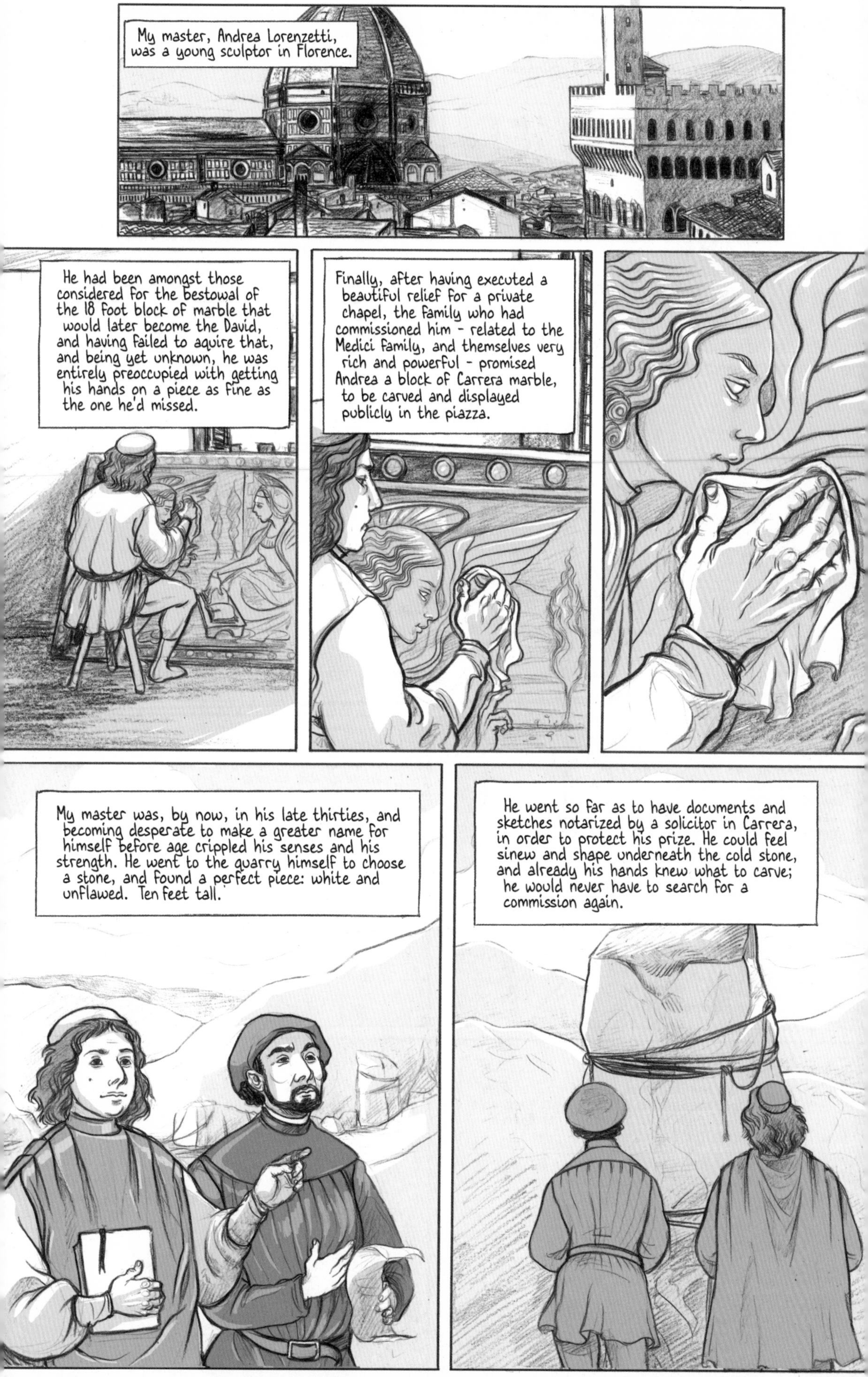

My master, Andrea Lorenzetti, was a young sculptor in Florence.
He had been amongst those considered for the bestowal of the 18 foot block of marble that would later become the David, and having failed to aquire that, and being yet unknown, he was entirely preoccupied with getting his hands on a piece as fine as the one he'd missed.
Finally, after having executed a beautiful relief for a private chapel, the family who had commissioned him - related to the Medici family, and themselves very rich and powerful - promised Andrea a block of Carrera marble, to be carved and displayed publicly in the piazza.
My master was, by now, in his late thirties, and becoming desperate to make a greater name for himself before age crippled his senses and his strength. He went to the quarry himself to choose a stone, and found a perfect piece: white and unflawed. Ten feet tall.
He went so far as to have documents and sketches notarized by a solicitor in Carrera, in order to protect his prize. He could feel sinew and shape underneath the cold stone, and already his hands knew what to carve; he would never have to search for a commission again.

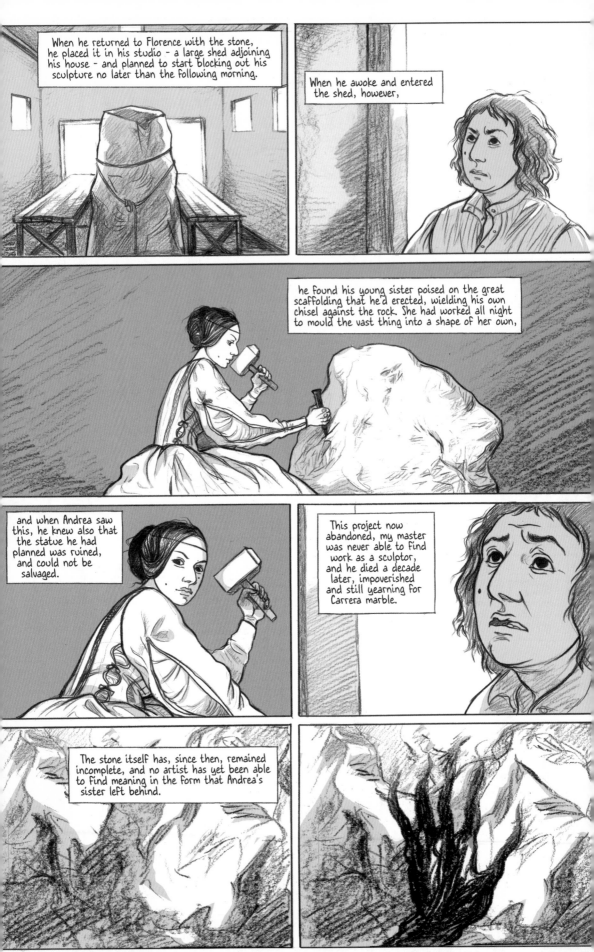

When he returned to Florence with the stone, he placed it in his studio — a large shed adjoining his house — and planned to start blocking out his sculpture no later than the following morning.

When he awoke and entered the shed, however,

he found his young sister poised on the great scaffolding that he'd erected, wielding his own chisel against the rock. She had worked all night to mould the vast thing into a shape of her own,

and when Andrea saw this, he knew also that the statue he had planned was ruined, and could not be salvaged.

This project now abandoned, my master was never able to find work as a sculptor, and he died a decade later, impoverished and still yearning for Carrera marble.

The stone itself has, since then, remained incomplete, and no artist has yet been able to find meaning in the form that Andrea's sister left behind.

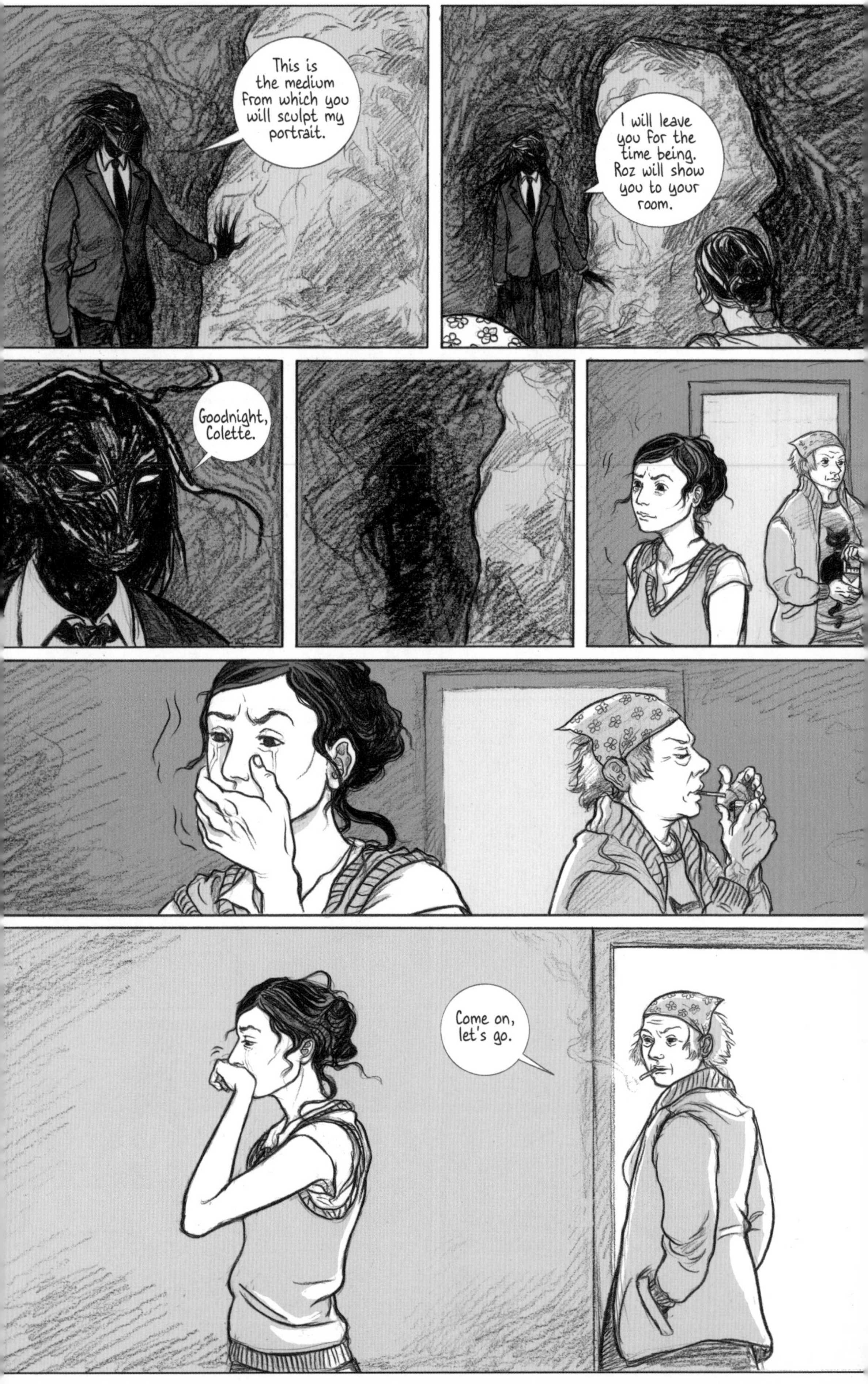
This is the medium from which you will sculpt my portrait.
I will leave you for the time being. Roz will show you to your room.
Goodnight, Colette.
Come on, let's go.

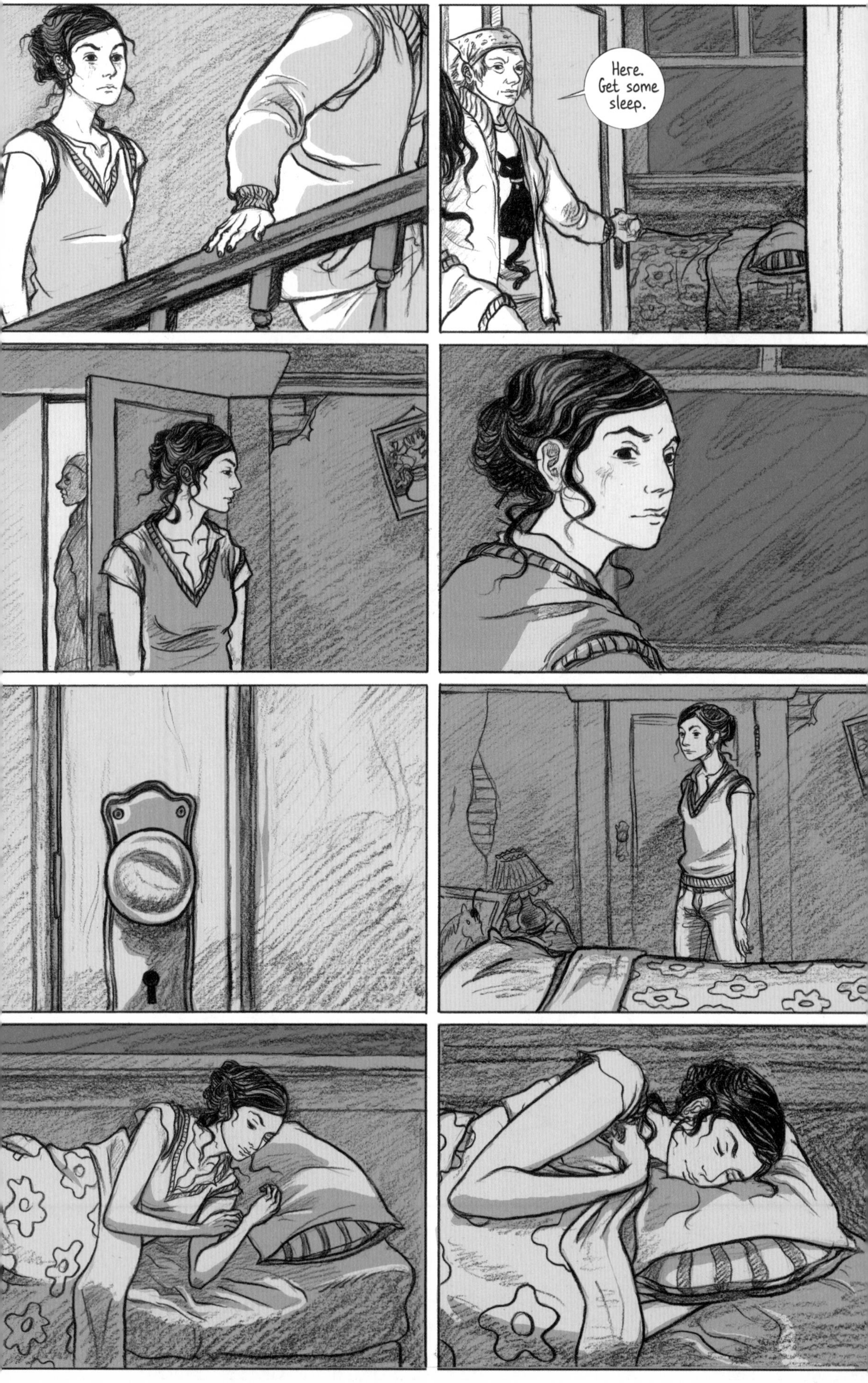
Here. Get some sleep.

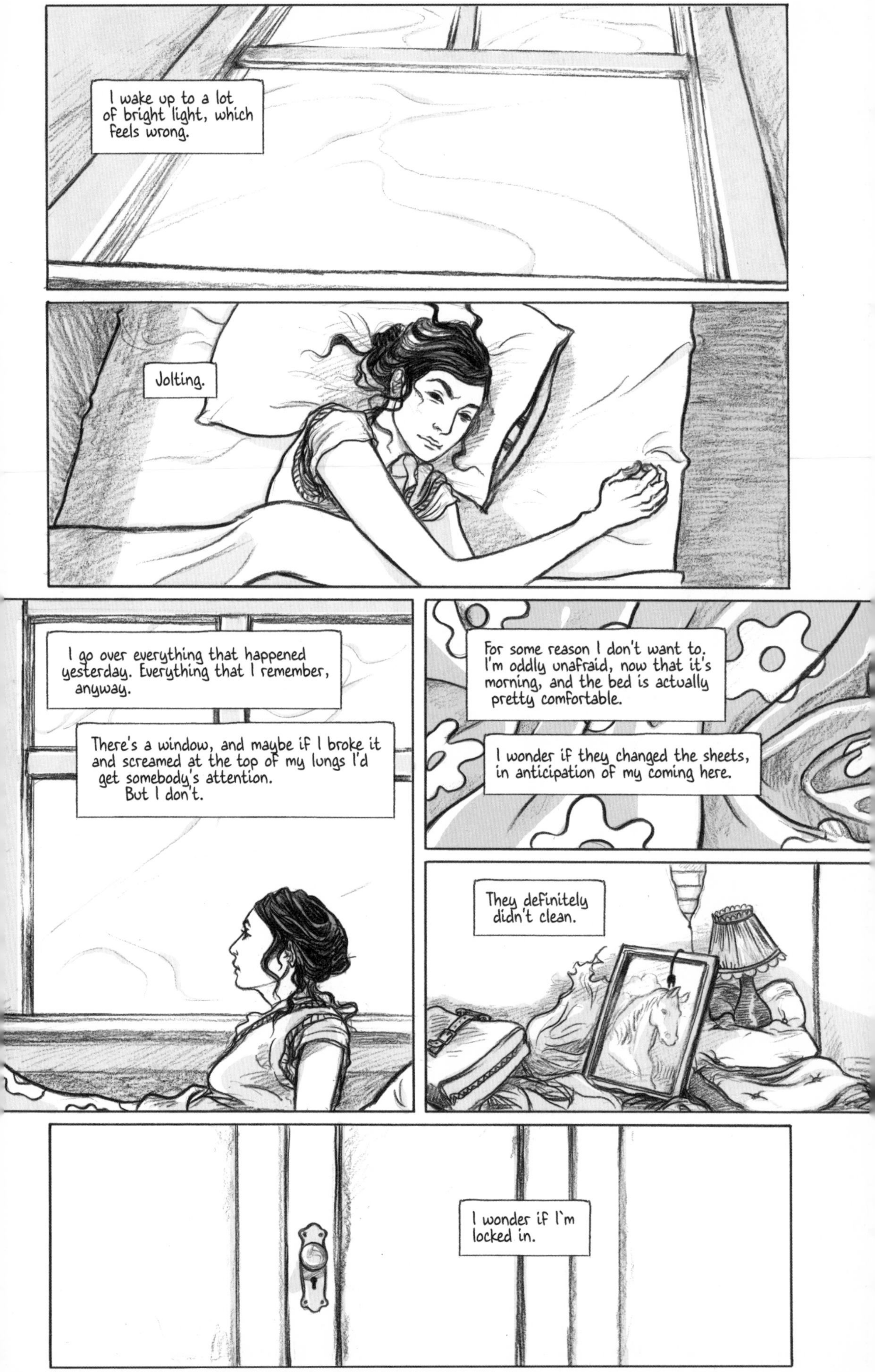

I wake up to a lot of bright light, which feels wrong.
Jolting.
I go over everything that happened yesterday. Everything that I remember, anyway.
There's a window, and maybe if I broke it and screamed at the top of my lungs I'd get somebody's attention. But I don't.
For some reason I don't want to. I'm oddly unafraid, now that it's morning, and the bed is actually pretty comfortable.
I wonder if they changed the sheets, in anticipation of my coming here.
They definitely didn't clean.
I wonder if I'm locked in.

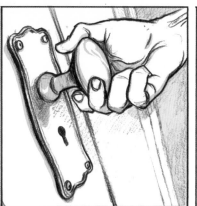

I'm not.

The house looks much smaller in the daytime. Just a house. Not a mansion, really, and certainly not whatever many-winged and multi-towered monstrosity I imagined last night.

I don't have much trouble retracing my steps back to the studio, even with my somewhat hazy recollection of where I was led.

The block of marble is still there. The room is brighter now, and I can see the walls are lined with shelves, with carving tools on them.

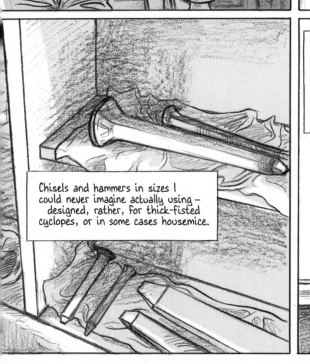

Chisels and hammers in sizes I could never imagine actually using — designed, rather, for thick-fisted cyclopes, or in some cases housemice.

I wonder if I'm meant to do this portrait from memory, and fairly unreliable memory at that. The shadowy thing isn't here, and I can't really imagine it — him — coming in and posing for me.

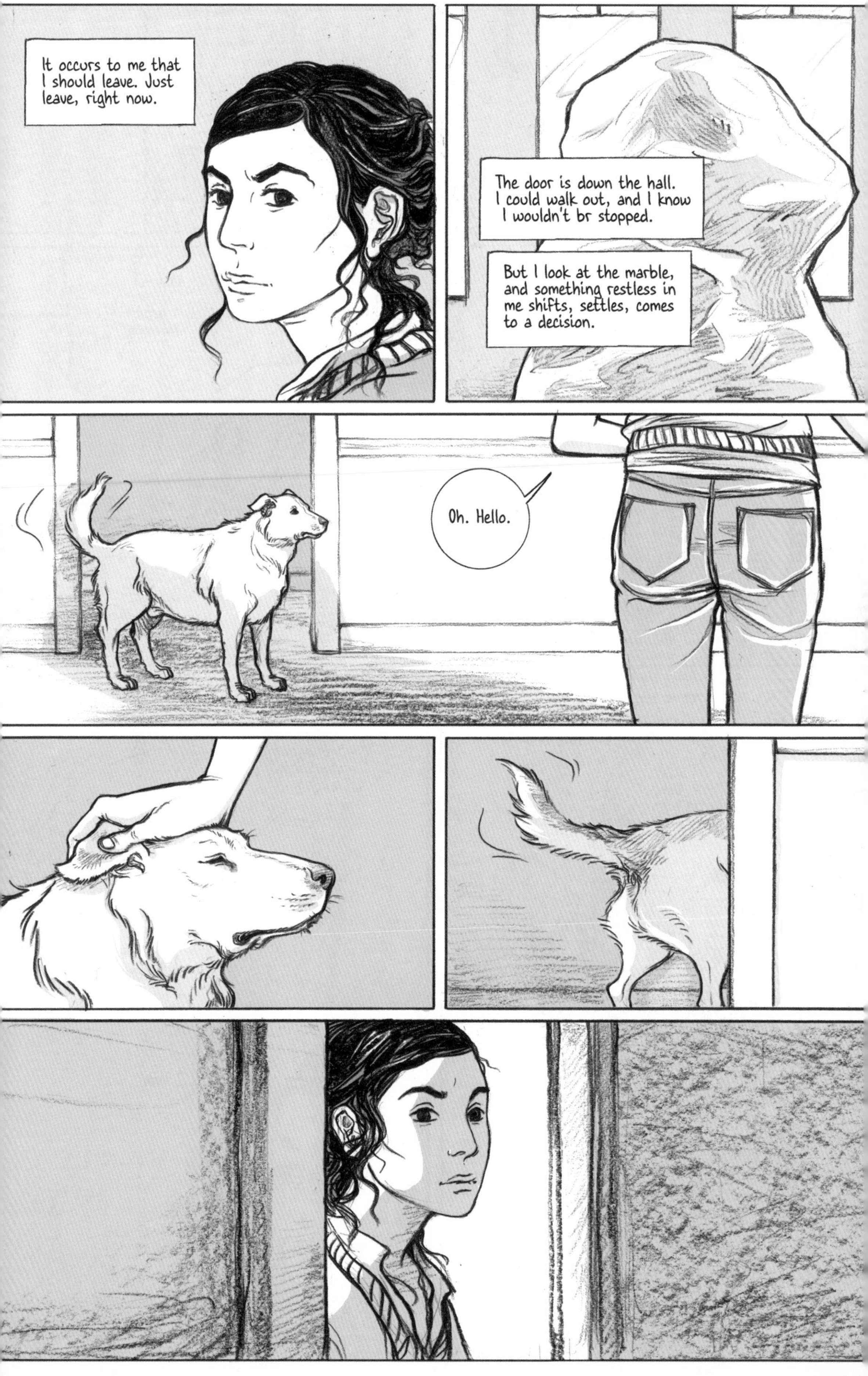
It occurs to me that I should leave. Just leave, right now.
The door is down the hall. I could walk out, and I know I wouldn't br stopped.
But I look at the marble, and something restless in me shifts, settles, comes to a decision.
Oh. Hello.

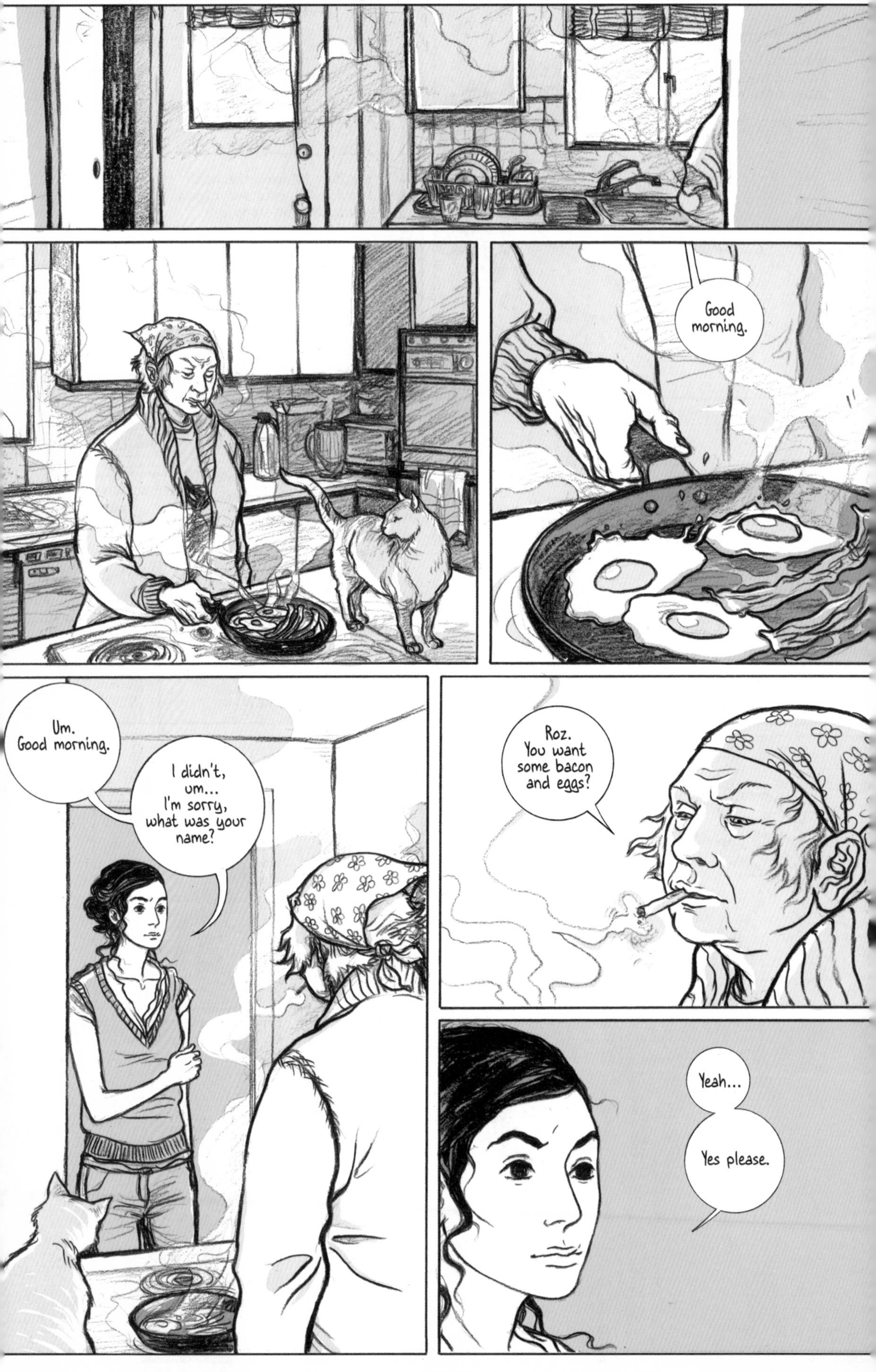
Good morning.
Um. Good morning.
I didn't, um... I'm sorry, what was your name?
Roz. You want some bacon and eggs?
Yeah...
Yes please.

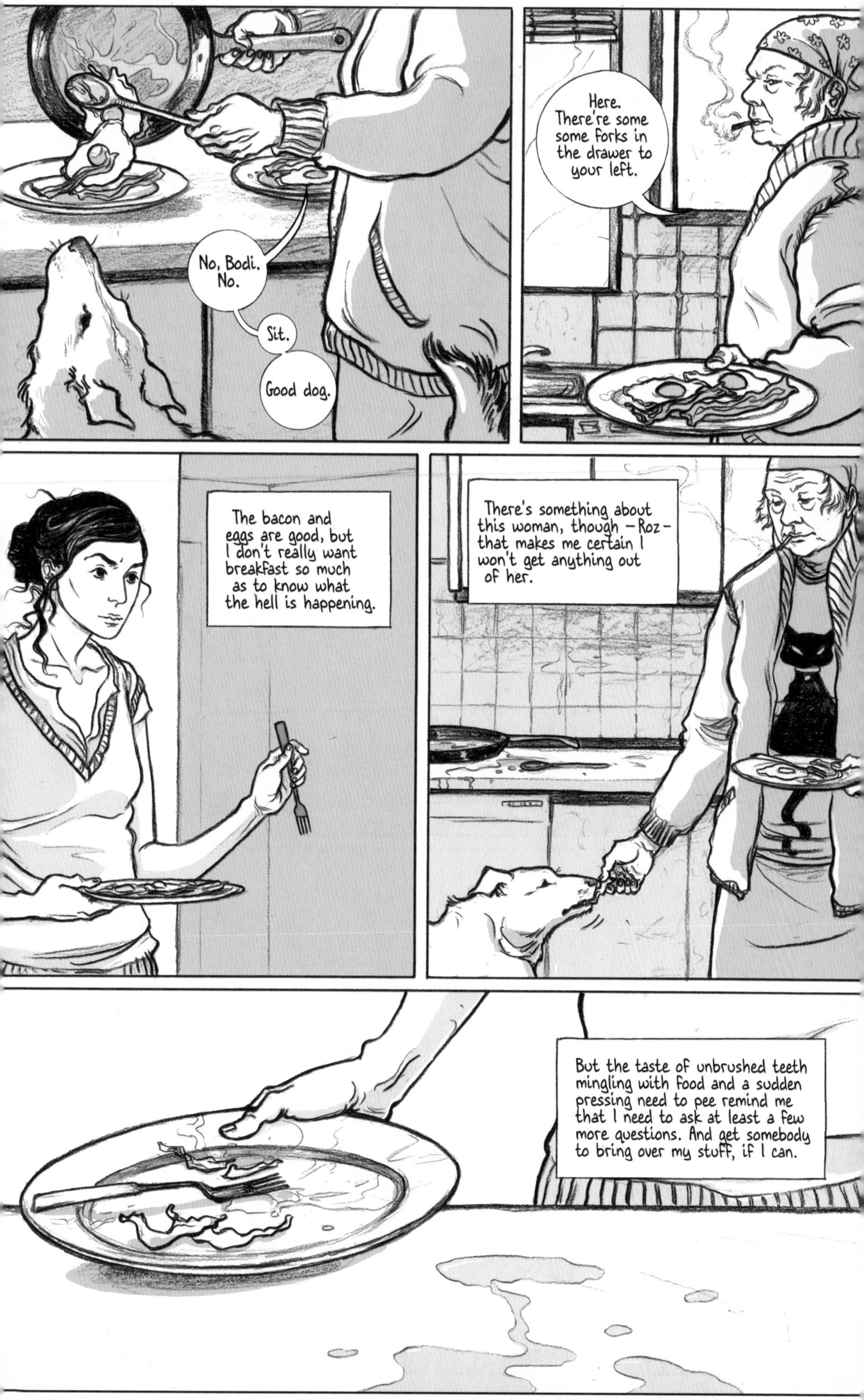
No, Bodi. No.
Sit.
Good dog.
Here. There're some some forks in the drawer to your left.
The bacon and eggs are good, but I don't really want breakfast so much as to know what the hell is happening.
There's something about this woman, though —Roz— that makes me certain I won't get anything out of her.
But the taste of unbrushed teeth mingling with food and a sudden pressing need to pee remind me that I need to ask at least a few more questions. And get somebody to bring over my stuff, if I can.

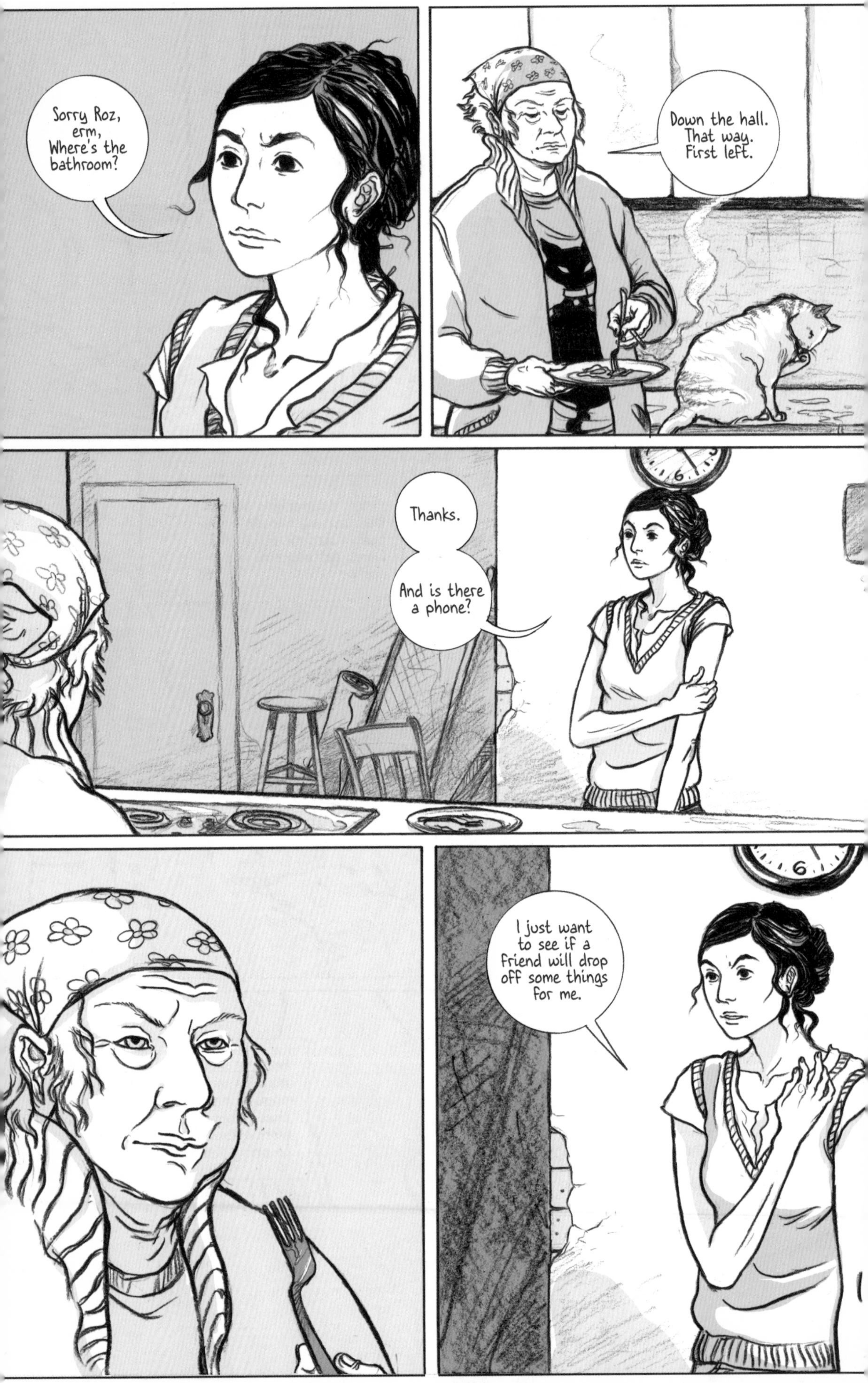
Sorry Roz, erm, Where's the bathroom?
Down the hall. That way. First left.
Thanks.
And is there a phone?
I just want to see if a friend will drop off some things for me.

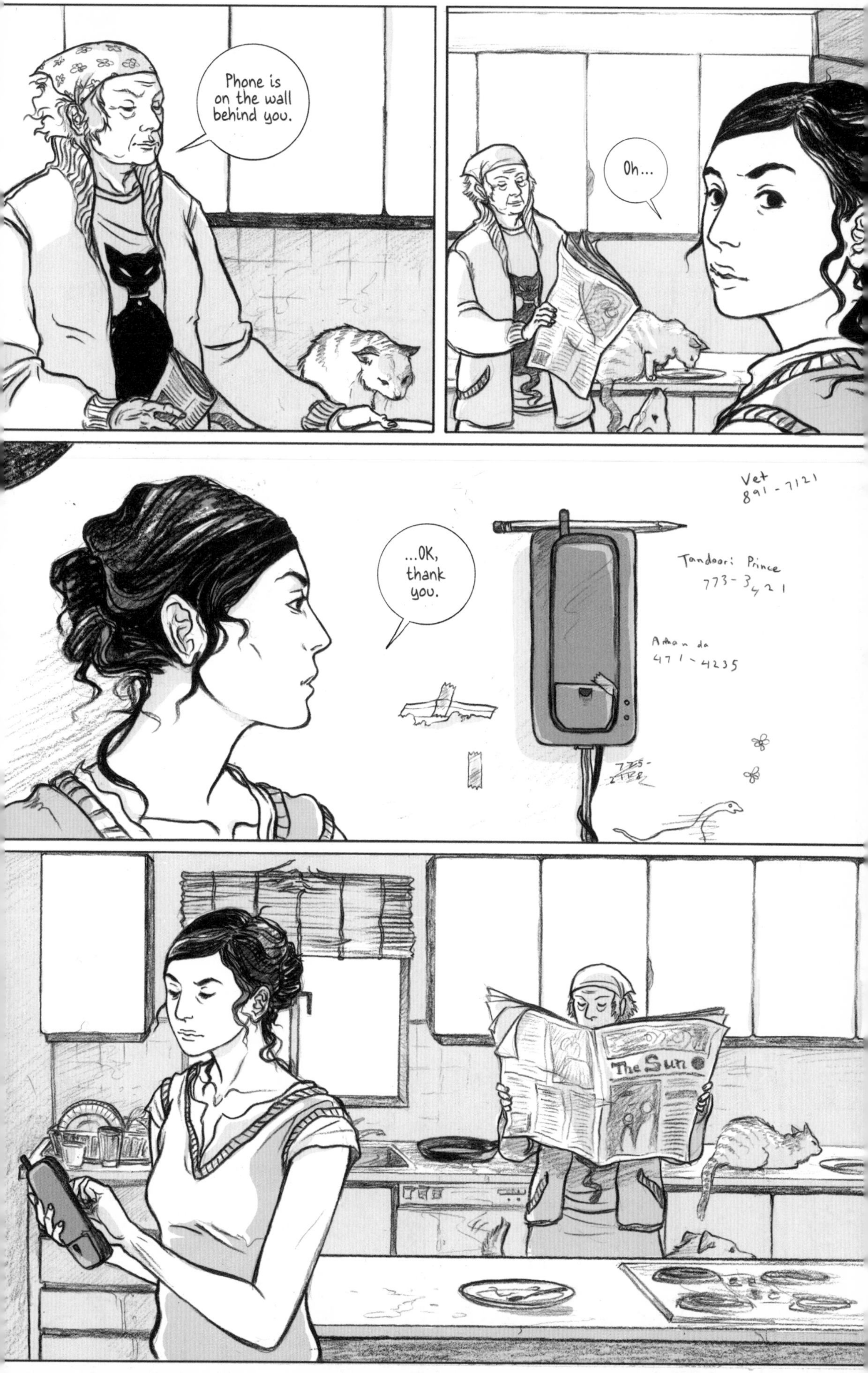

Phone is on the wall behind you.
Oh...
Vet
891-7121
Tandoori Prince
773-3421
Amanda
471-4235
...OK, thank you.
The Sun

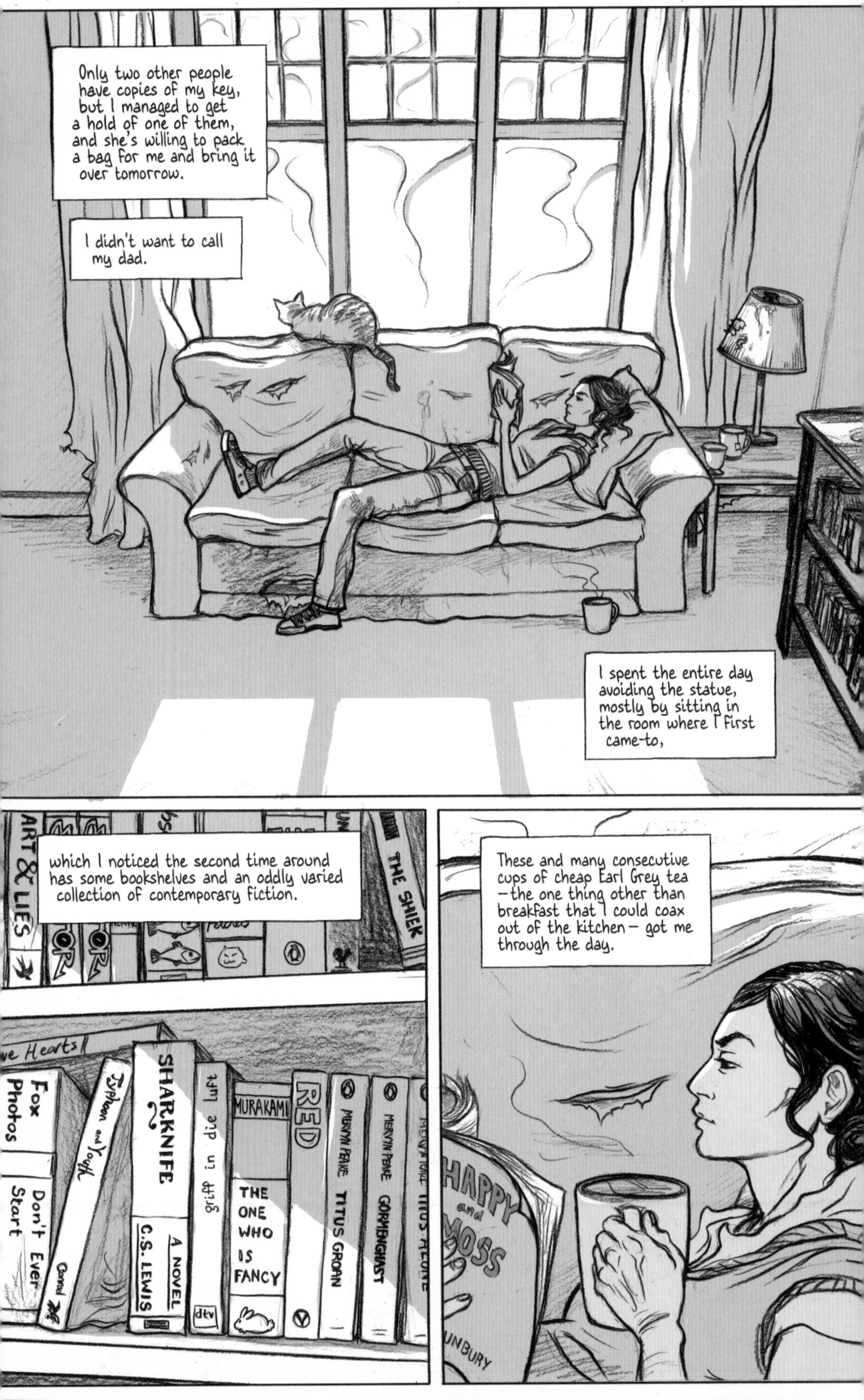
Only two other people have copies of my key, but I managed to get a hold of one of them, and she's willing to pack a bag for me and bring it over tomorrow.
I didn't want to call my dad.
I spent the entire day avoiding the statue, mostly by sitting in the room where I first came-to,
which I noticed the second time around has some bookshelves and an oddly varied collection of contemporary fiction.
ART & LIES
THE SHIEK
Fox Photos
Don't Ever Start
Typhoon and Youth
Conrad
SHARKNIFE
A NOVEL
C.S. LEWIS
griff in die luft
dtv
MURAKAMI
THE ONE WHO IS FANCY
RED
MERVYN PEAKE
TITUS GROAN
MERVYN PEAKE
GORMENGHAST
TITUS ALONE
These and many consecutive cups of cheap Earl Grey tea —the one thing other than breakfast that I could coax out of the kitchen— got me through the day.
HAPPY and MOSS

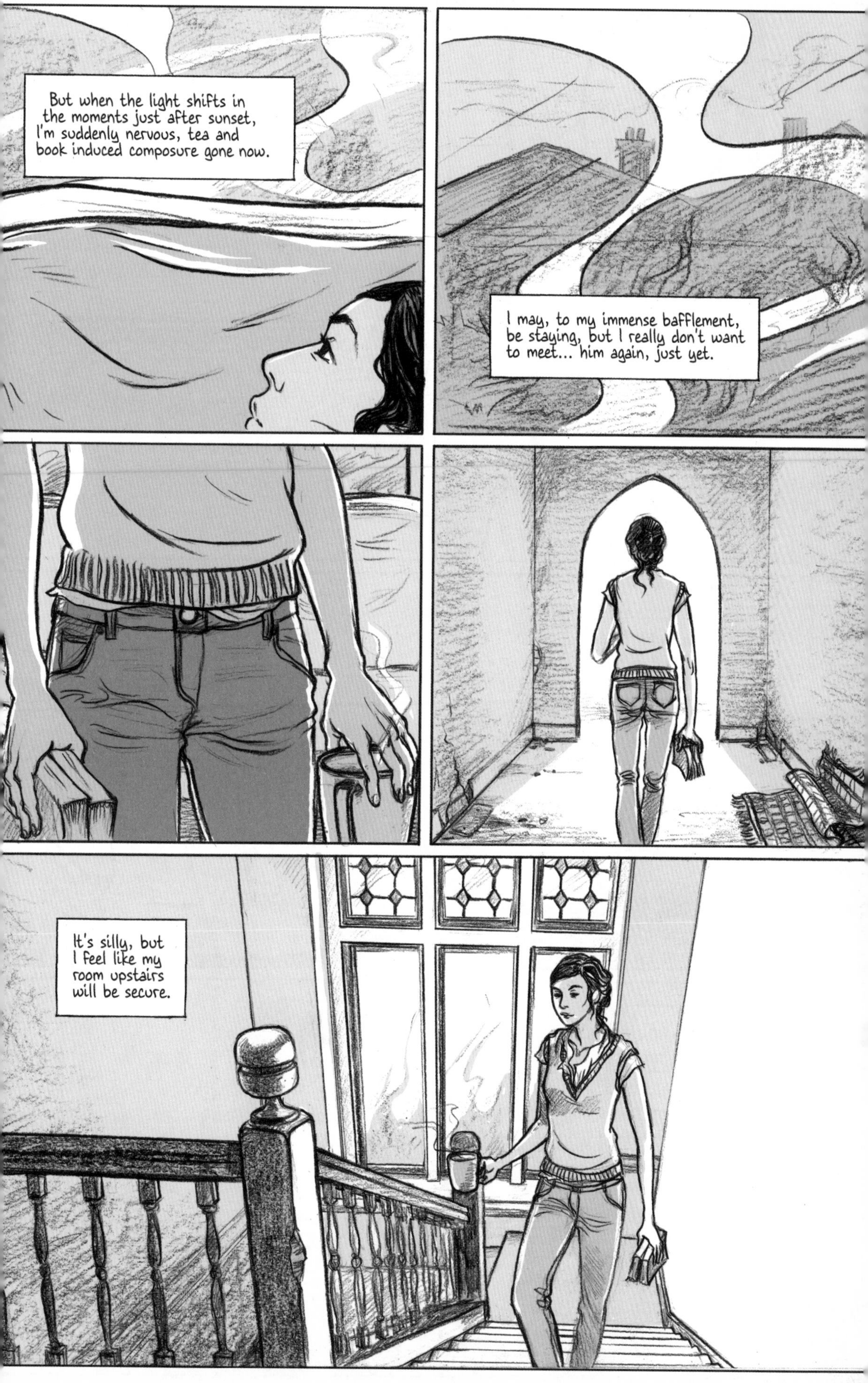
But when the light shifts in the moments just after sunset, I'm suddenly nervous, tea and book induced composure gone now.
I may, to my immense bafflement, be staying, but I really don't want to meet... him again, just yet.
It's silly, but I feel like my room upstairs will be secure.

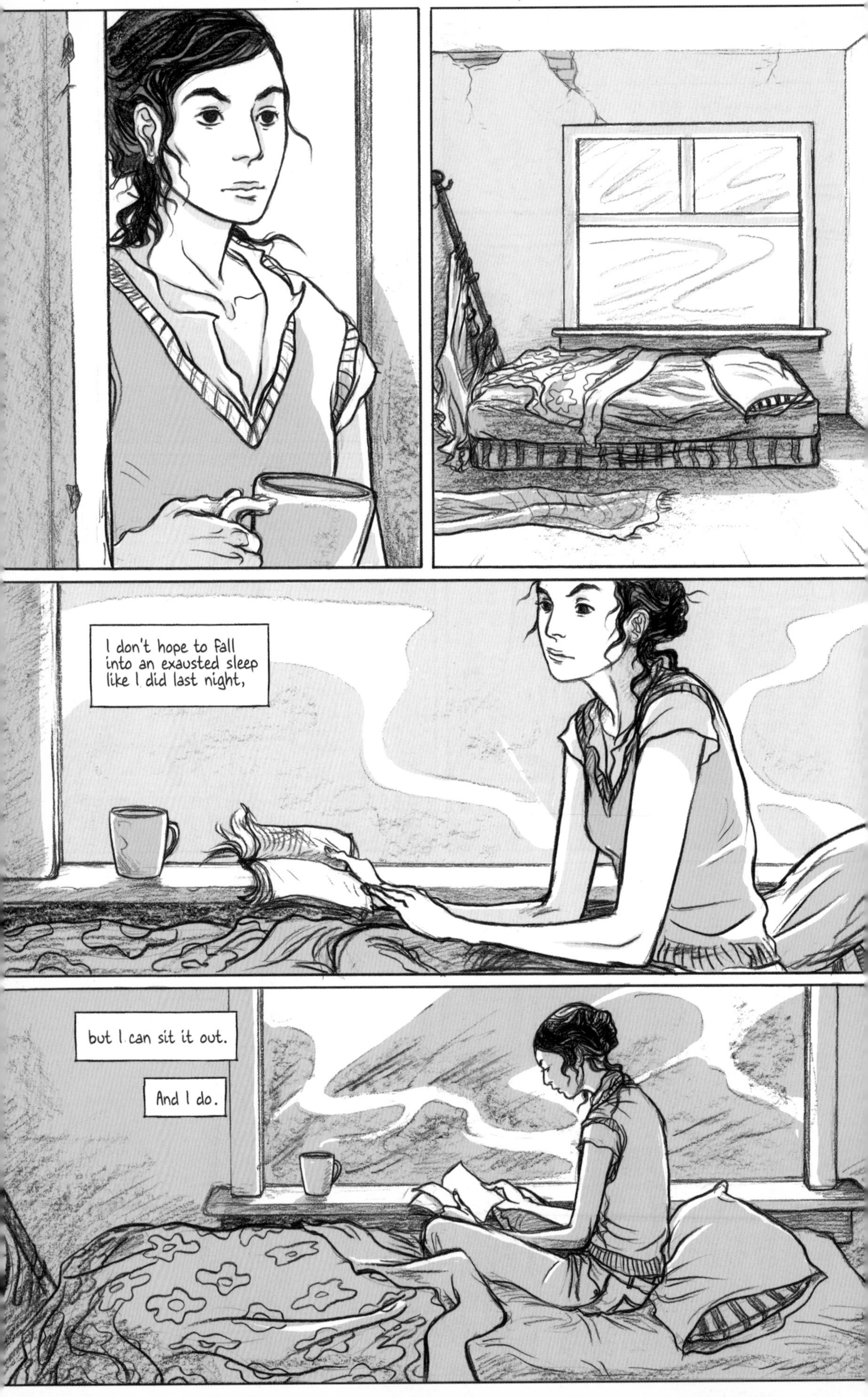
I don't hope to fall into an exausted sleep like I did last night,
but I can sit it out.
And I do.

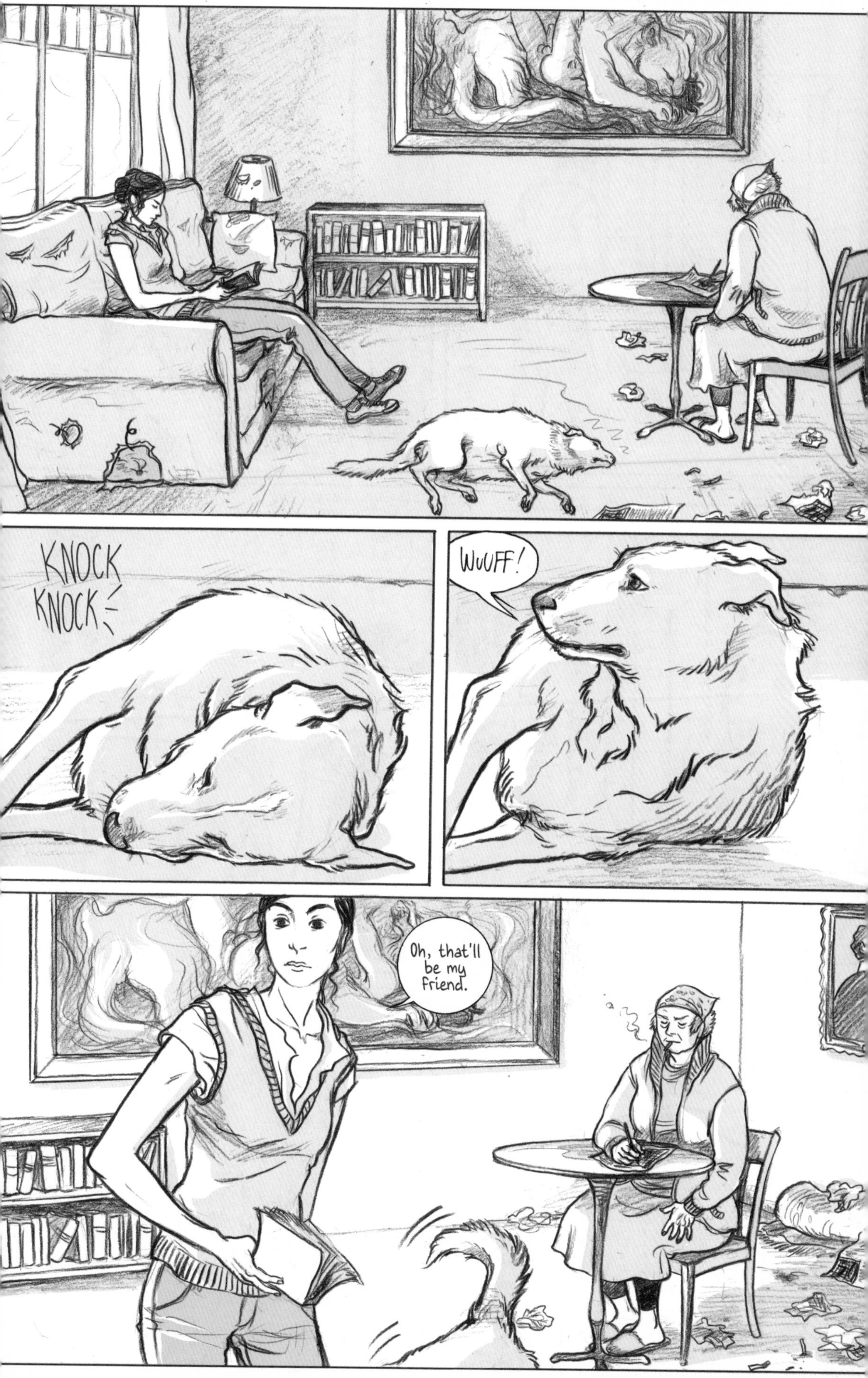
KNOCK
KNOCK
WUUFF!
Oh, that'll be my friend.

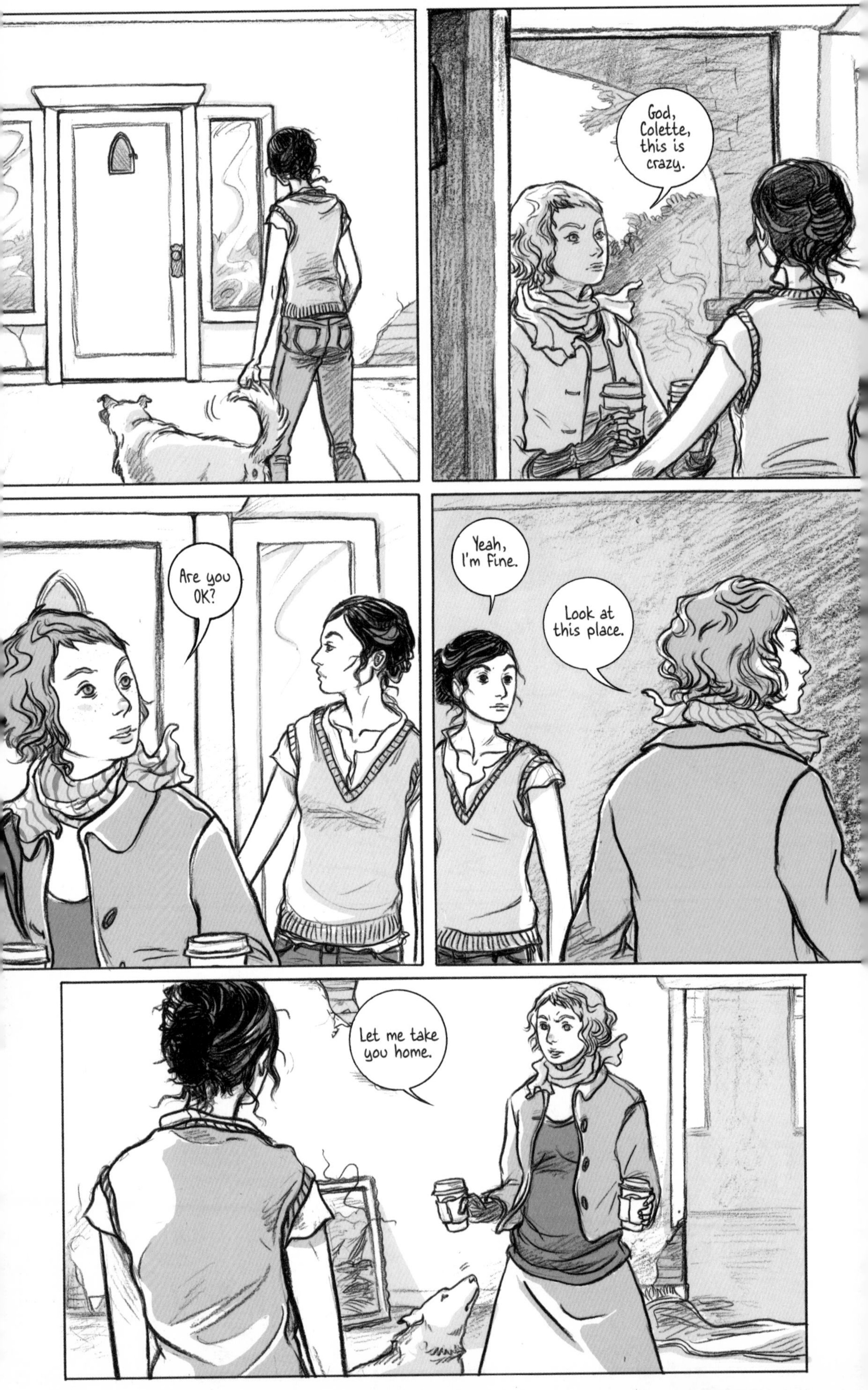
God, Colette, this is crazy.
Are you OK?
Yeah, I'm fine.
Look at this place.
Let me take you home.

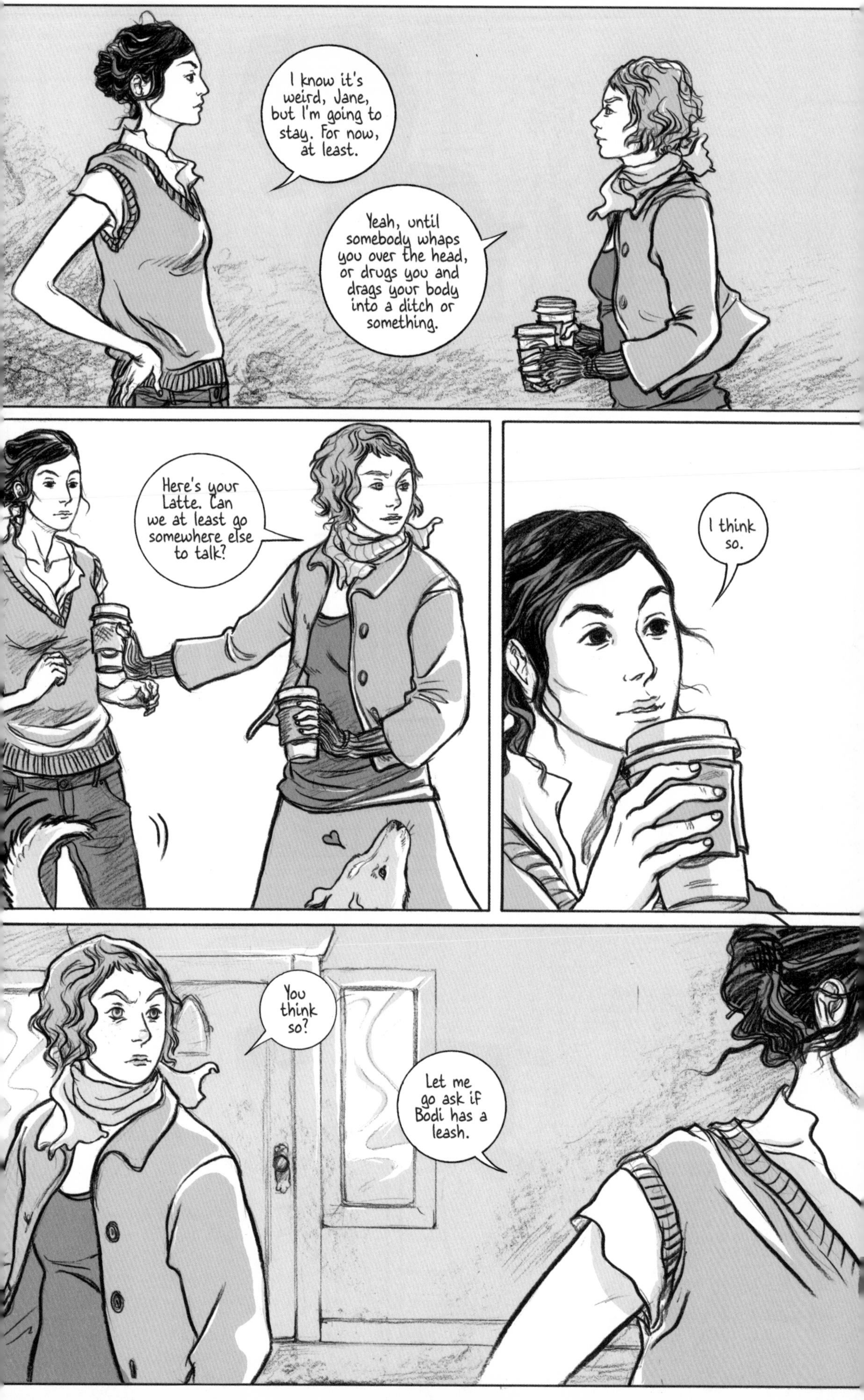
I know it's weird, Jane, but I'm going to stay. For now, at least.
Yeah, until somebody whaps you over the head, or drugs you and drags your body into a ditch or something.
Here's your Latte. Can we at least go somewhere else to talk?
I think so.
You think so?
Let me go ask if Bodi has a leash.

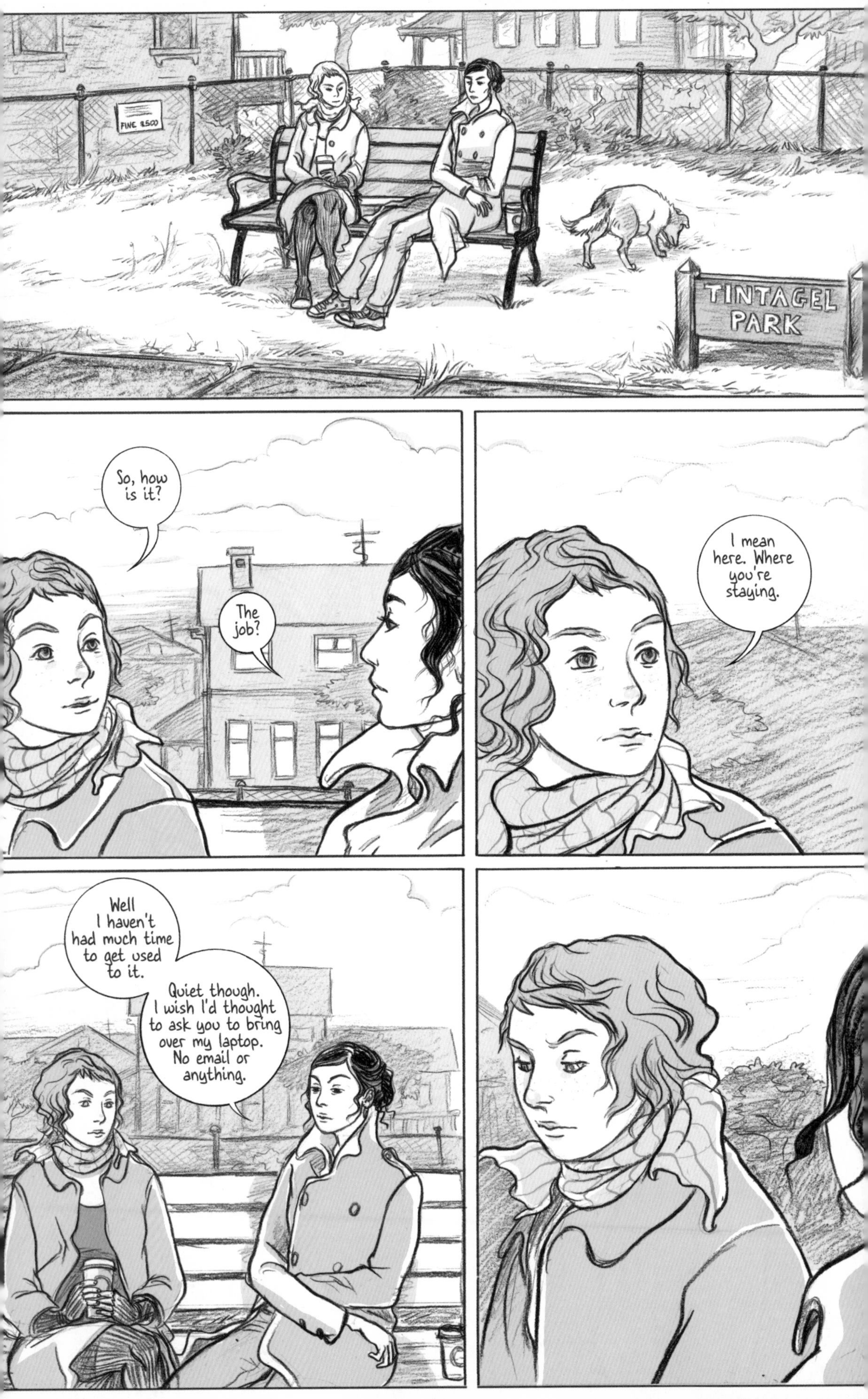
FINE $500
TINTAGEL PARK
So, how is it?
The job?
I mean here. Where you're staying.
Well I haven't had much time to get used to it.
Quiet though. I wish I'd thought to ask you to bring over my laptop. No email or anything.

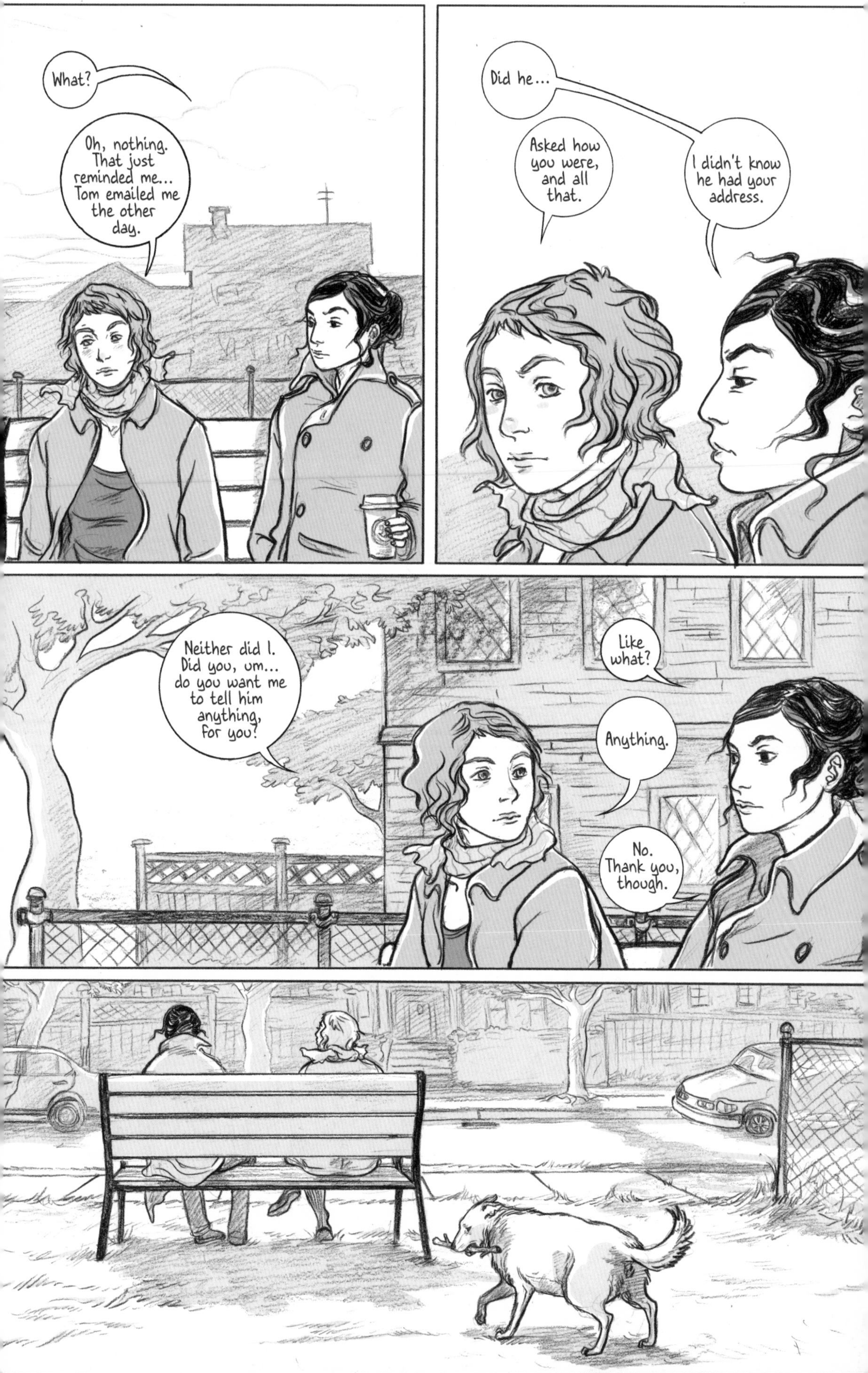
What?
Oh, nothing. That just reminded me... Tom emailed me the other day.
Did he...
Asked how you were, and all that.
I didn't know he had your address.
Neither did I. Did you, um... do you want me to tell him anything, for you?
Like what?
Anything.
No. Thank you, though.

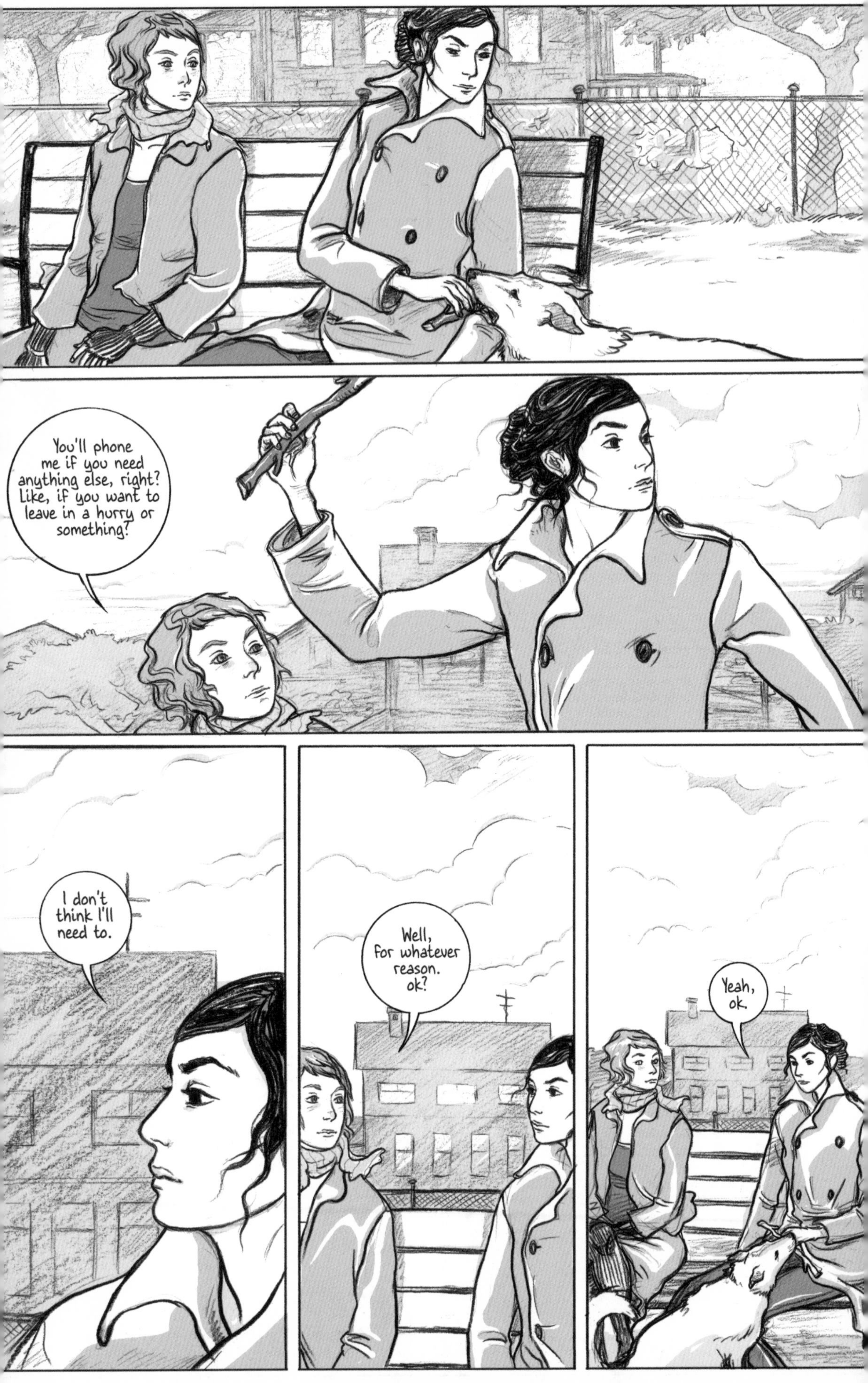
You'll phone me if you need anything else, right? Like, if you want to leave in a hurry or something?
I don't think I'll need to.
Well, for whatever reason. ok?
Yeah, ok.

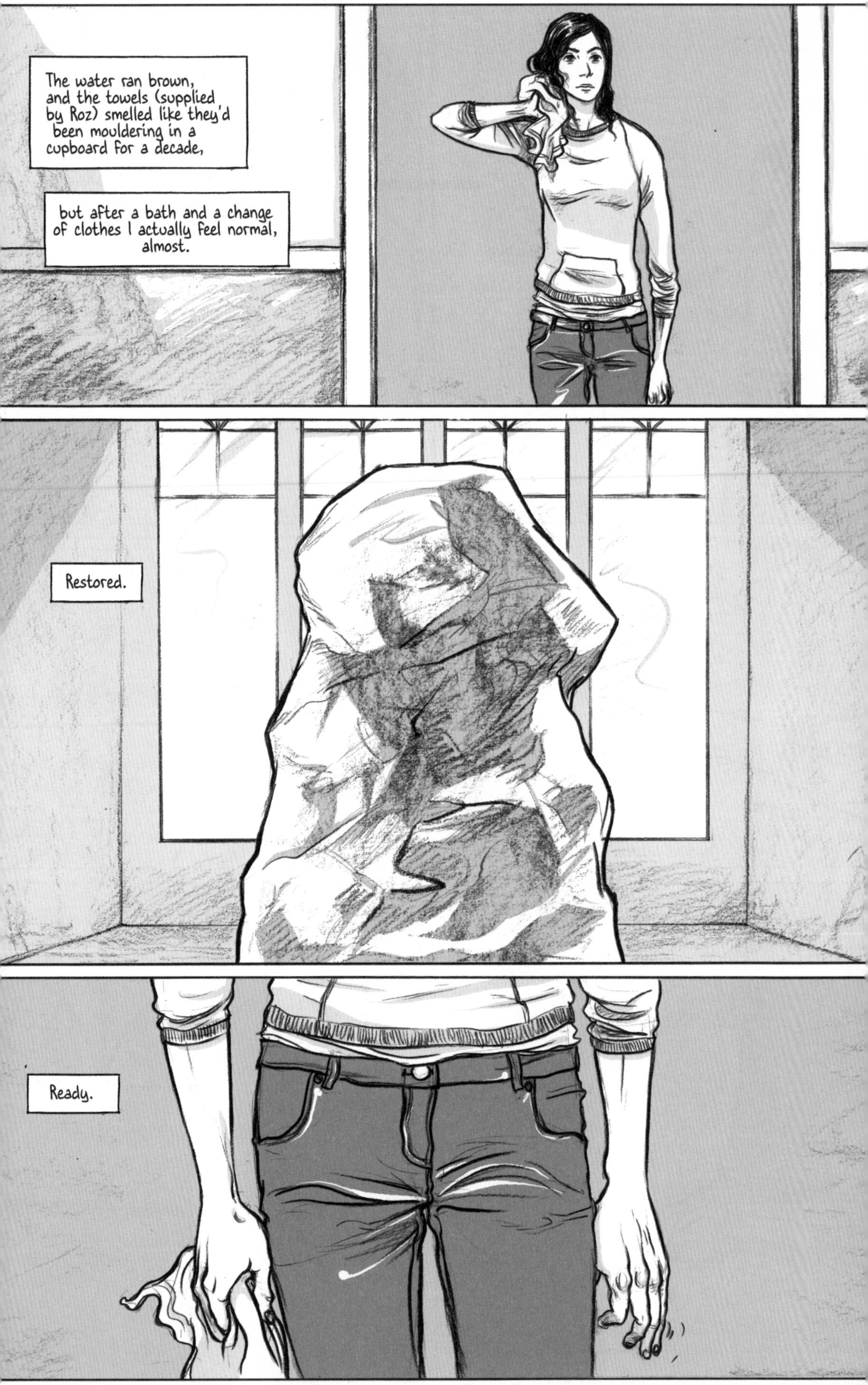
The water ran brown, and the towels (supplied by Roz) smelled like they'd been mouldering in a cupboard for a decade,
but after a bath and a change of clothes I actually feel normal, almost.
Restored.
Ready.

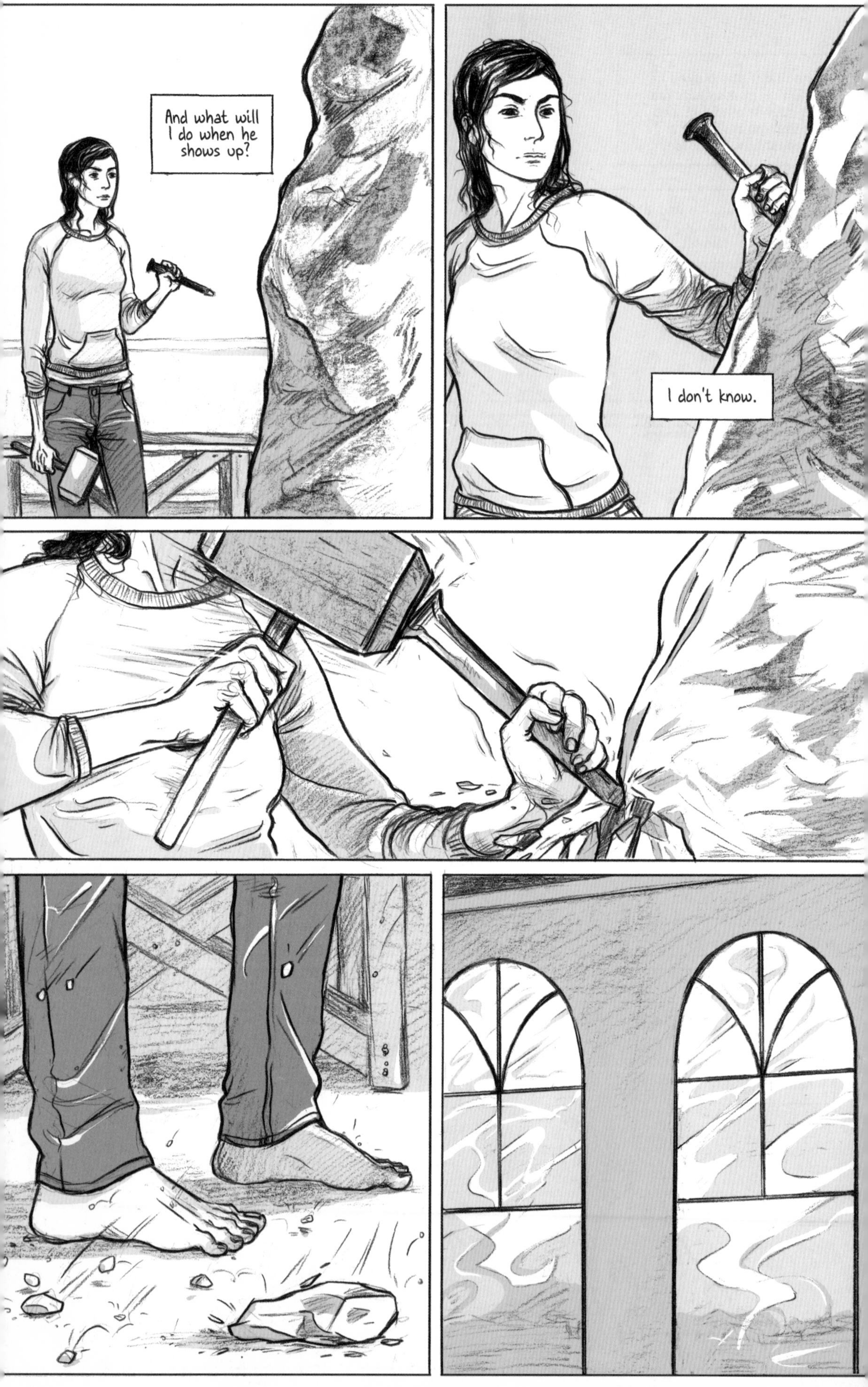
And what will I do when he shows up?
I don't know.

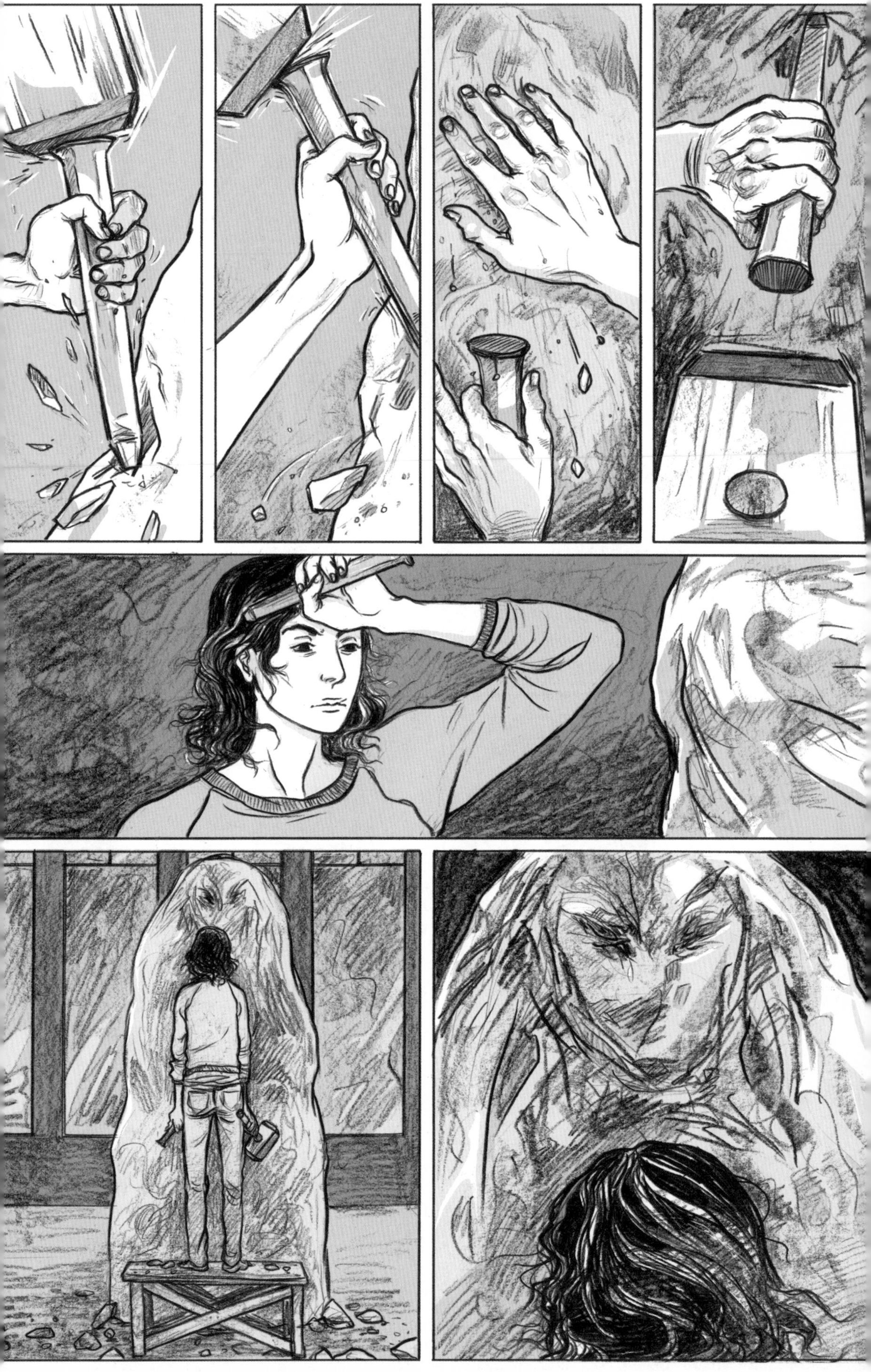

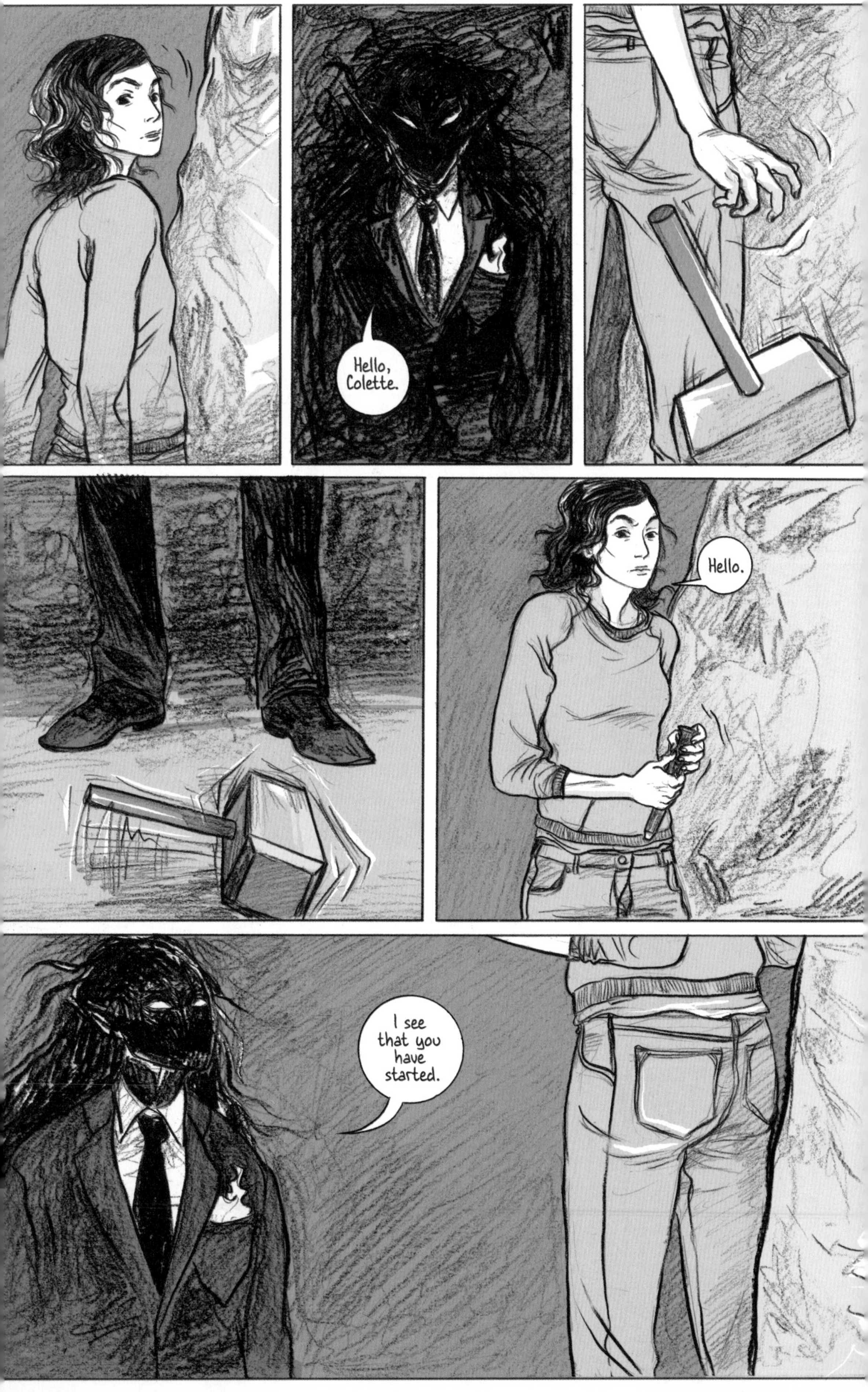
Hello, Colette.
Hello.
I see that you have started.

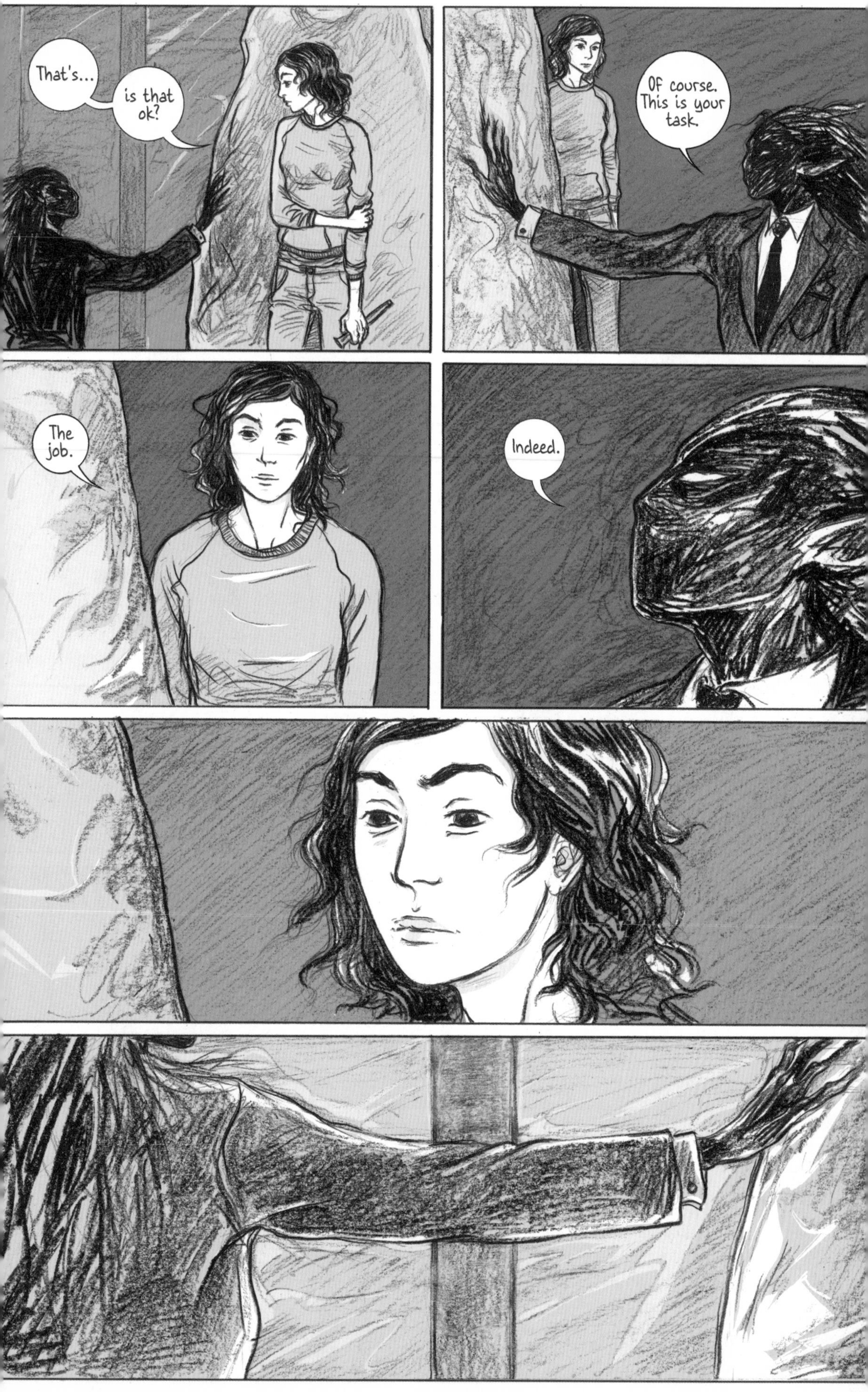
That's...
is that ok?
Of course. This is your task.
The job.
Indeed.

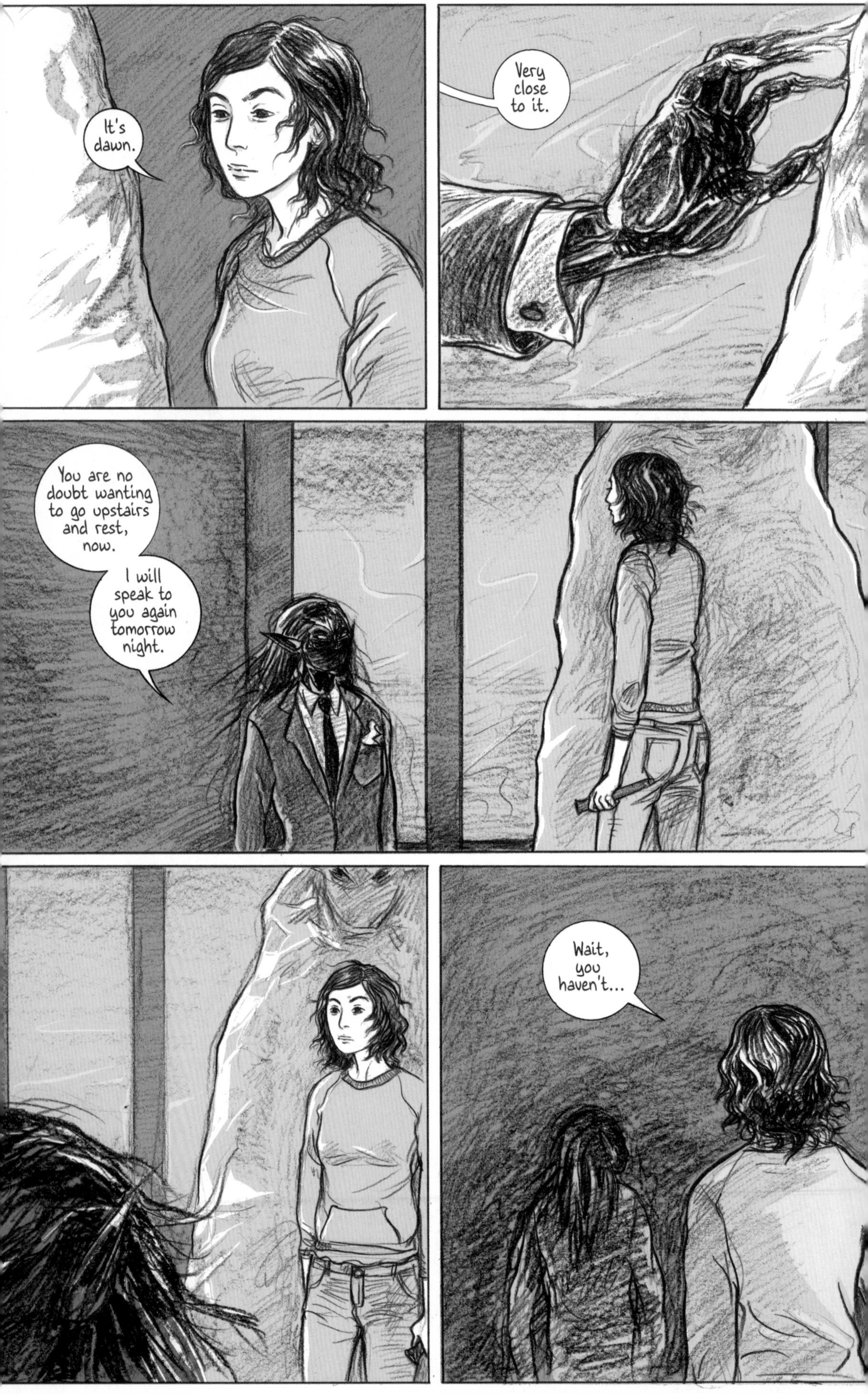
It's dawn.
Very close to it.
You are no doubt wanting to go upstairs and rest, now.
I will speak to you again tomorrow night.
Wait, you haven't...

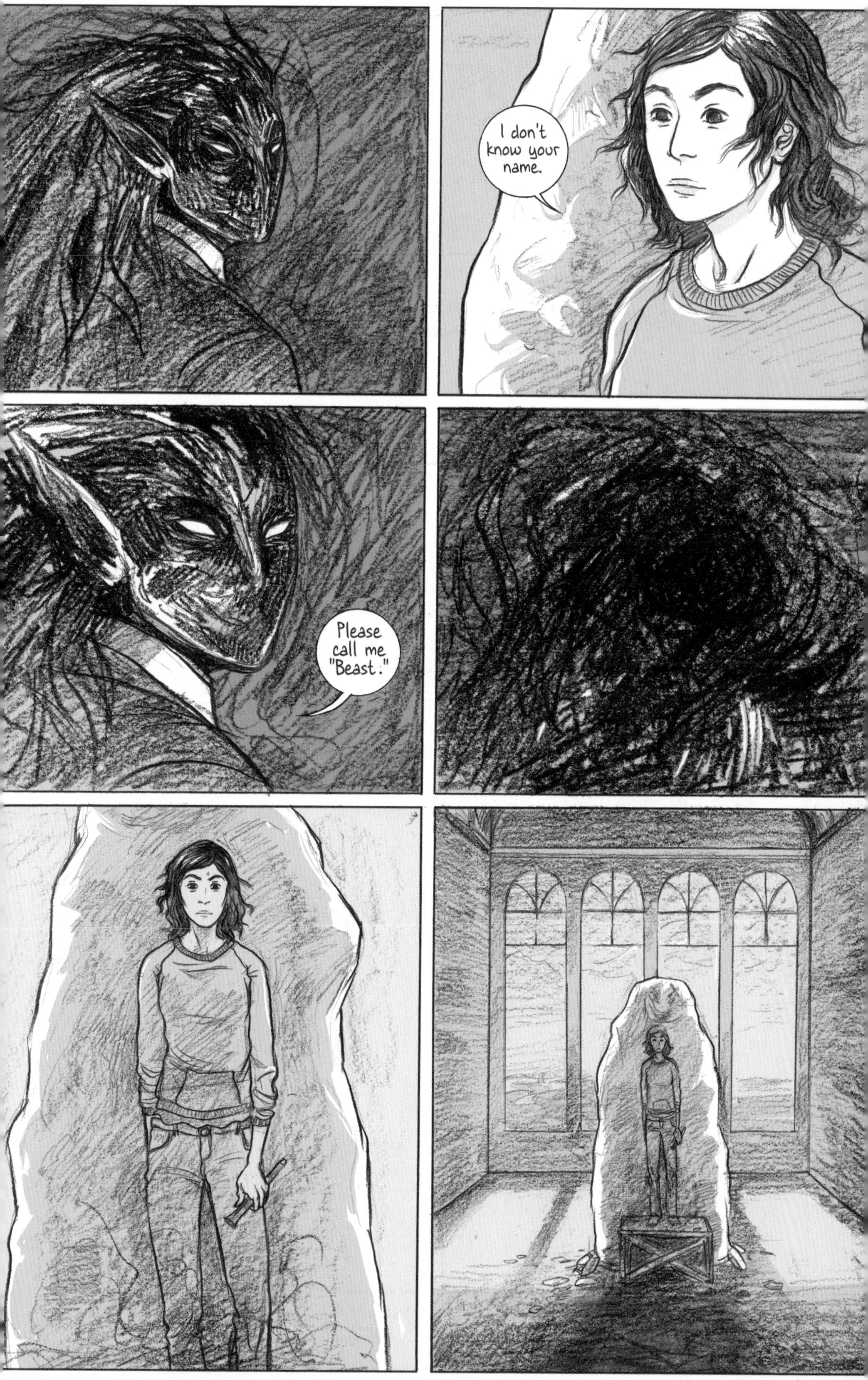
I don't know your name.
Please call me "Beast."

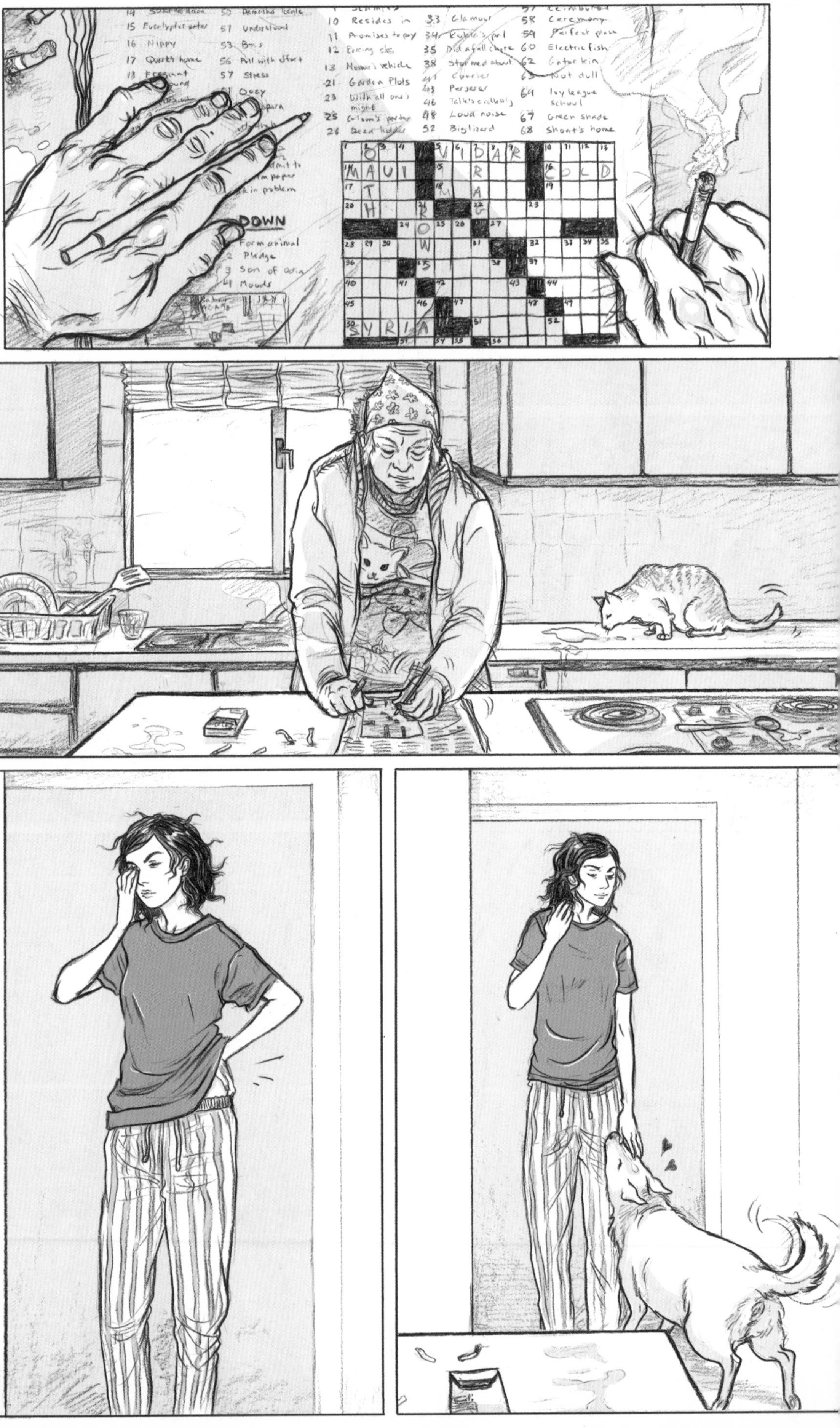

15 Eucalyptus eater
16 Nippy
17 Quark's home
56 Pull with effort
57 Stress
61 Oozy
10 Resides in
11 Promises to pay
21 Garden Plots
23 With all one's might
33 Glamour
35 Did a fall chore
38 Stormed about
48 Loud noise
52 Big lizard
58 Ceremony
59 Perfect place
60 Electric fish
62 Gator kin
63 Not dull
64 Ivy league school
67 Green shade
68 Shoat's home
DOWN
2 Pledge
3 Son of Odin
4 Moods

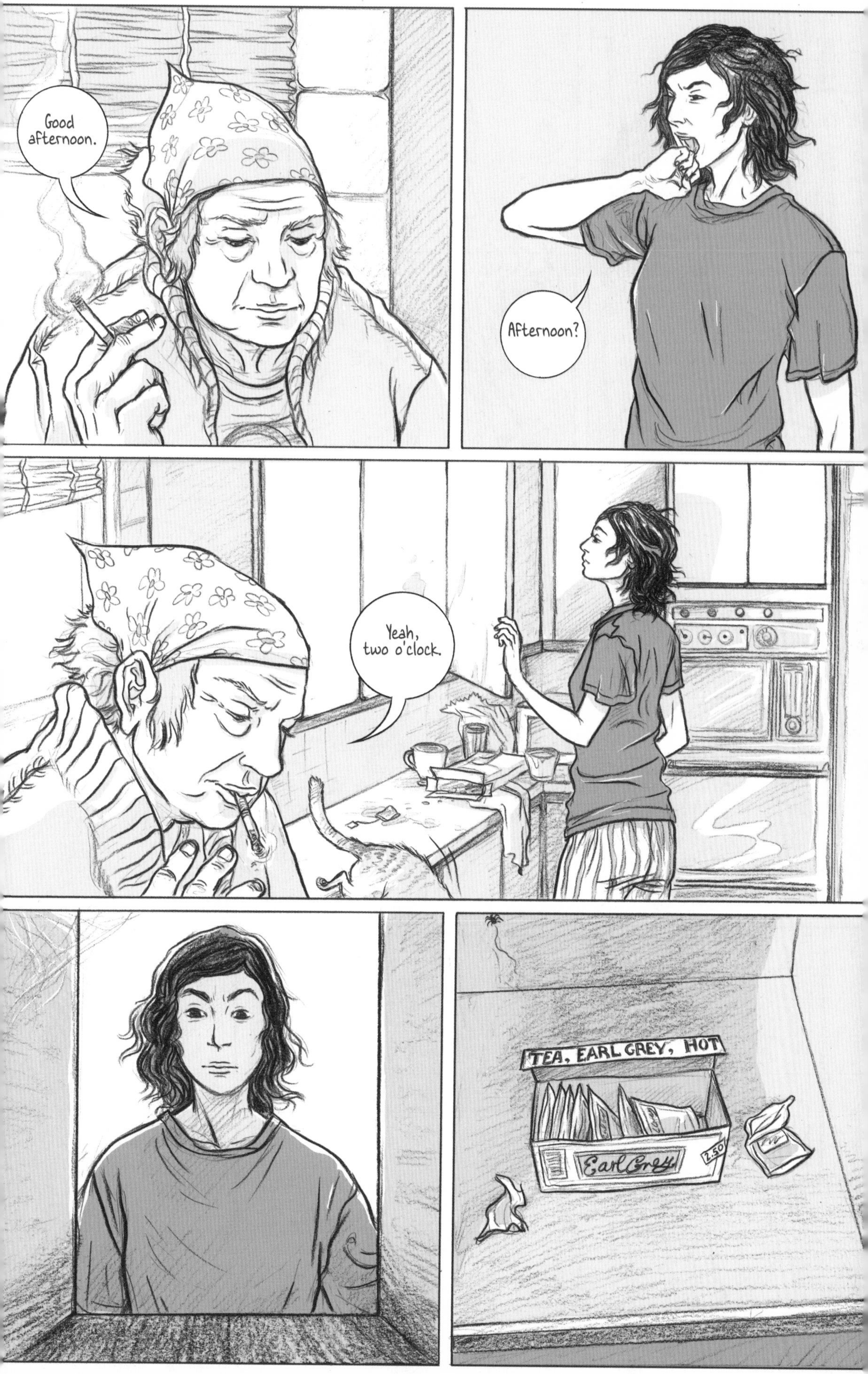
Good afternoon.
Afternoon?
Yeah, two o'clock.
TEA, EARL GREY, HOT
Earl Grey
2.50

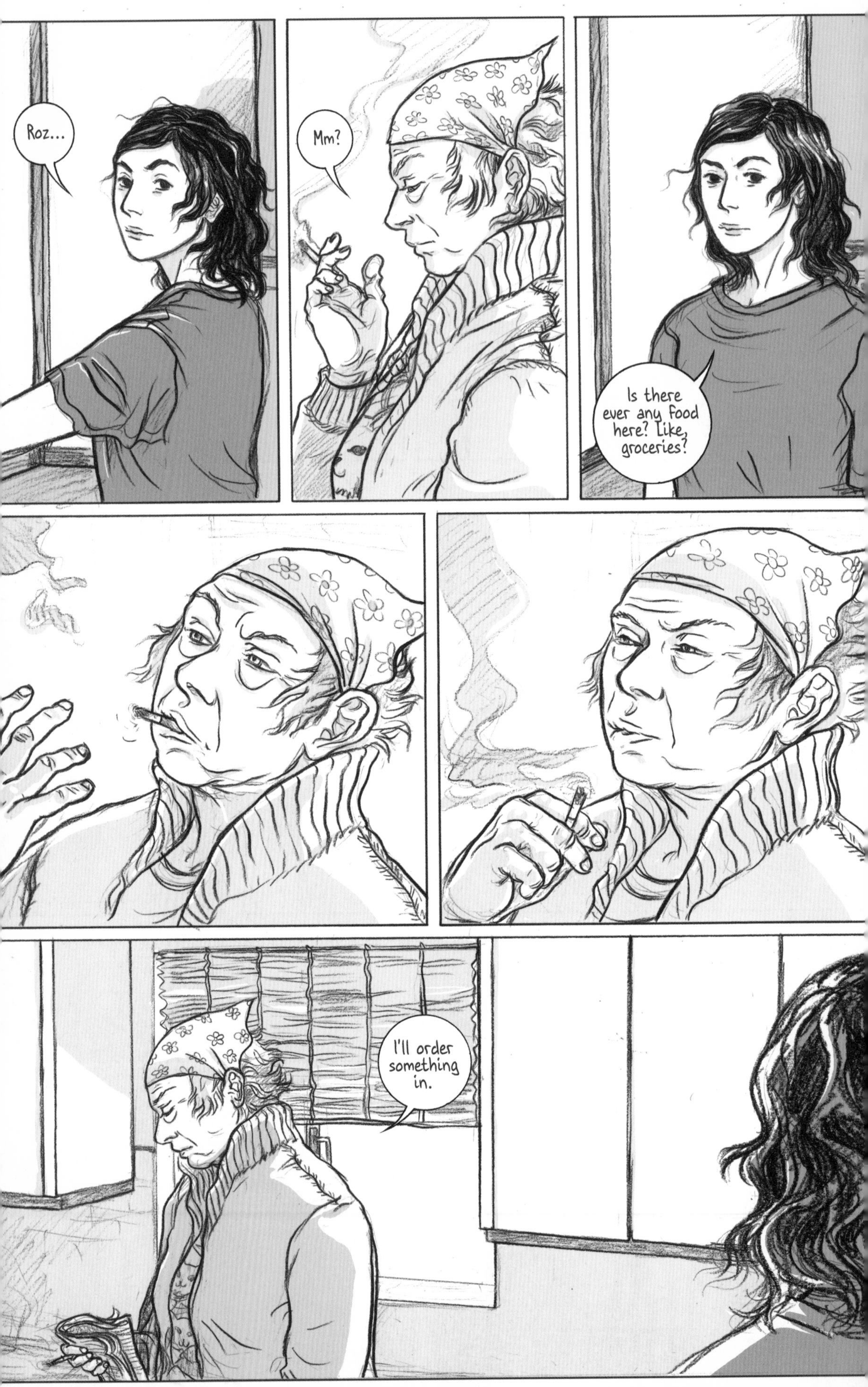
Roz...
Mm?
Is there ever any food here? Like, groceries?
I'll order something in.

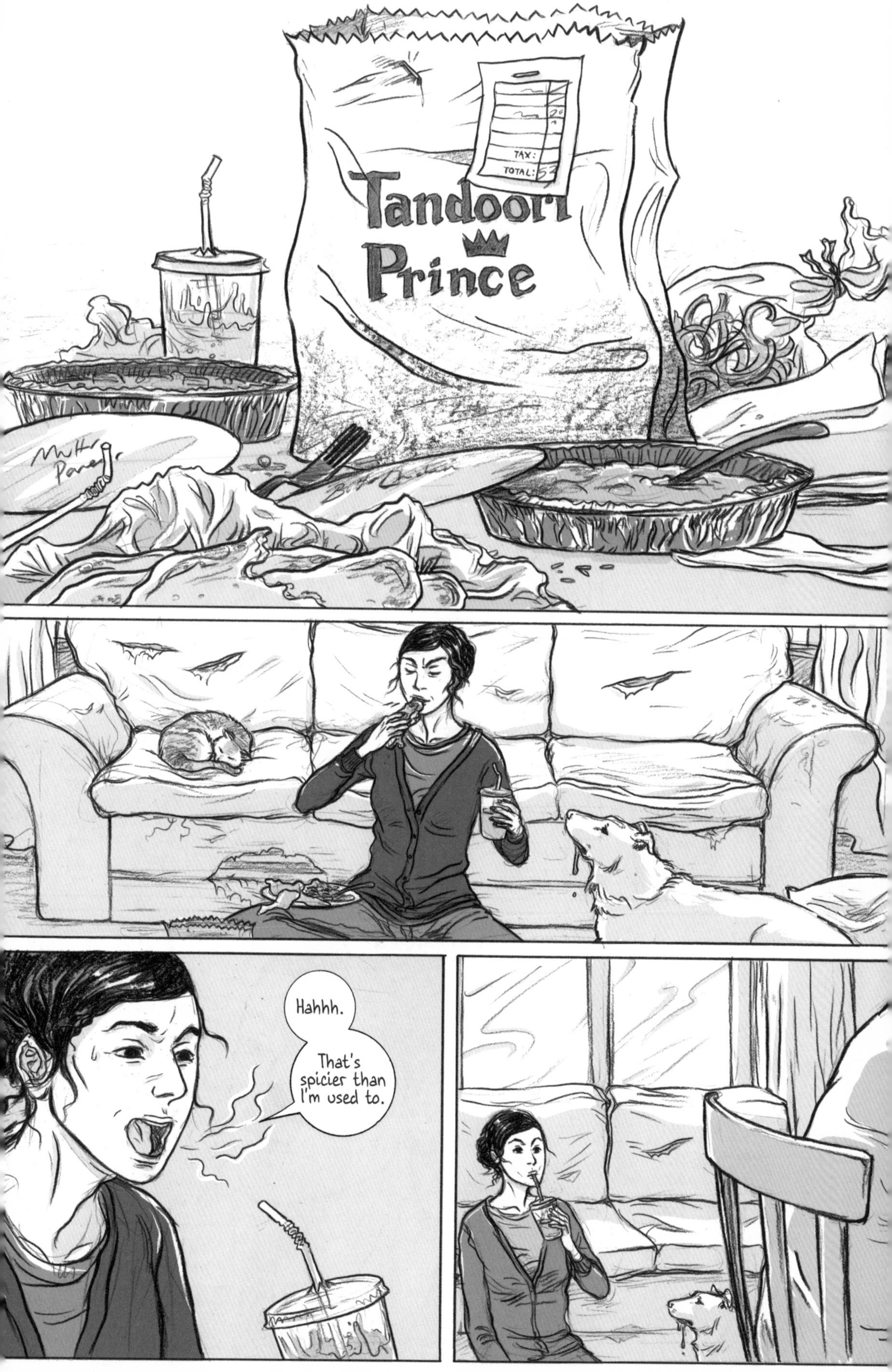
Tandoori Prince
TAX:
TOTAL:
Hahhh.
That's spicier than I'm used to.

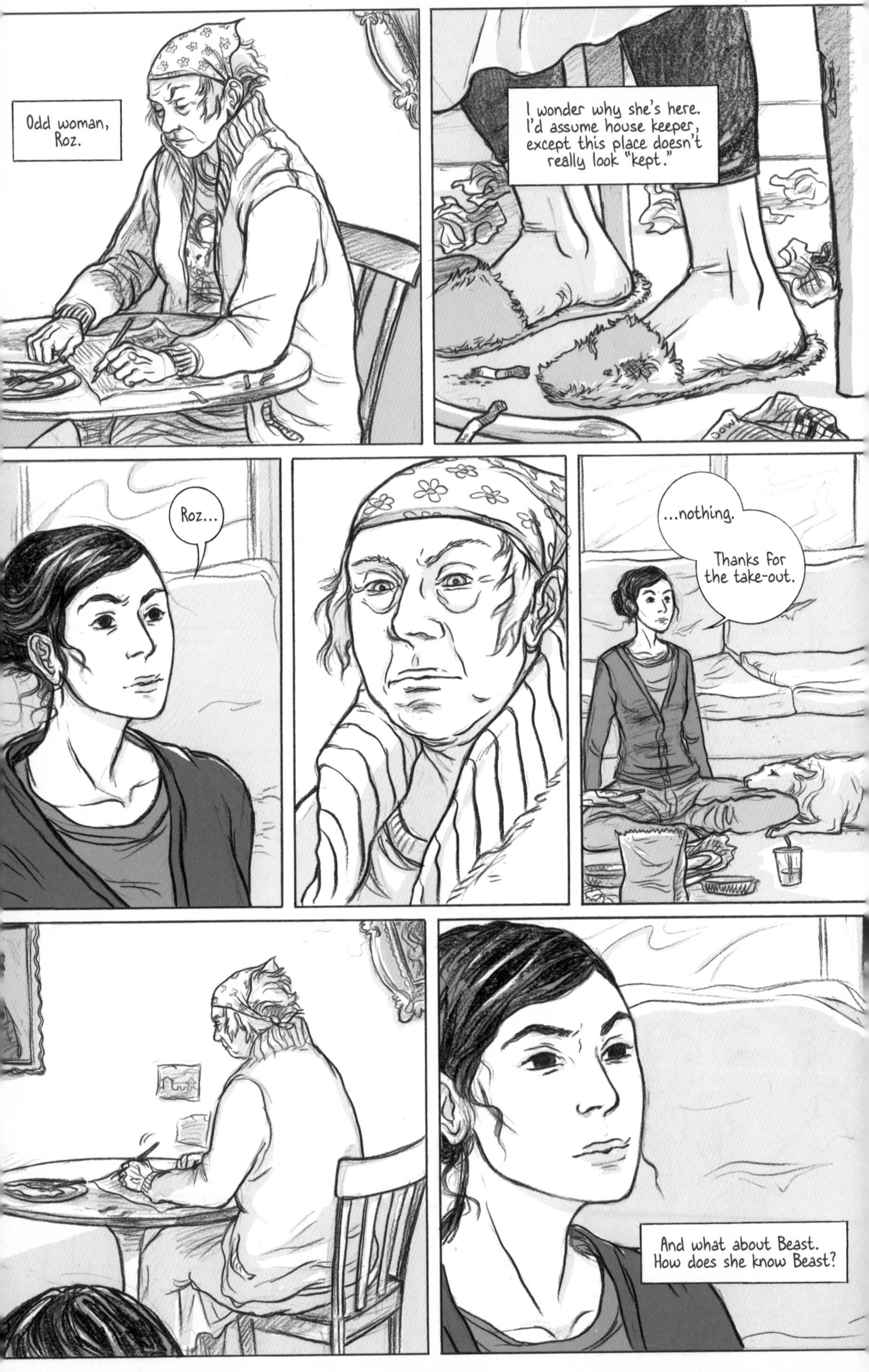
Odd woman, Roz.
I wonder why she's here. I'd assume house keeper, except this place doesn't really look "kept."
Roz...
...nothing.
Thanks for the take-out.
And what about Beast. How does she know Beast?

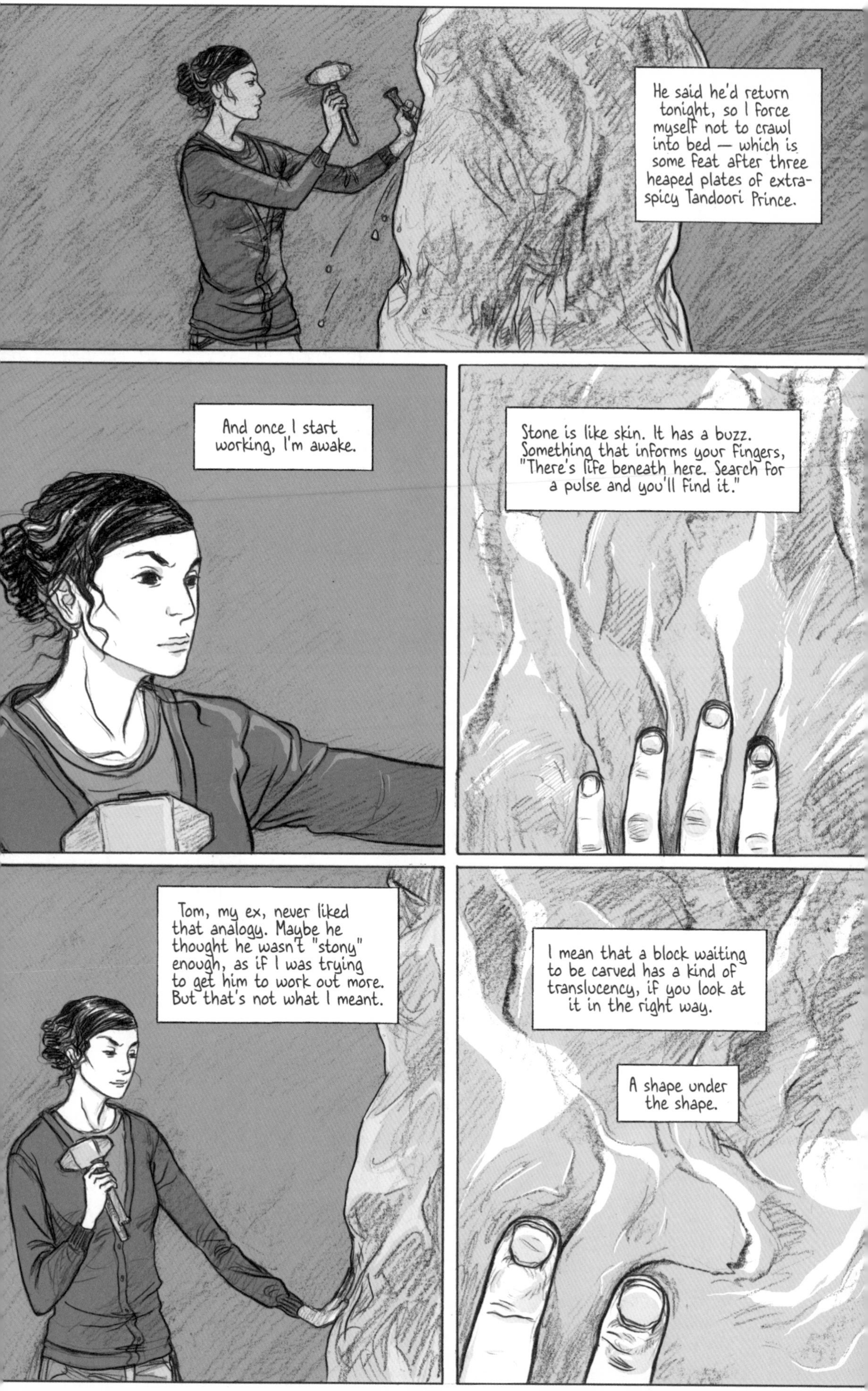
He said he'd return tonight, so I force myself not to crawl into bed — which is some feat after three heaped plates of extra-spicy Tandoori Prince.
And once I start working, I'm awake.
Stone is like skin. It has a buzz. Something that informs your fingers, "There's life beneath here. Search for a pulse and you'll find it."
Tom, my ex, never liked that analogy. Maybe he thought he wasn't "stony" enough, as if I was trying to get him to work out more. But that's not what I meant.
I mean that a block waiting to be carved has a kind of translucency, if you look at it in the right way.
A shape under the shape.

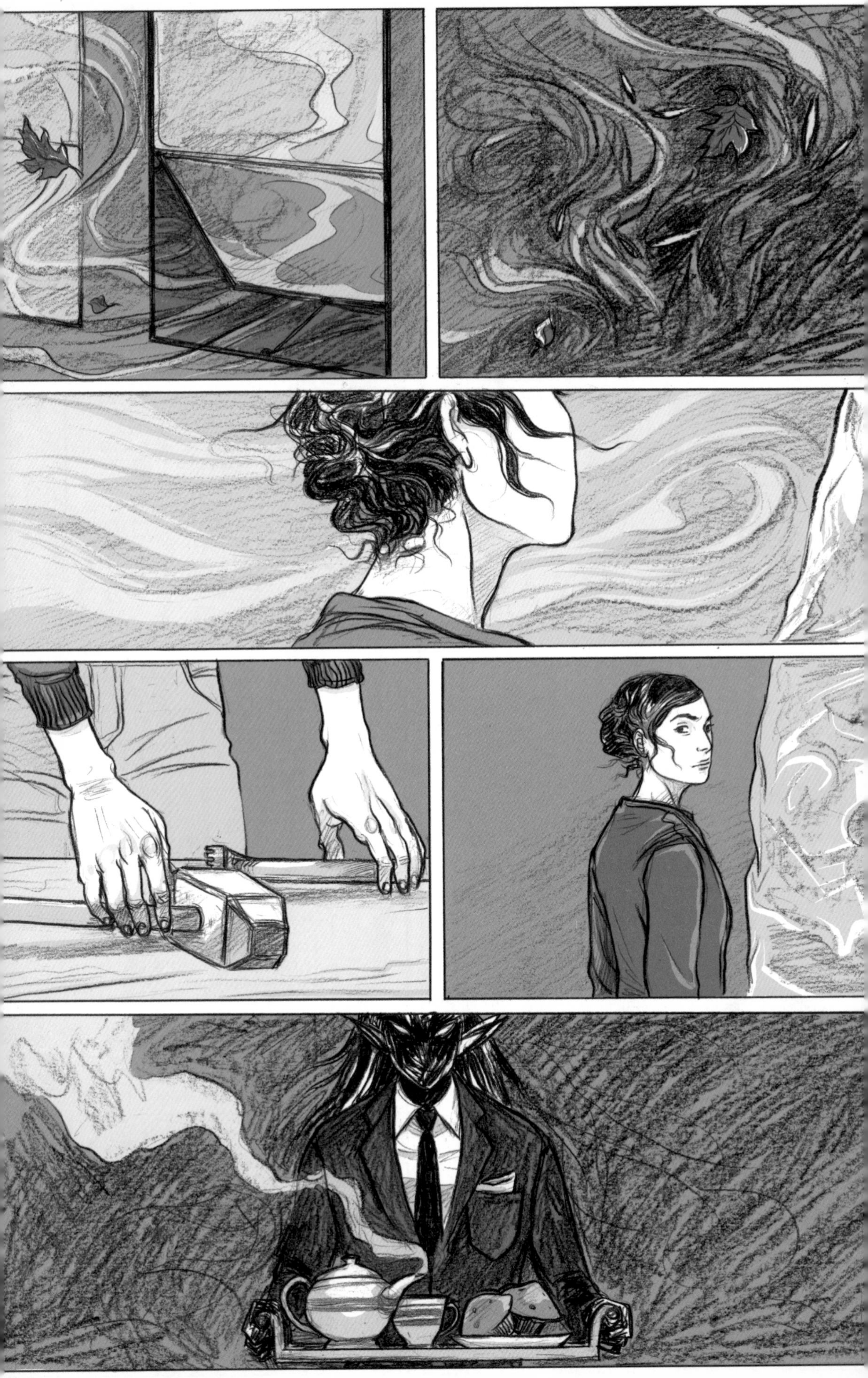

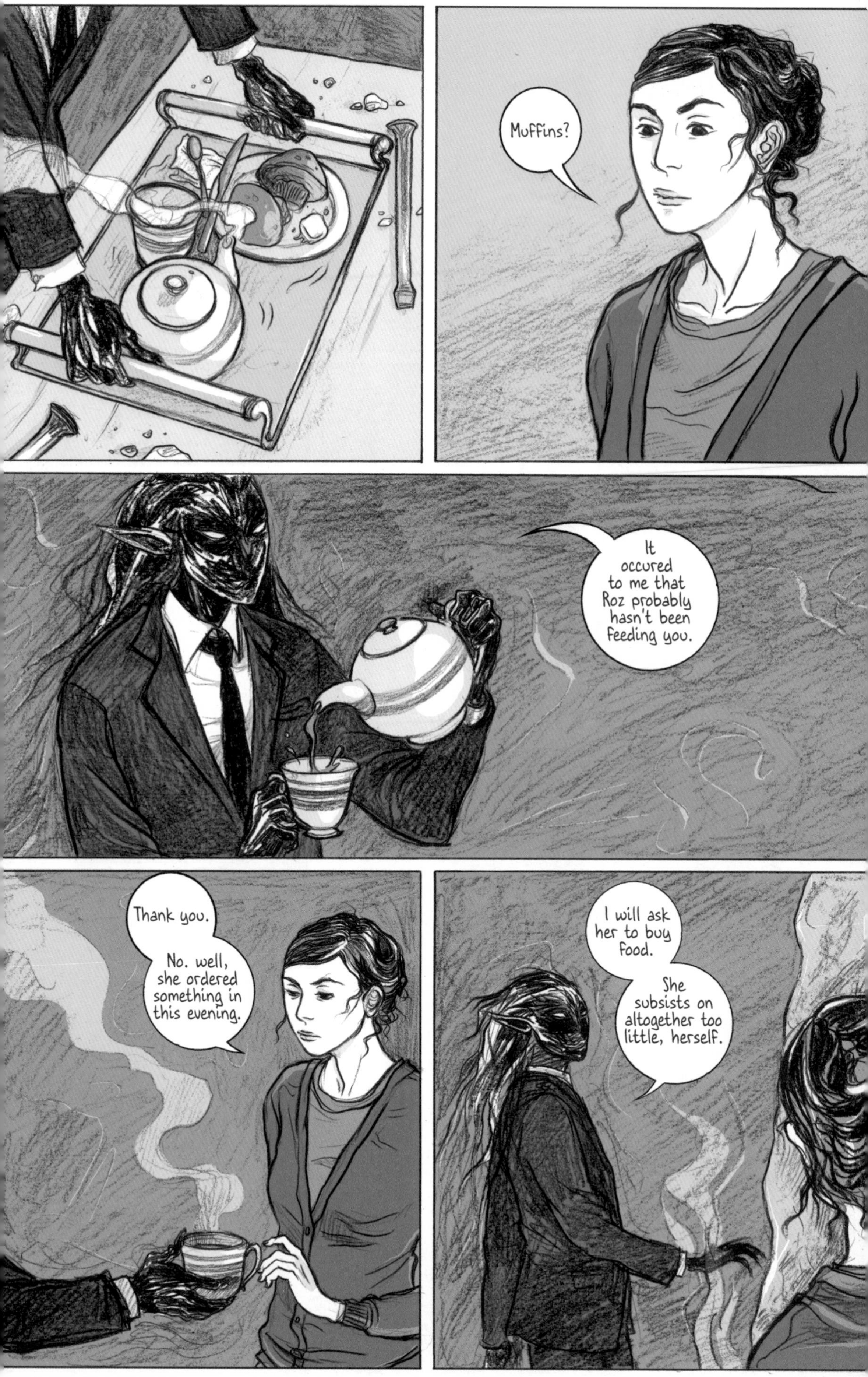
Muffins?
It occured to me that Roz probably hasn't been feeding you.
Thank you.
No. well, she ordered something in this evening.
I will ask her to buy food.
She subsists on altogether too little, herself.

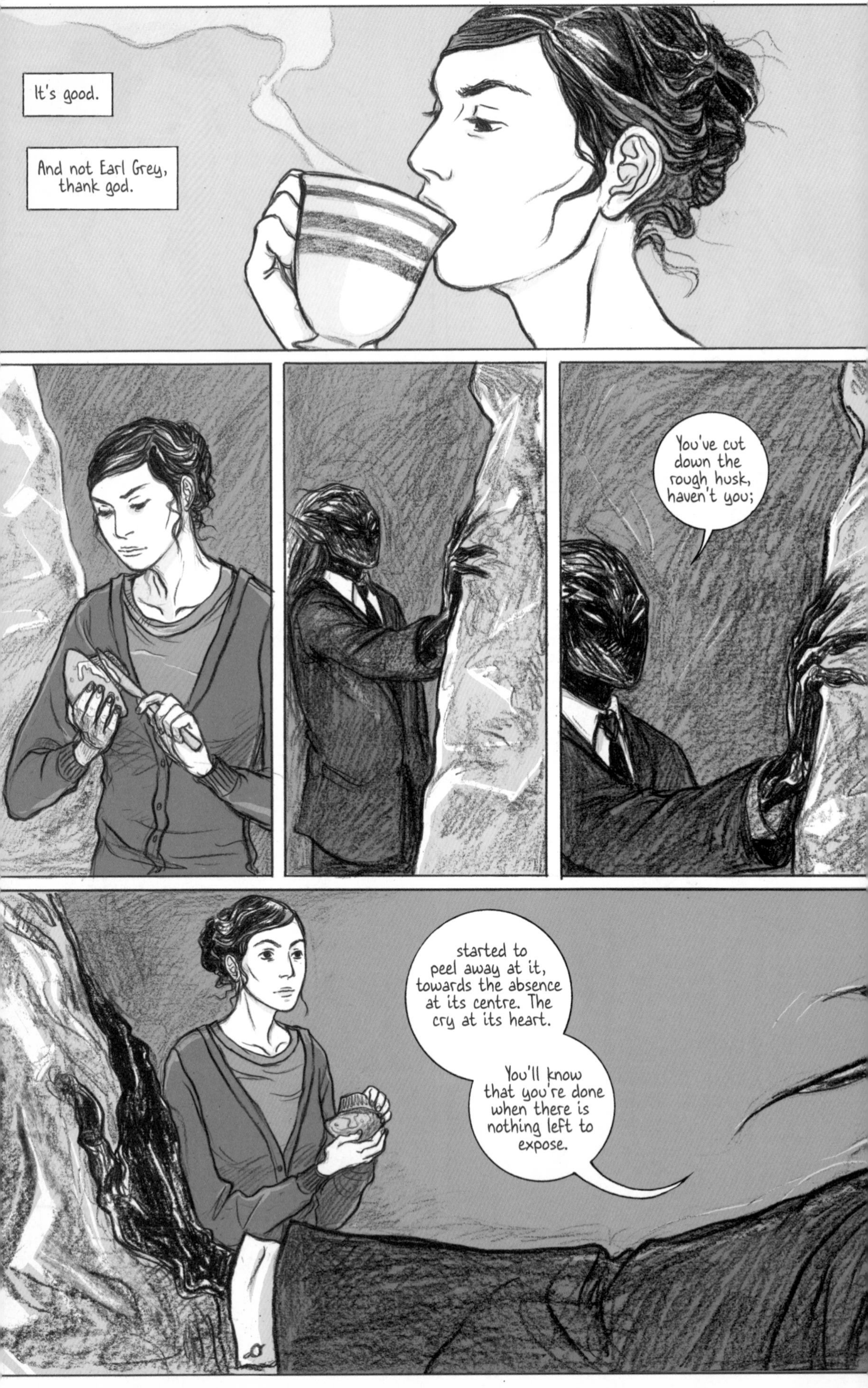
It's good.
And not Earl Grey, thank god.
You've cut down the rough husk, haven't you;
started to peel away at it, towards the absence at its centre. The cry at its heart.
You'll know that you're done when there is nothing left to expose.

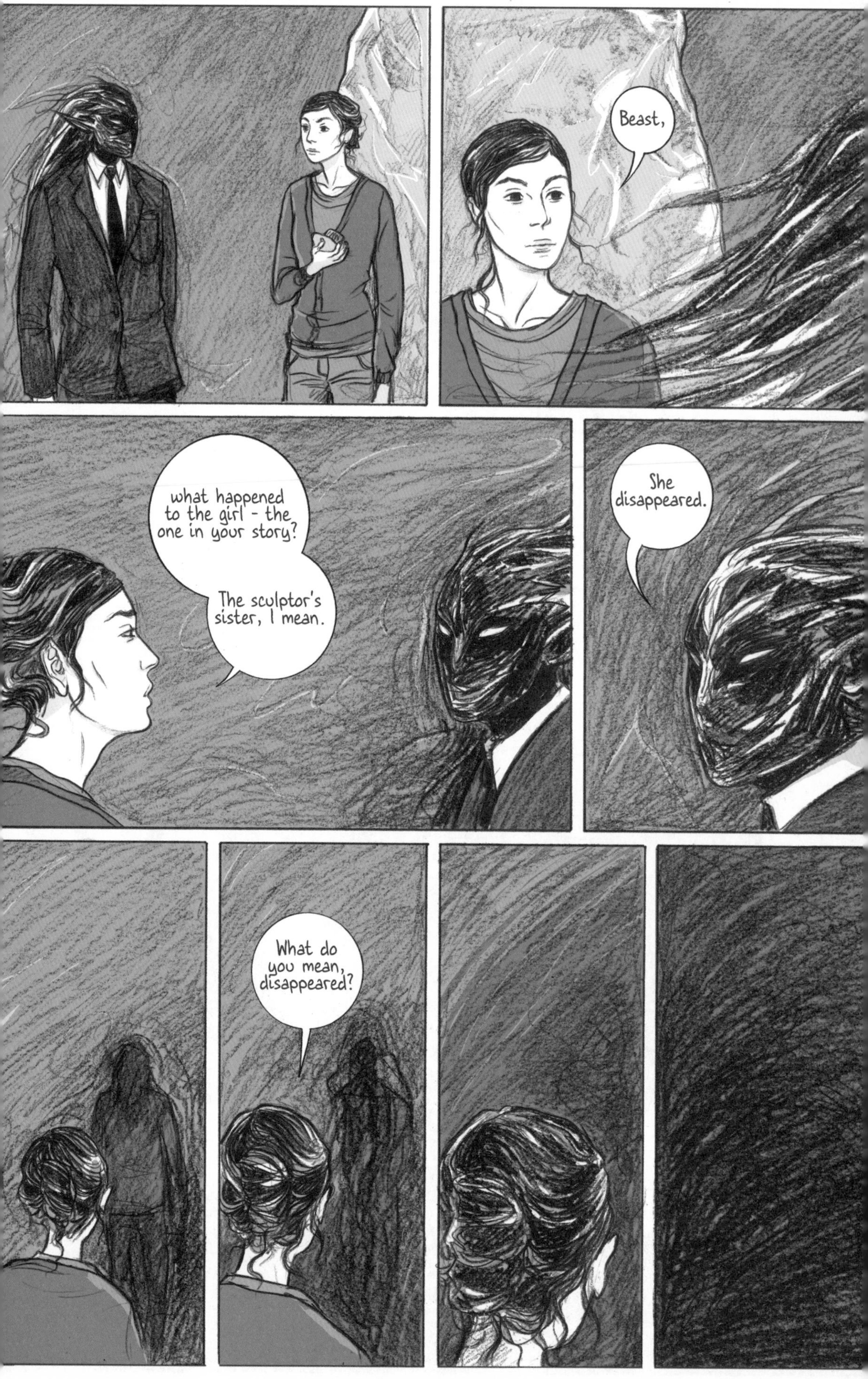
Beast,
what happened to the girl - the one in your story?
The sculptor's sister, I mean.
She disappeared.
What do you mean, disappeared?

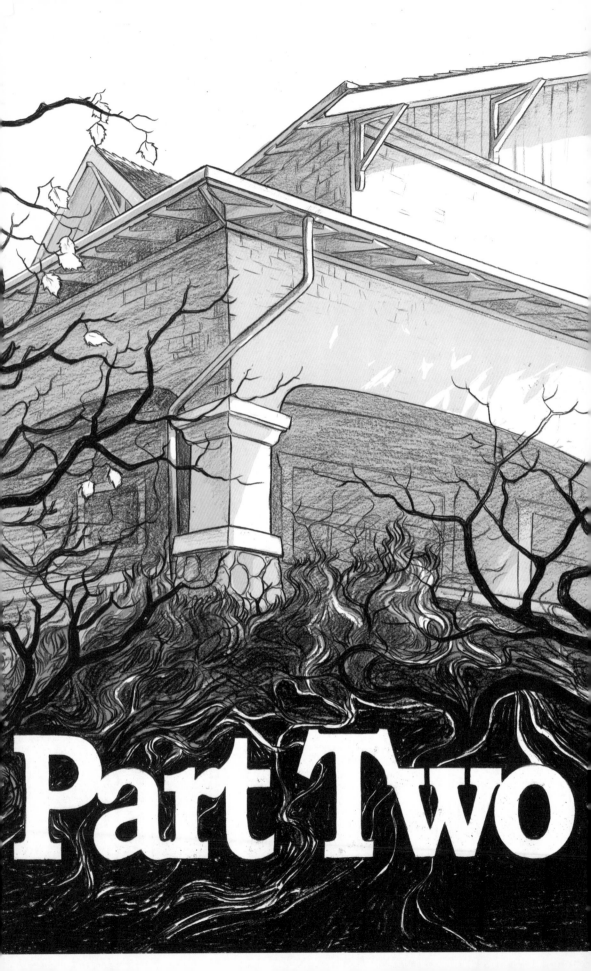

Part Two

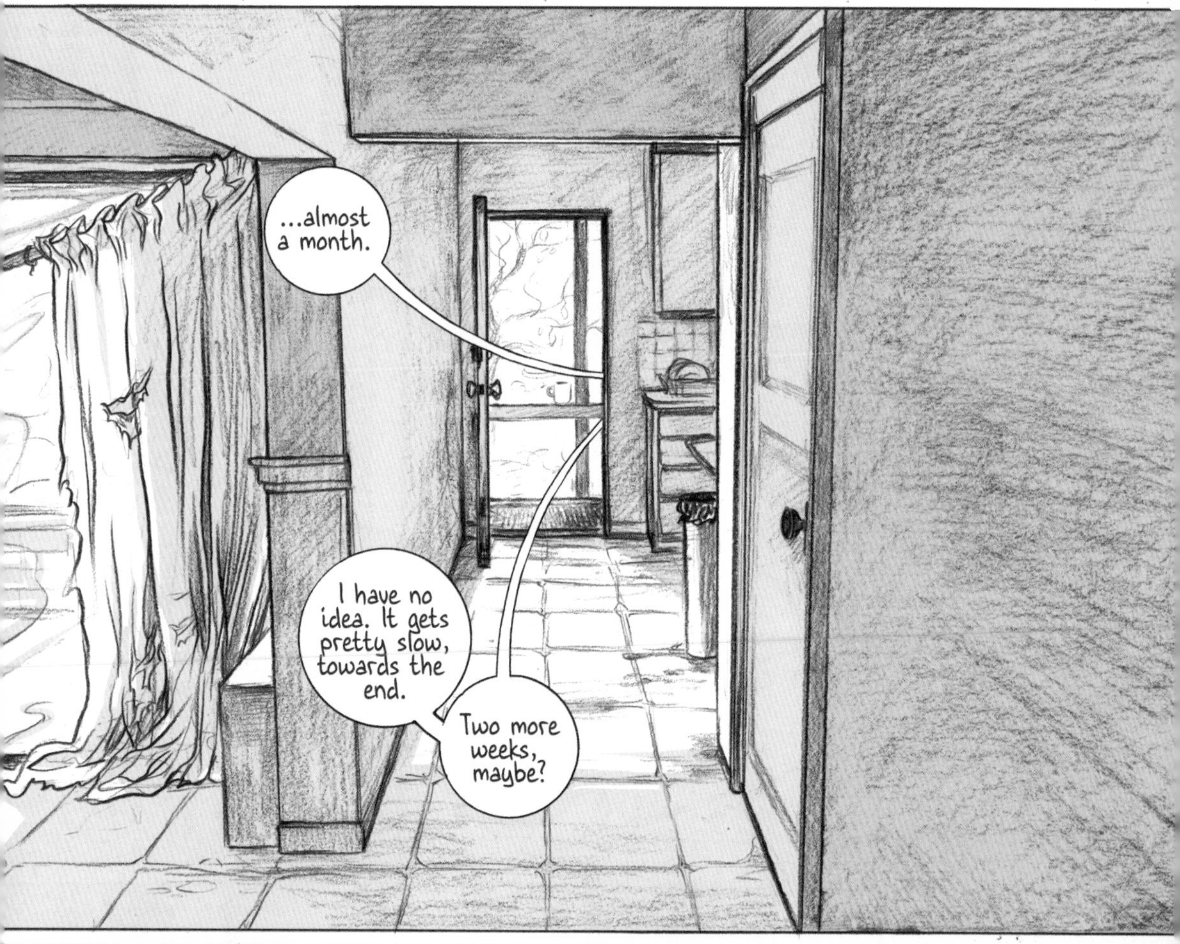
...almost a month.
I have no idea. It gets pretty slow, towards the end.
Two more weeks, maybe?

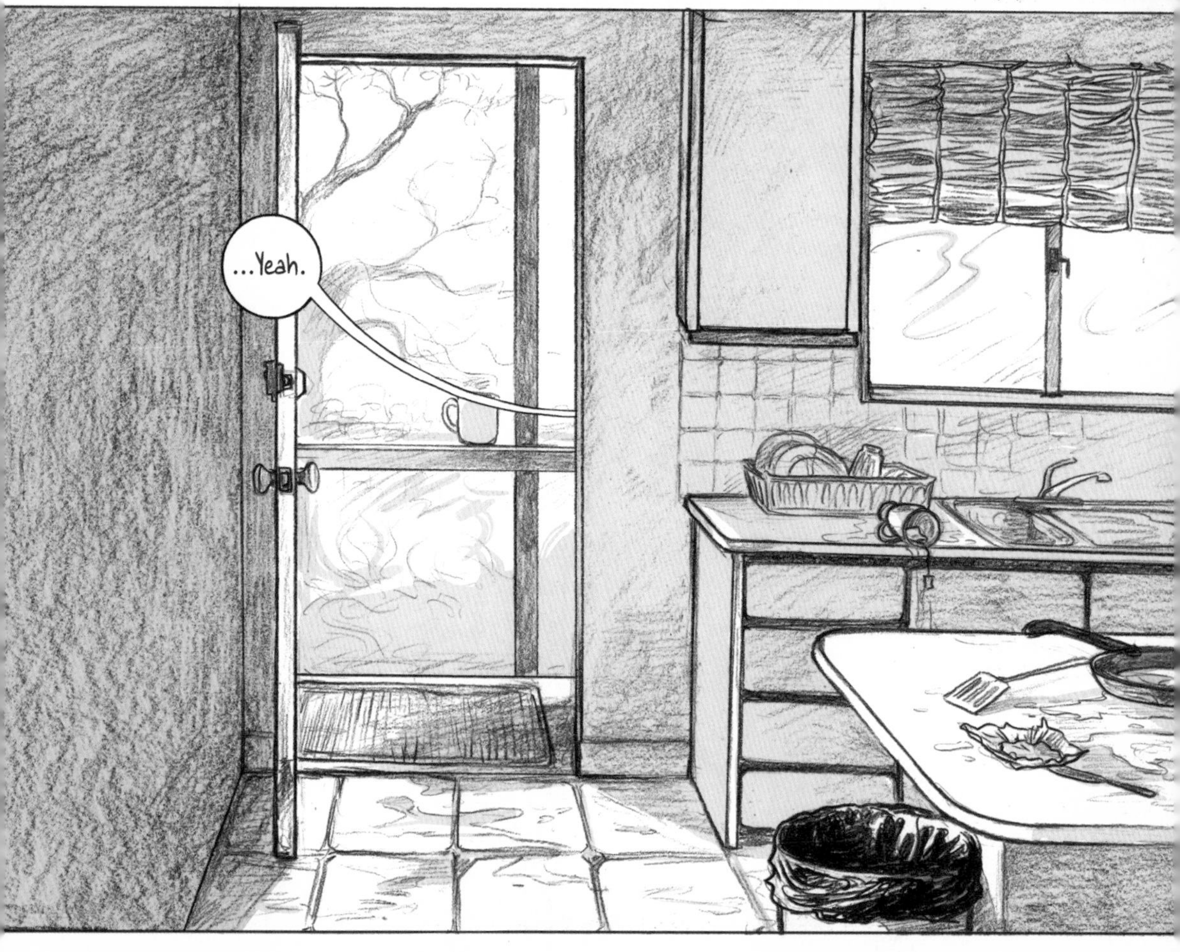
...Yeah.

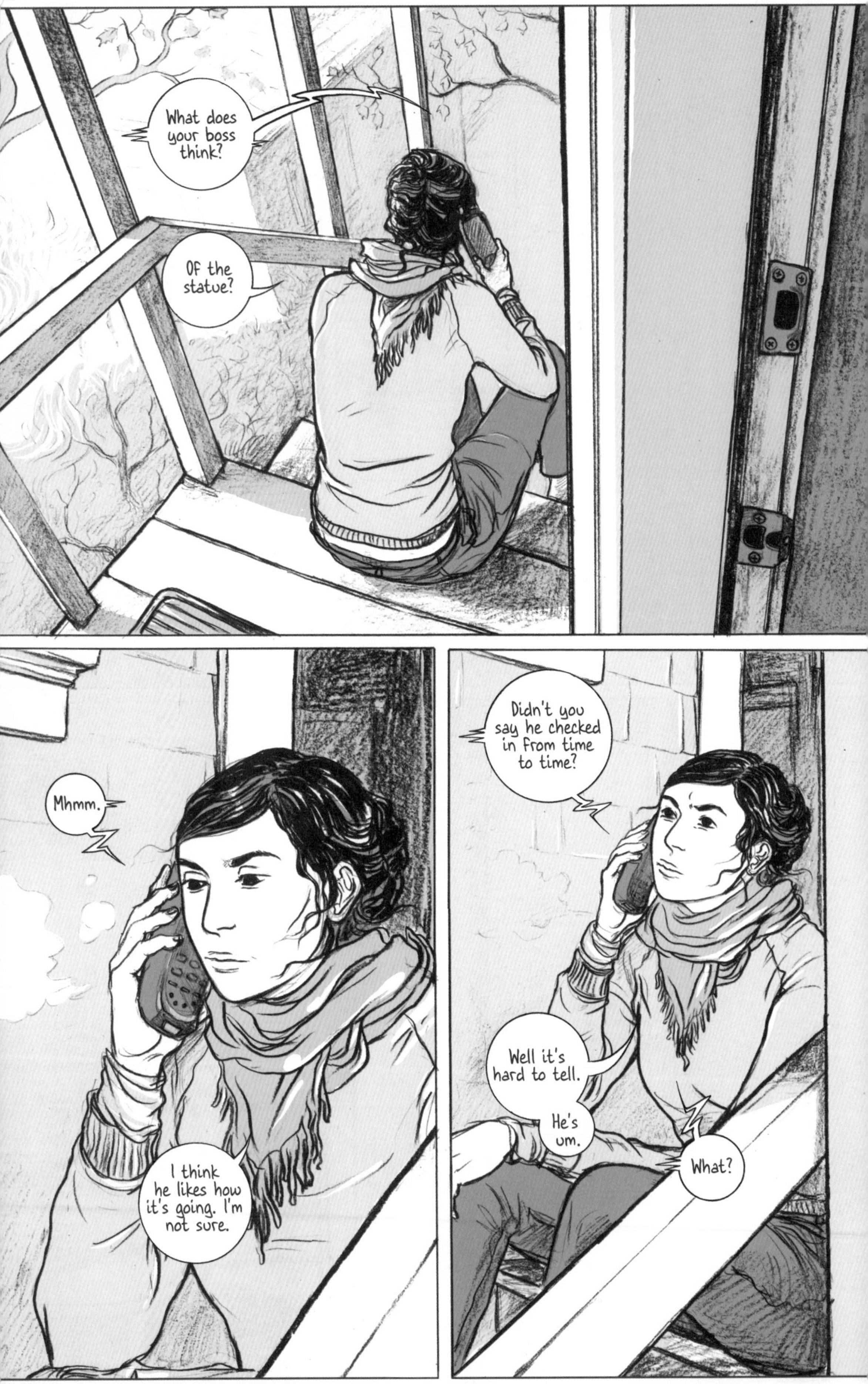
What does your boss think?
Of the statue?
Mhmm.
I think he likes how it's going. I'm not sure.
Didn't you say he checked in from time to time?
Well it's hard to tell.
He's um.
What?

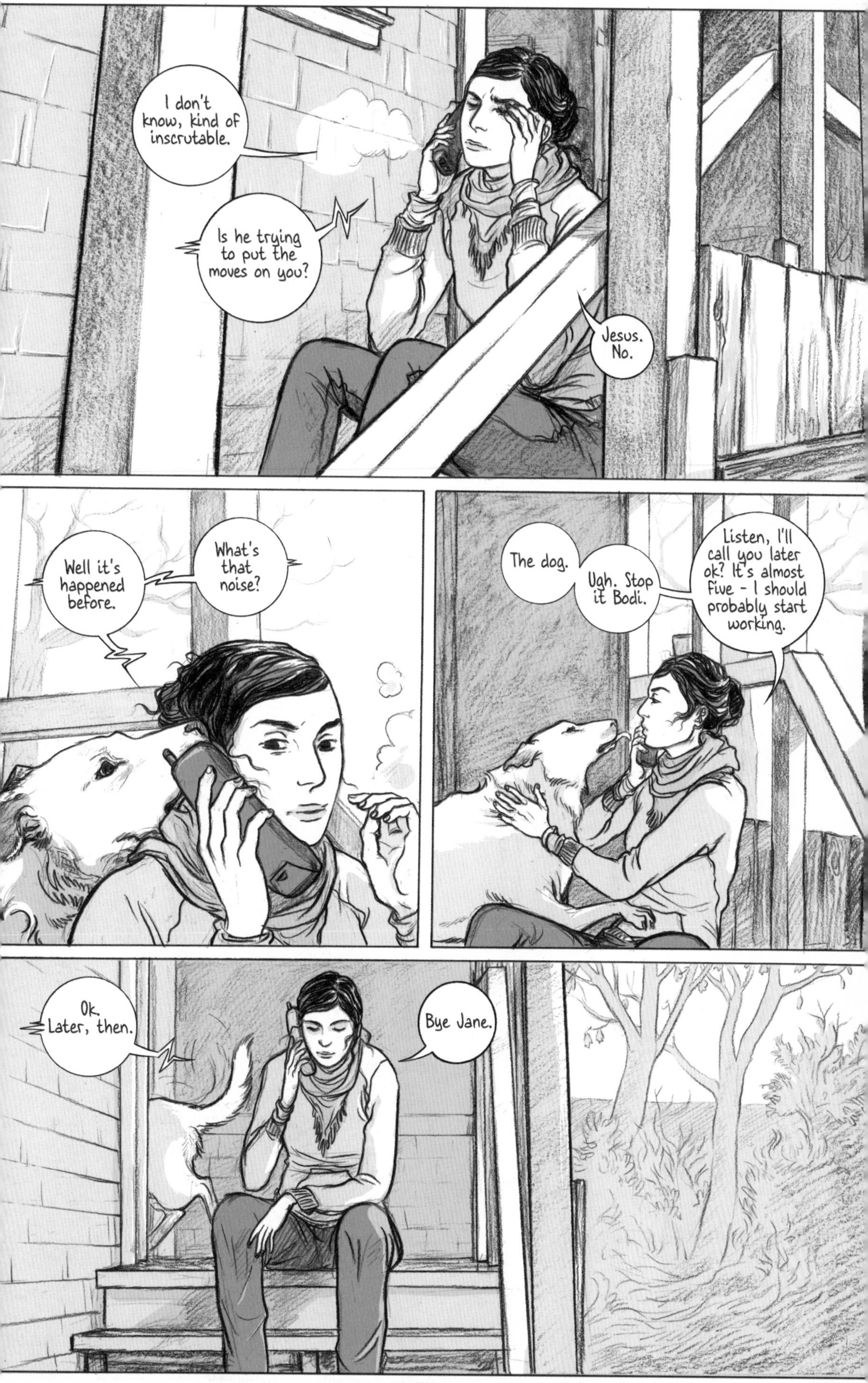
I don't know, kind of inscrutable.
Is he trying to put the moves on you?
Jesus. No.
Well it's happened before.
What's that noise?
The dog.
Ugh. Stop it Bodi.
Listen, I'll call you later ok? It's almost five - I should probably start working.
Ok. Later, then.
Bye Jane.

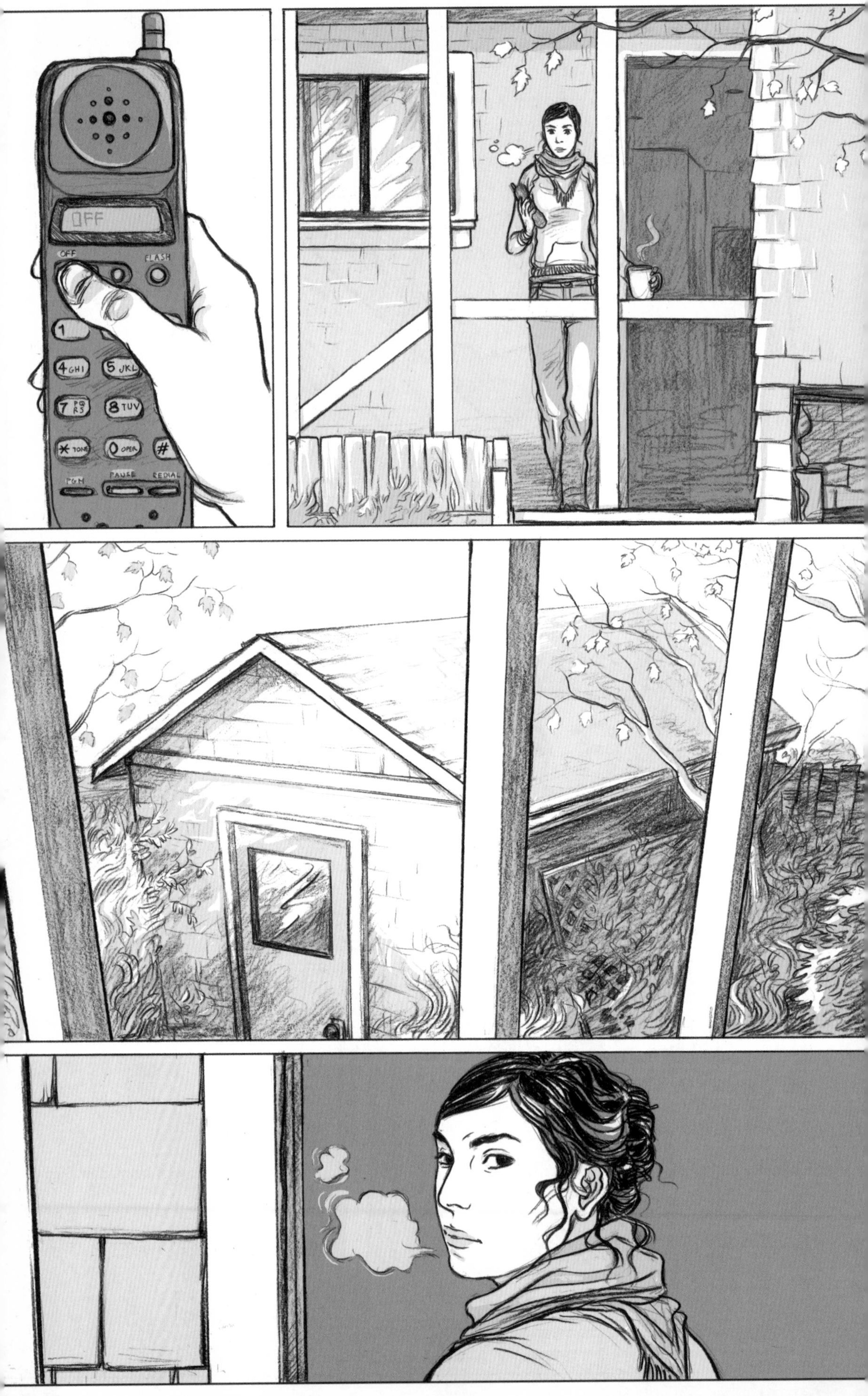
OFF
OFF
FLASH
1
4 GHI
5 JKL
8 TUV
0 OPER
#
PGM
PAUSE
REDIAL

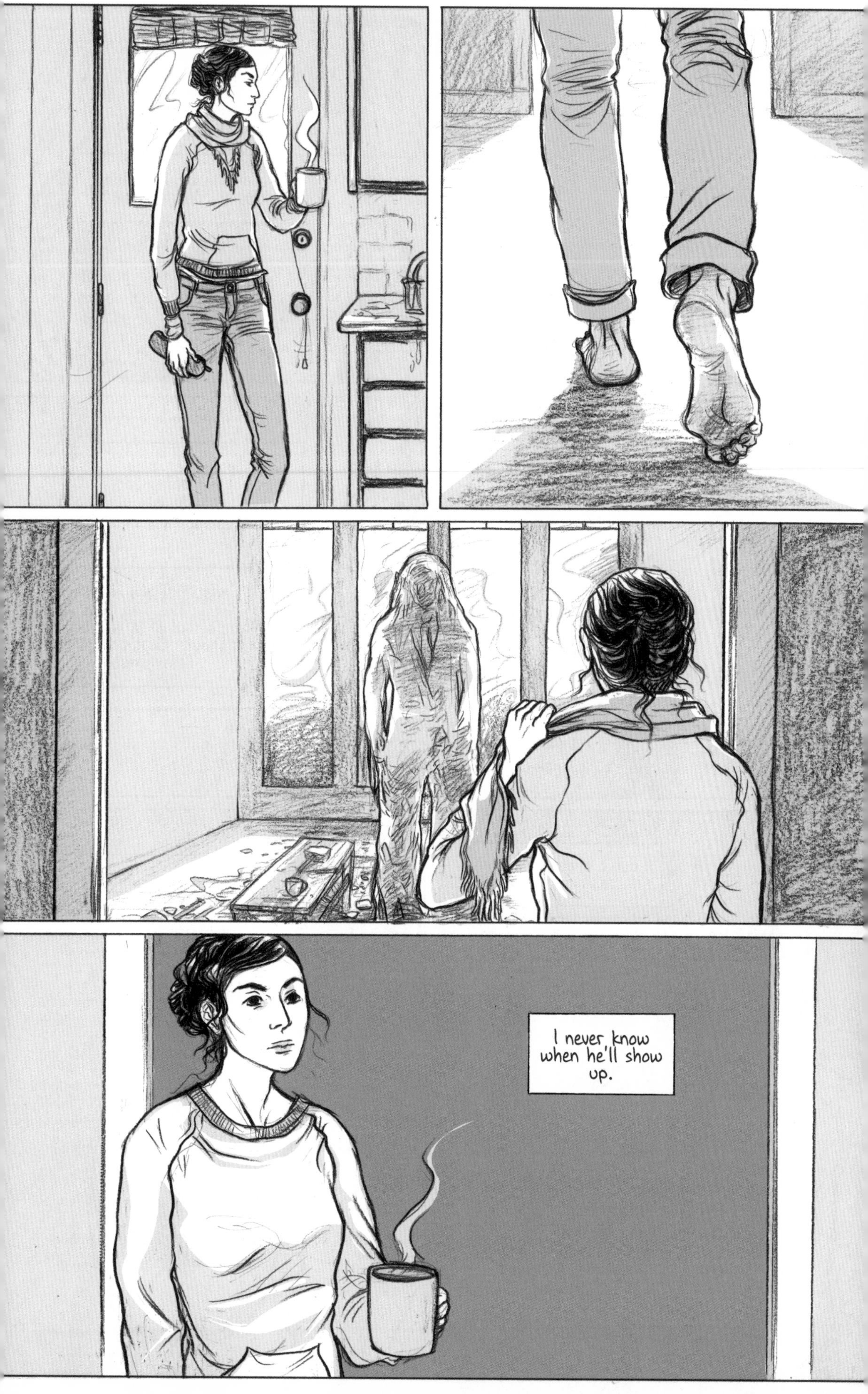
I never know when he'll show up.

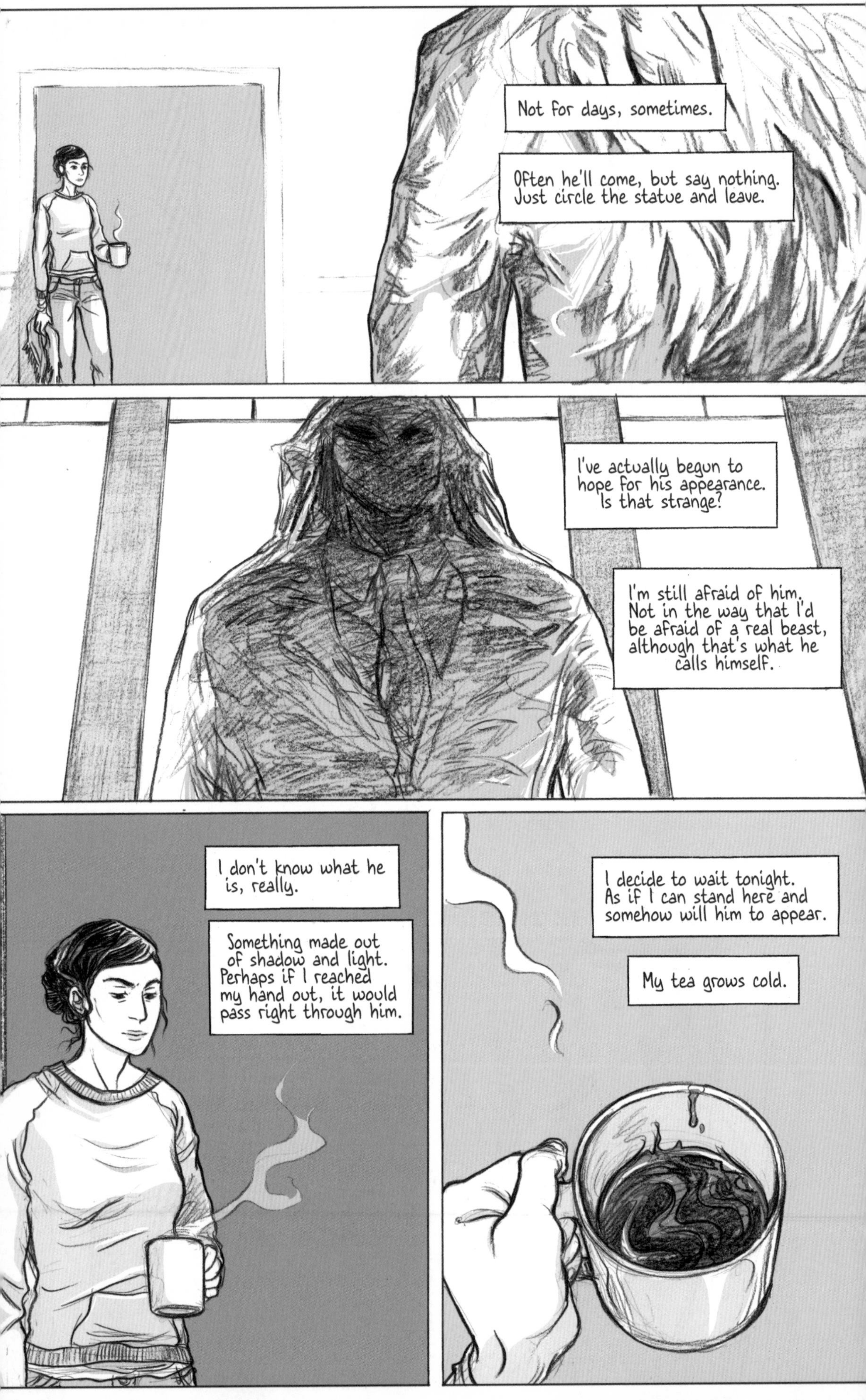
Not for days, sometimes.
Often he'll come, but say nothing. Just circle the statue and leave.
I've actually begun to hope for his appearance. Is that strange?
I'm still afraid of him. Not in the way that I'd be afraid of a real beast, although that's what he calls himself.
I don't know what he is, really.
Something made out of shadow and light. Perhaps if I reached my hand out, it would pass right through him.
I decide to wait tonight. As if I can stand here and somehow will him to appear.
My tea grows cold.

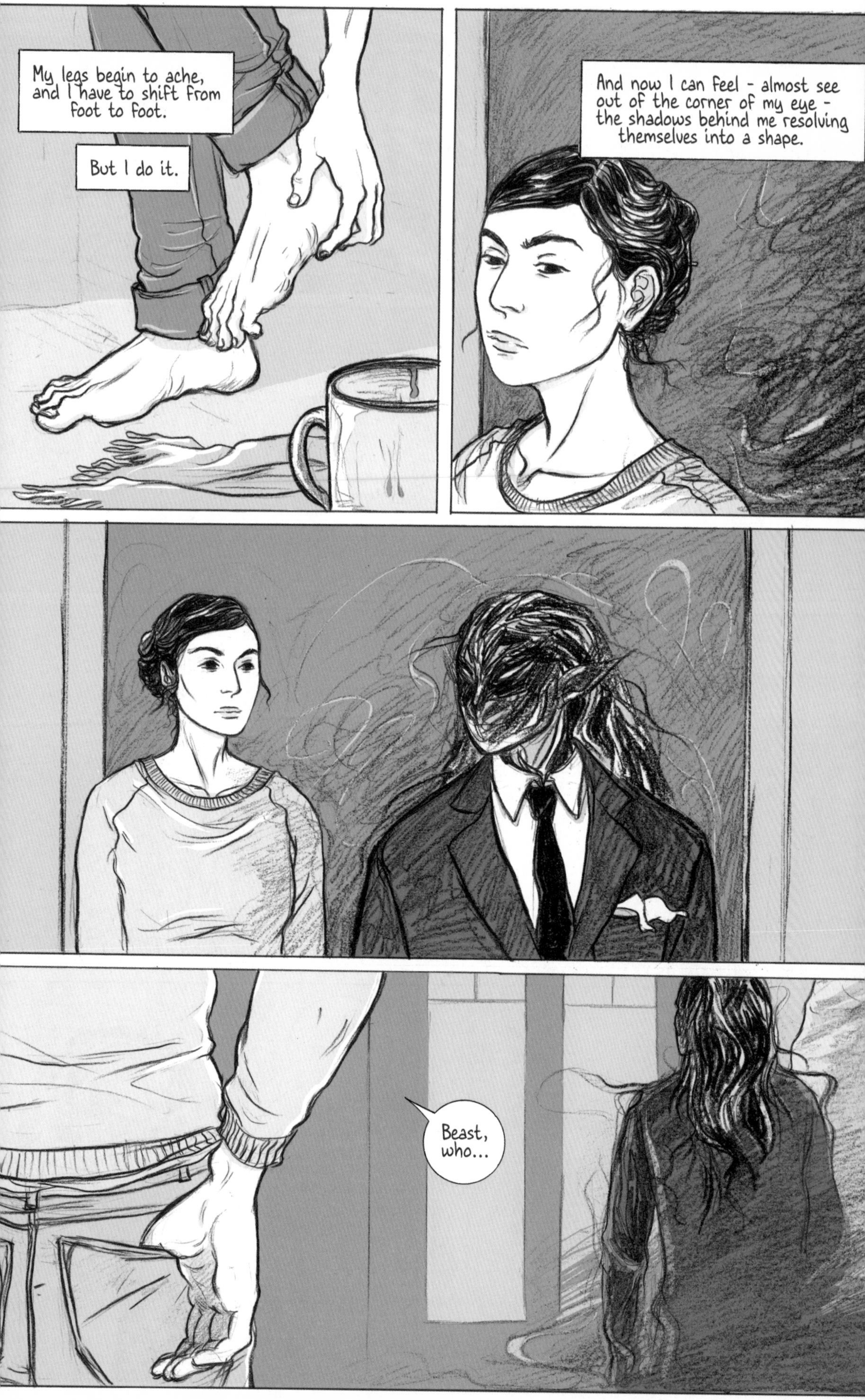
My legs begin to ache, and I have to shift from foot to foot.
But I do it.
And now I can feel - almost see out of the corner of my eye - the shadows behind me resolving themselves into a shape.
Beast, who...

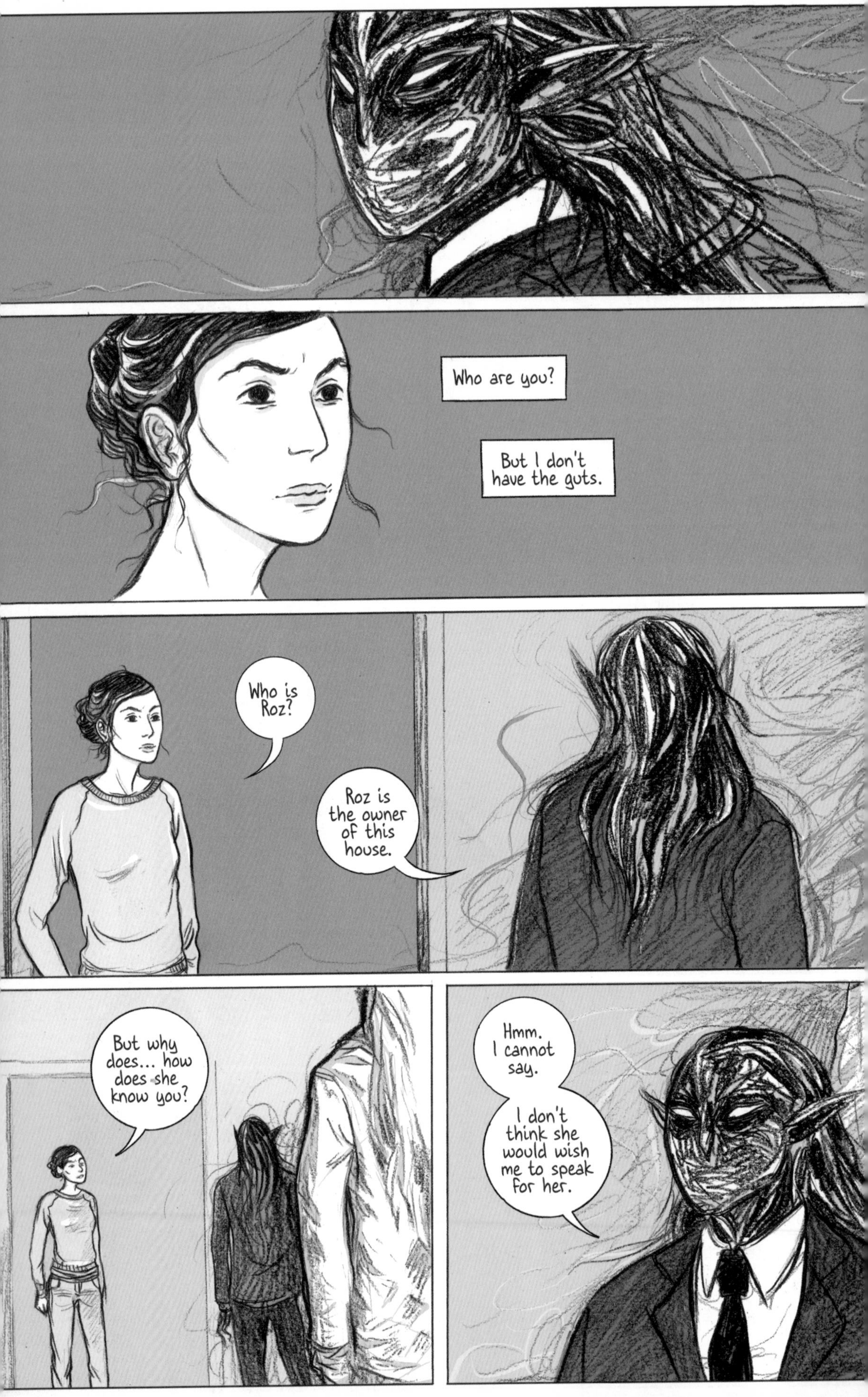
Who are you?
But I don't have the guts.
Who is Roz?
Roz is the owner of this house.
But why does... how does she know you?
Hmm. I cannot say.
I don't think she would wish me to speak for her.

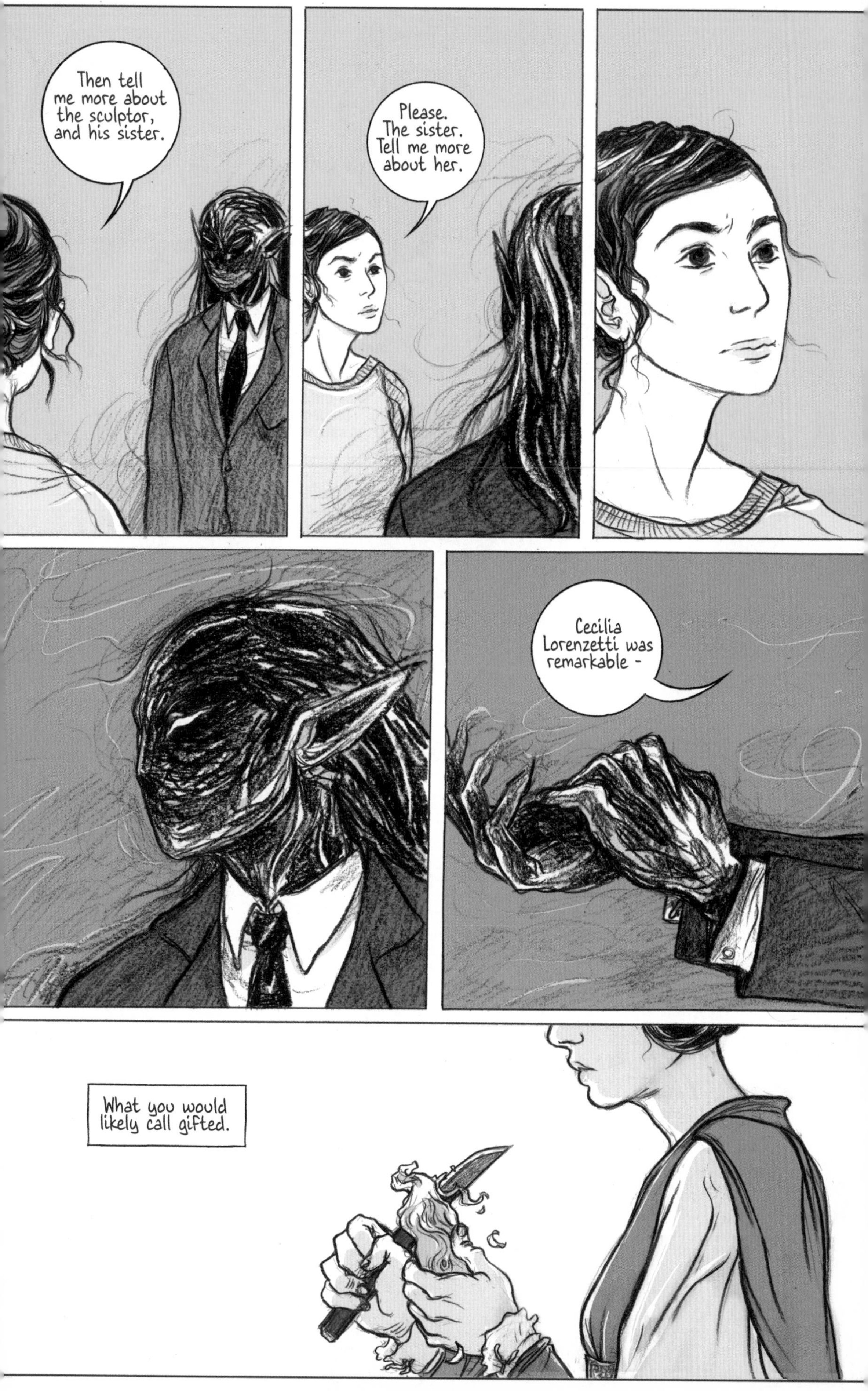
Then tell me more about the sculptor, and his sister.
Please. The sister. Tell me more about her.
Cecilia Lorenzetti was remarkable -
What you would likely call gifted.

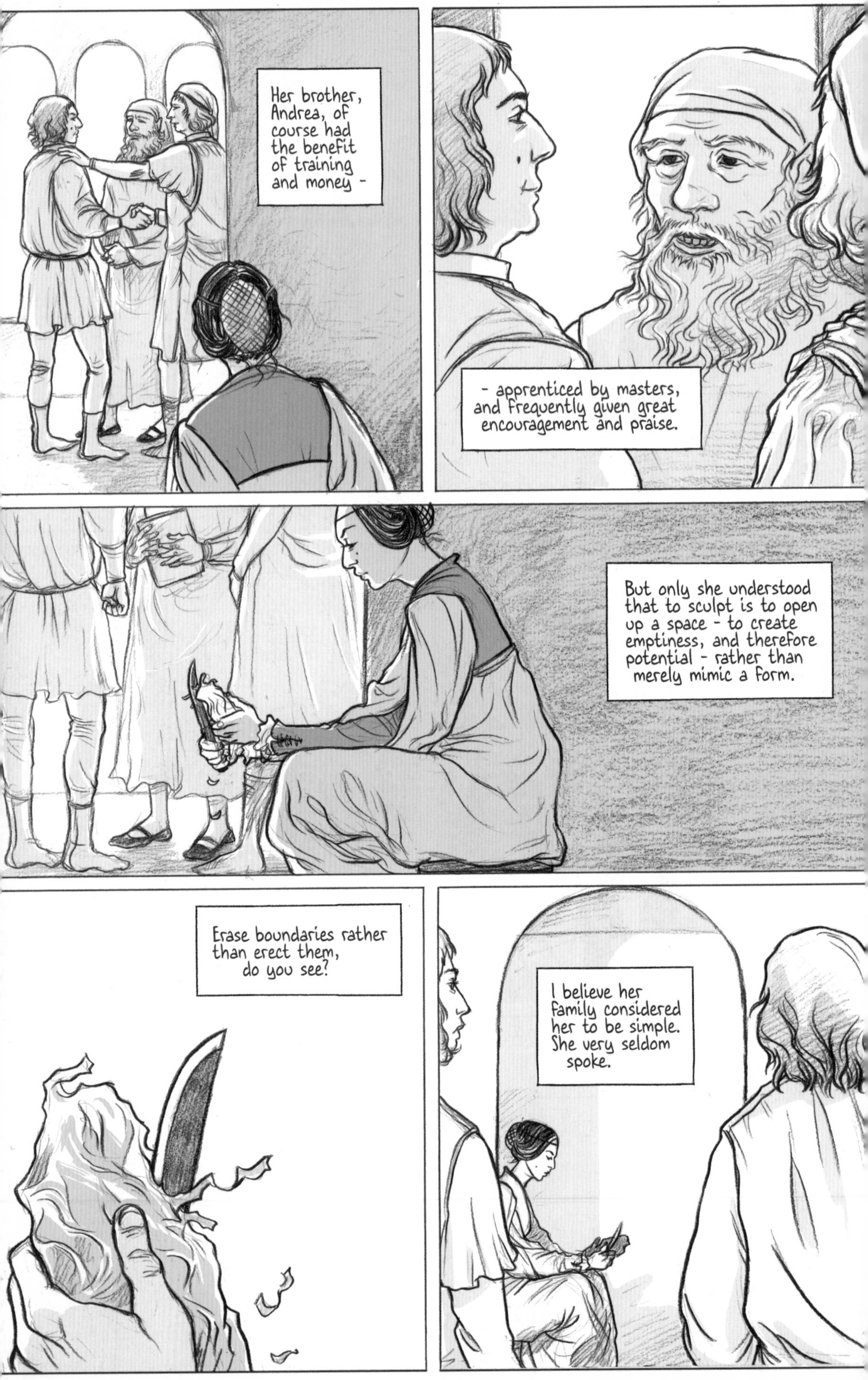
Her brother, Andrea, of course had the benefit of training and money -
- apprenticed by masters, and frequently given great encouragement and praise.
But only she understood that to sculpt is to open up a space - to create emptiness, and therefore potential - rather than merely mimic a form.
Erase boundaries rather than erect them, do you see?
I believe her family considered her to be simple. She very seldom spoke.

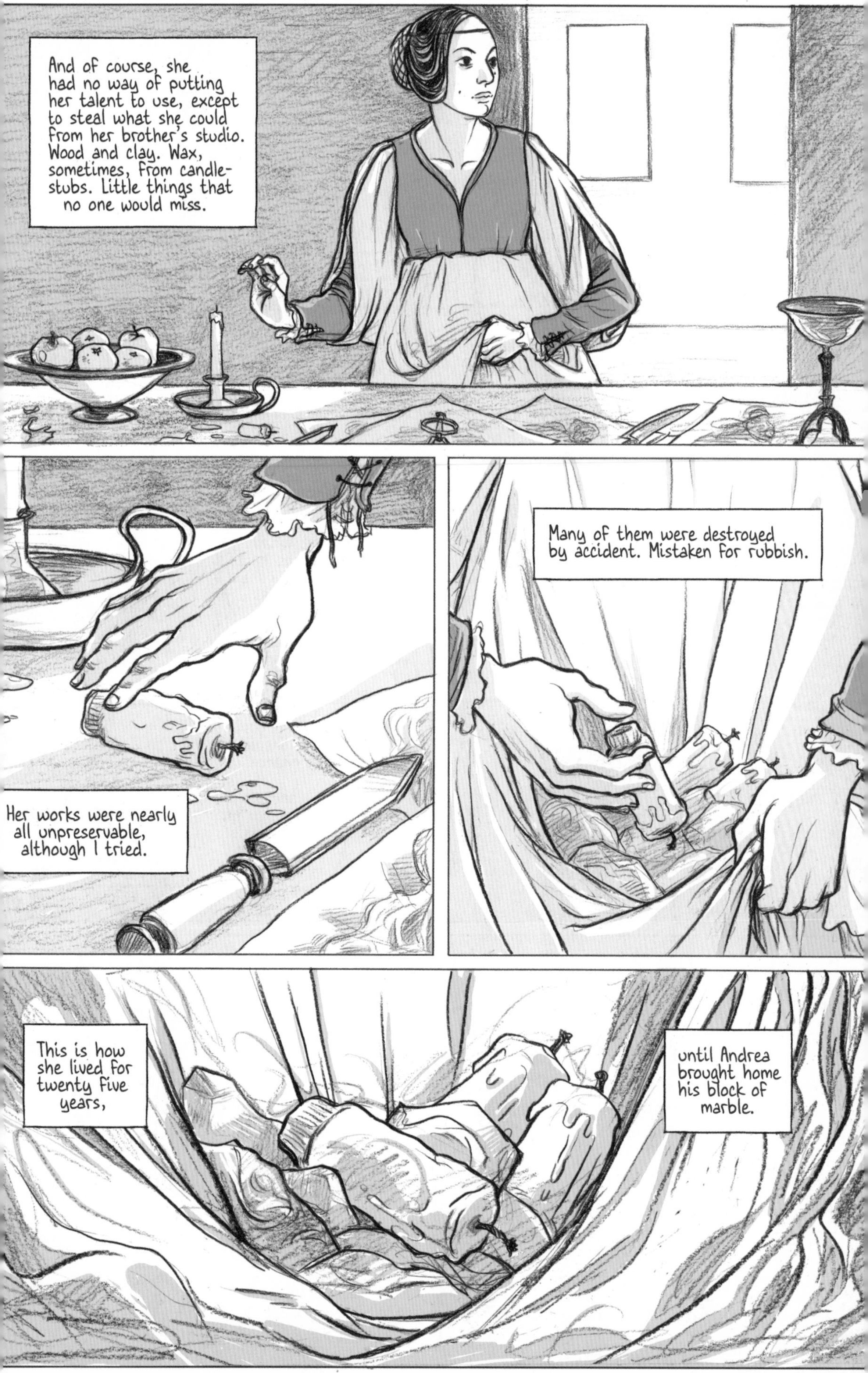
And of course, she had no way of putting her talent to use, except to steal what she could from her brother's studio. Wood and clay. Wax, sometimes, from candle-stubs. Little things that no one would miss.
Her works were nearly all unpreservable, although I tried.
Many of them were destroyed by accident. Mistaken for rubbish.
This is how she lived for twenty five years,
until Andrea brought home his block of marble.

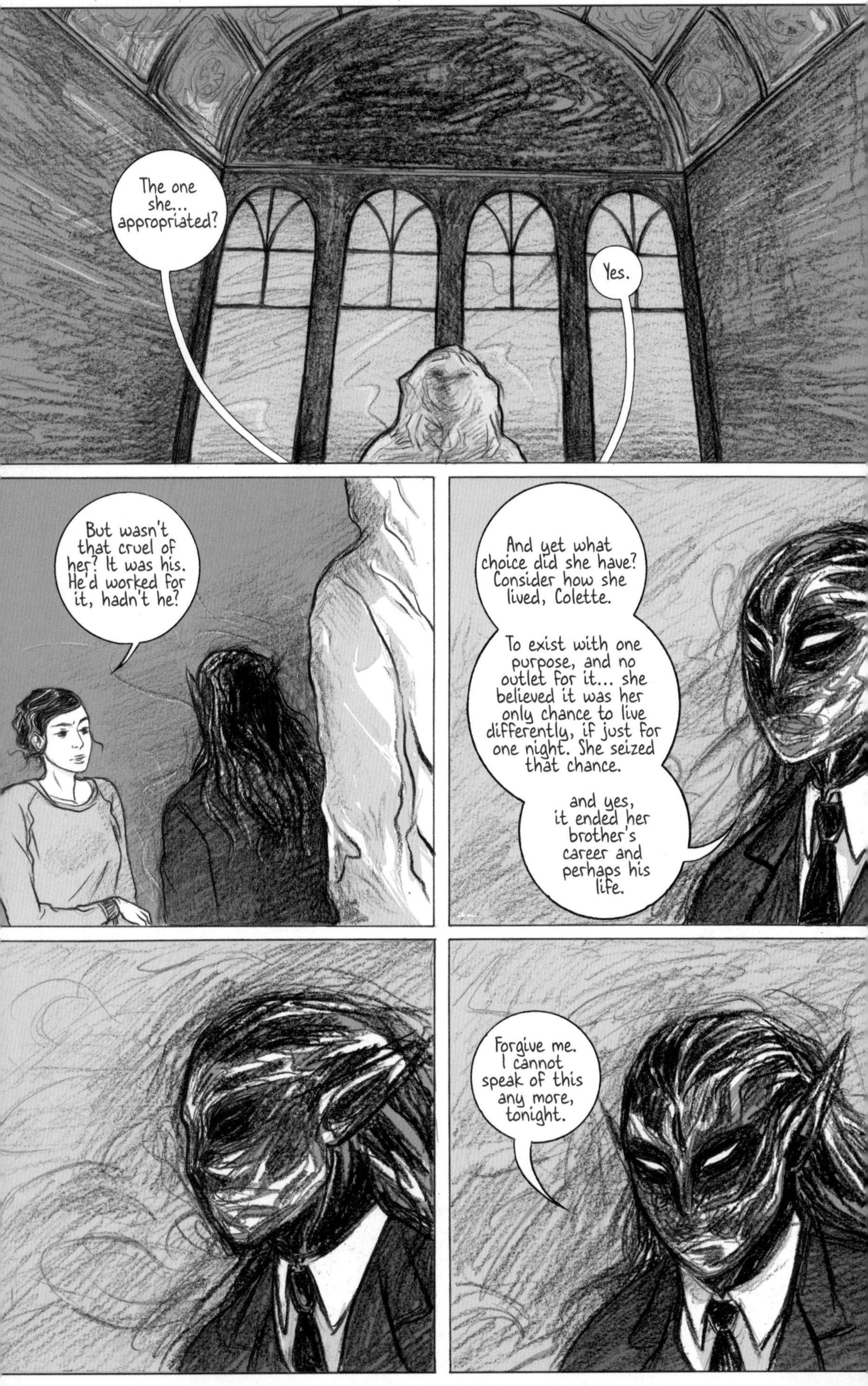
The one she... appropriated?
Yes.
But wasn't that cruel of her? It was his. He'd worked for it, hadn't he?
And yet what choice did she have? Consider how she lived, Colette.
To exist with one purpose, and no outlet for it... she believed it was her only chance to live differently, if just for one night. She seized that chance.
and yes, it ended her brother's career and perhaps his life.
Forgive me. I cannot speak of this any more, tonight.

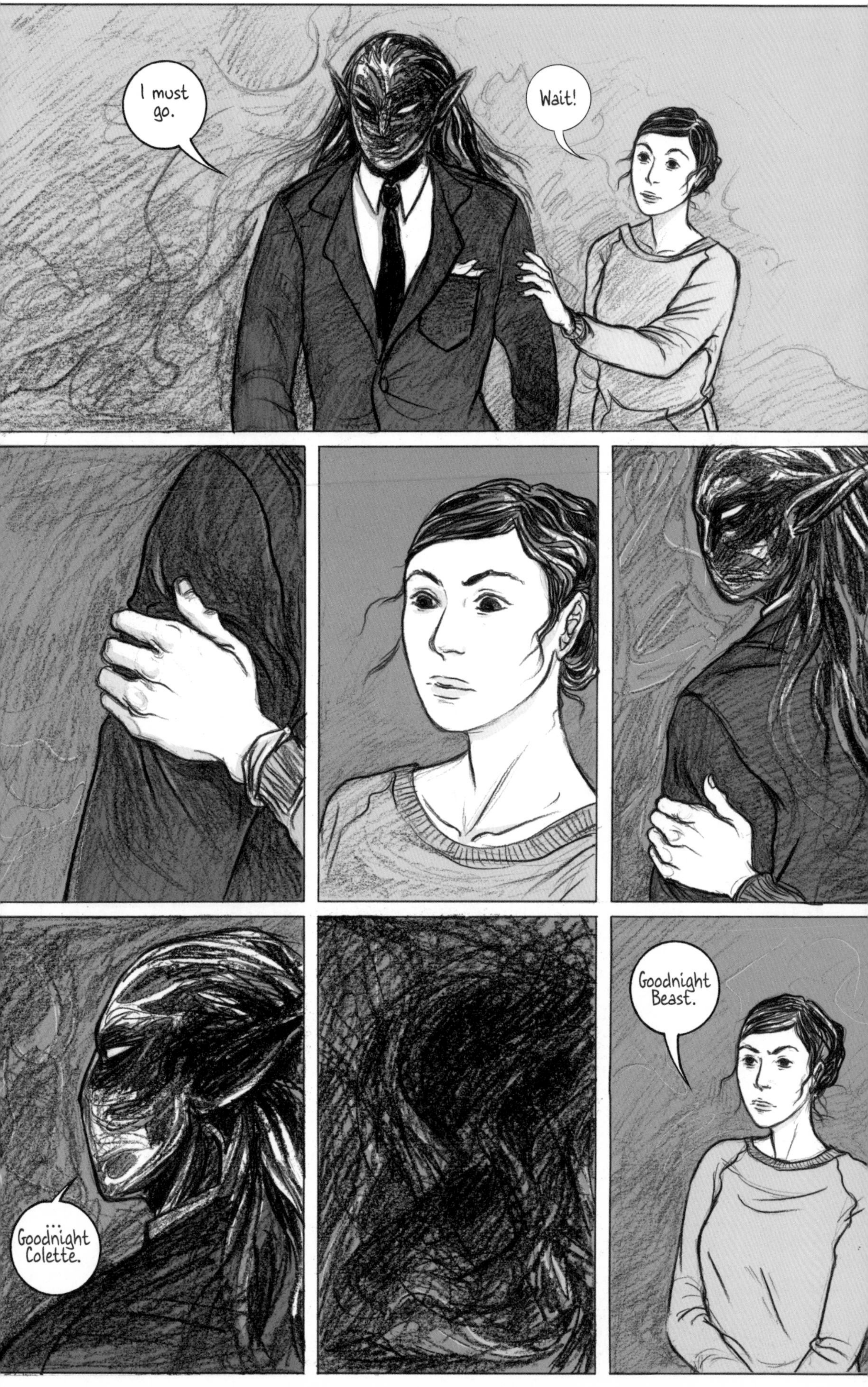
I must go.
Wait!
...Goodnight Colette.
Goodnight Beast.

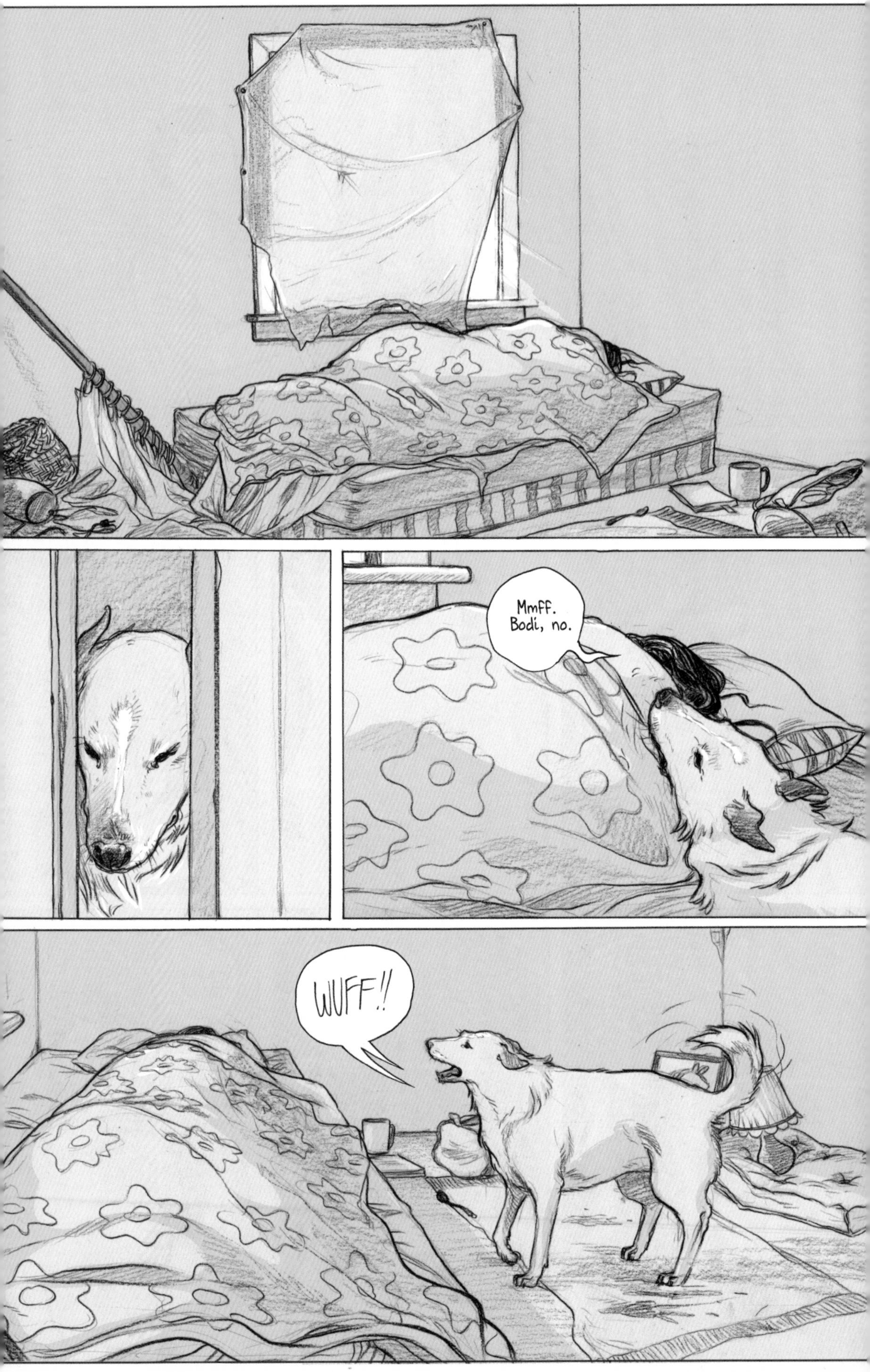
Mmff.
Bodi, no.
WUFF!!

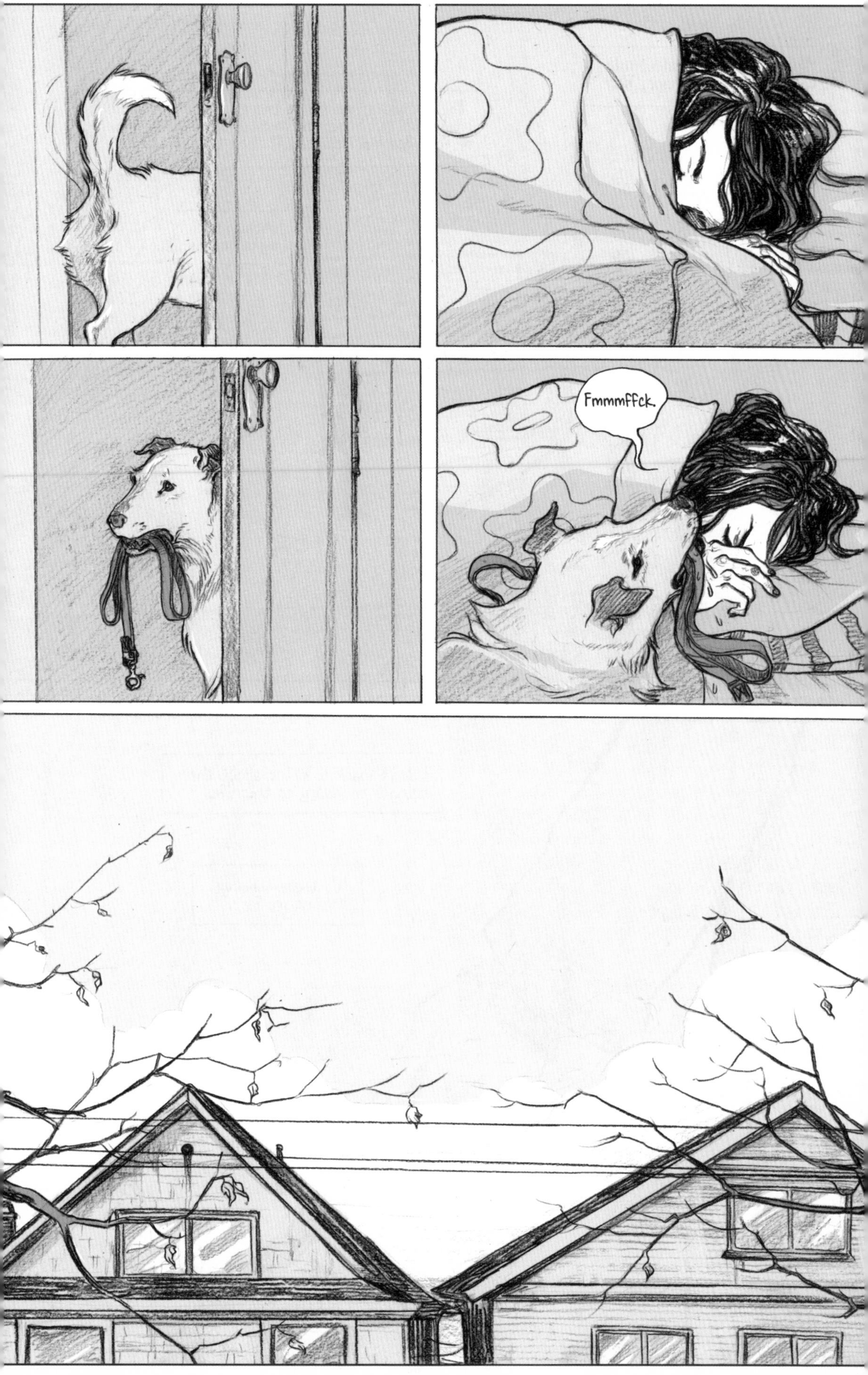
Fmmmffck.

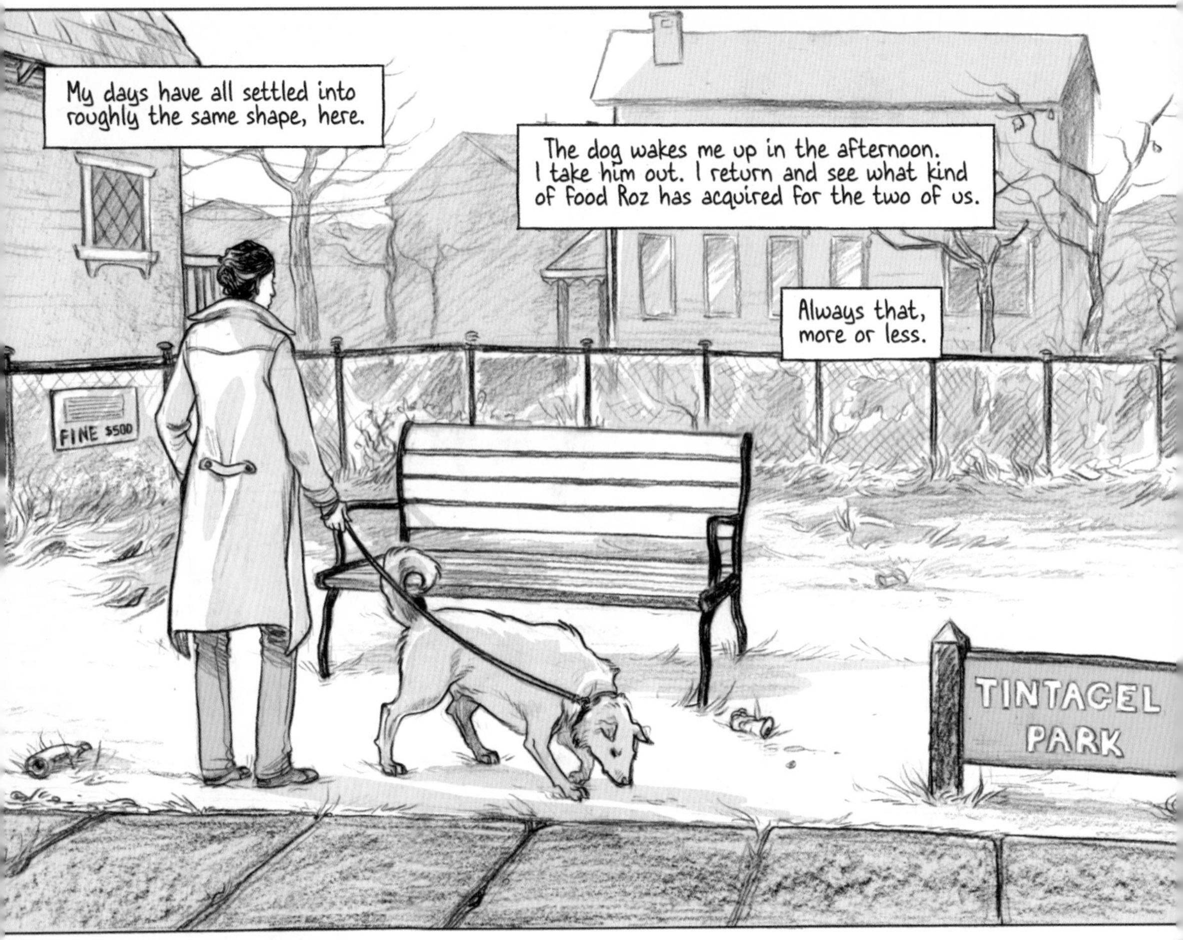
My days have all settled into roughly the same shape, here.
The dog wakes me up in the afternoon. I take him out. I return and see what kind of food Roz has acquired for the two of us.
Always that, more or less.
FINE $500
TINTAGEL PARK

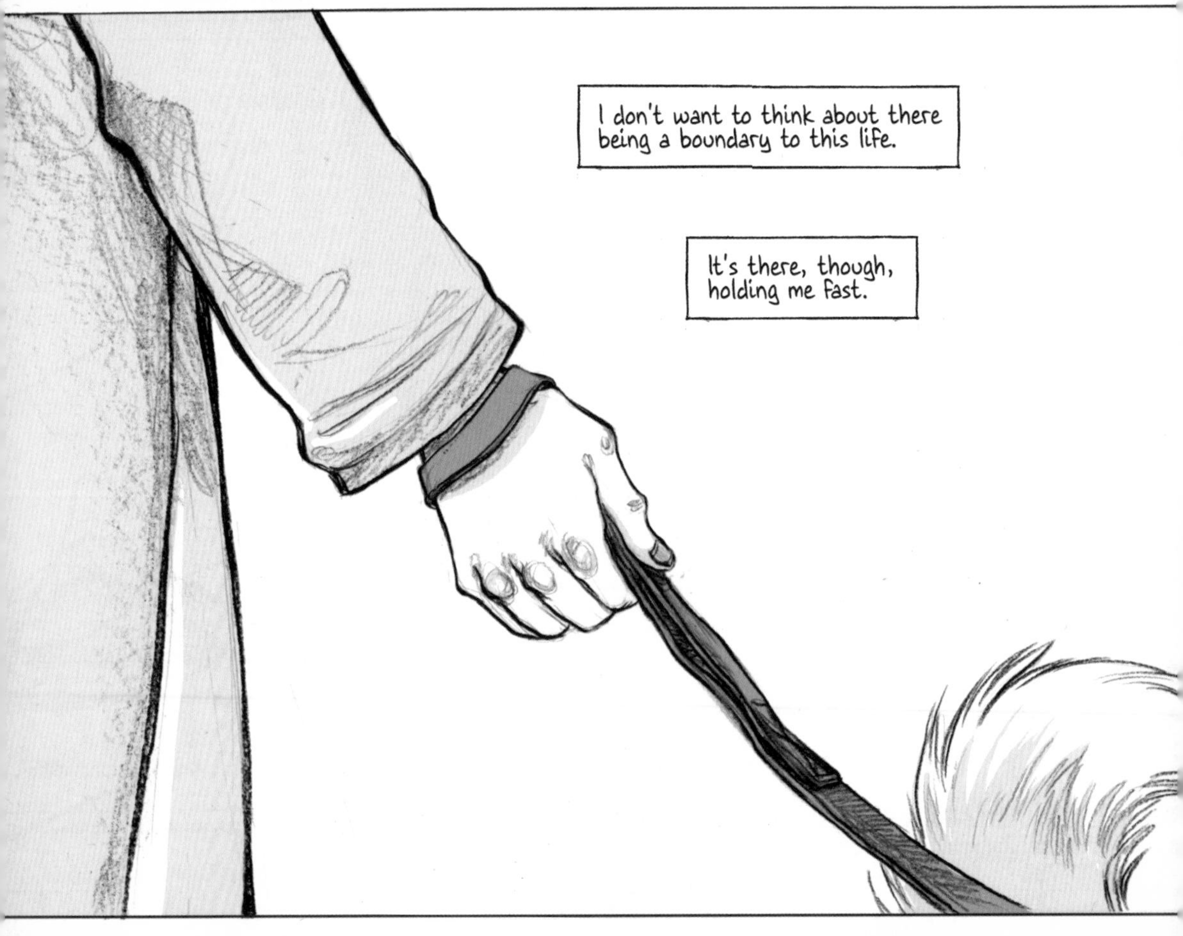
I don't want to think about there being a boundary to this life.
It's there, though, holding me fast.

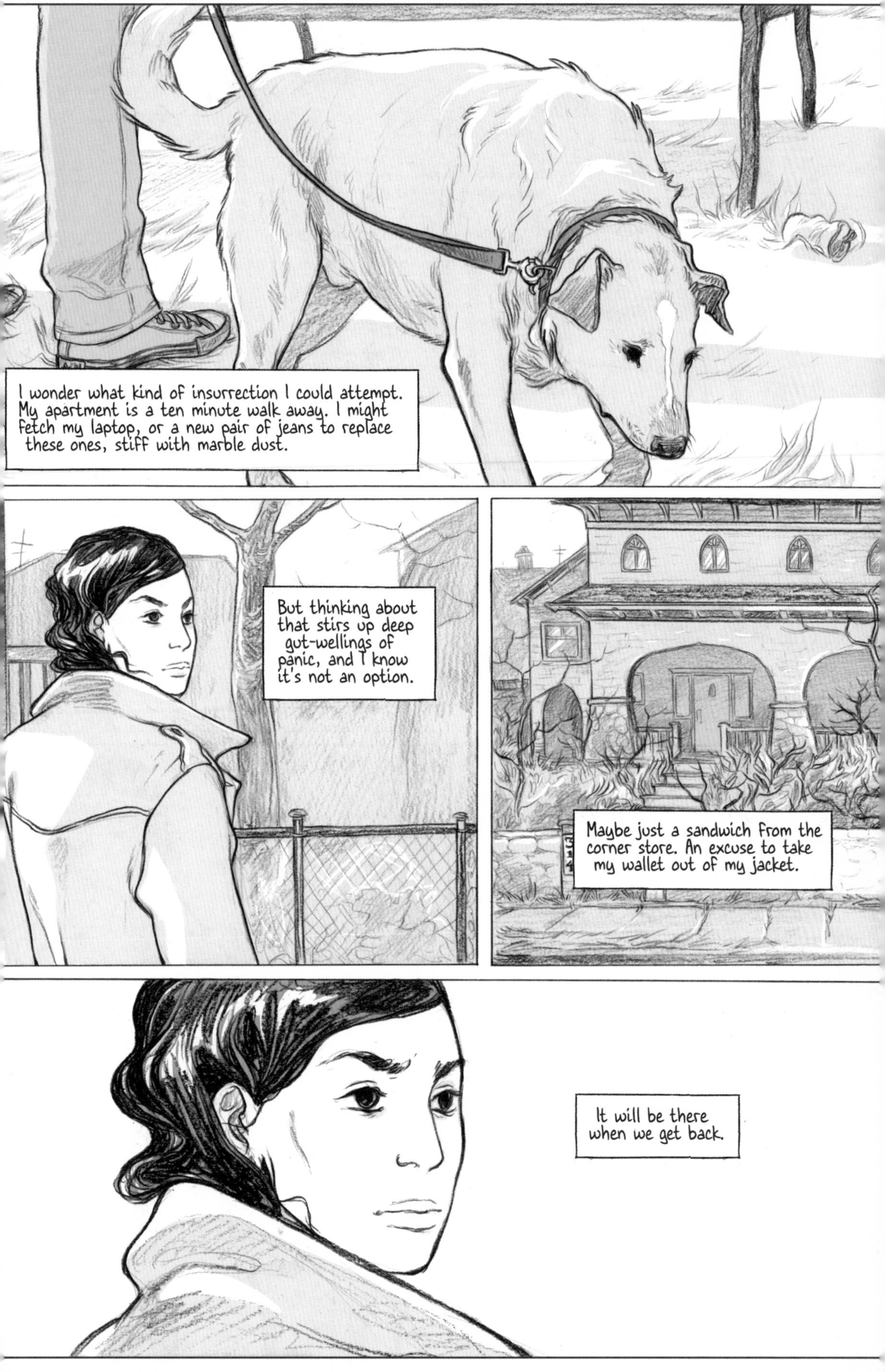
I wonder what kind of insurrection I could attempt. My apartment is a ten minute walk away. I might fetch my laptop, or a new pair of jeans to replace these ones, stiff with marble dust.
But thinking about that stirs up deep gut-wellings of panic, and I know it's not an option.
Maybe just a sandwich from the corner store. An excuse to take my wallet out of my jacket.
It will be there when we get back.

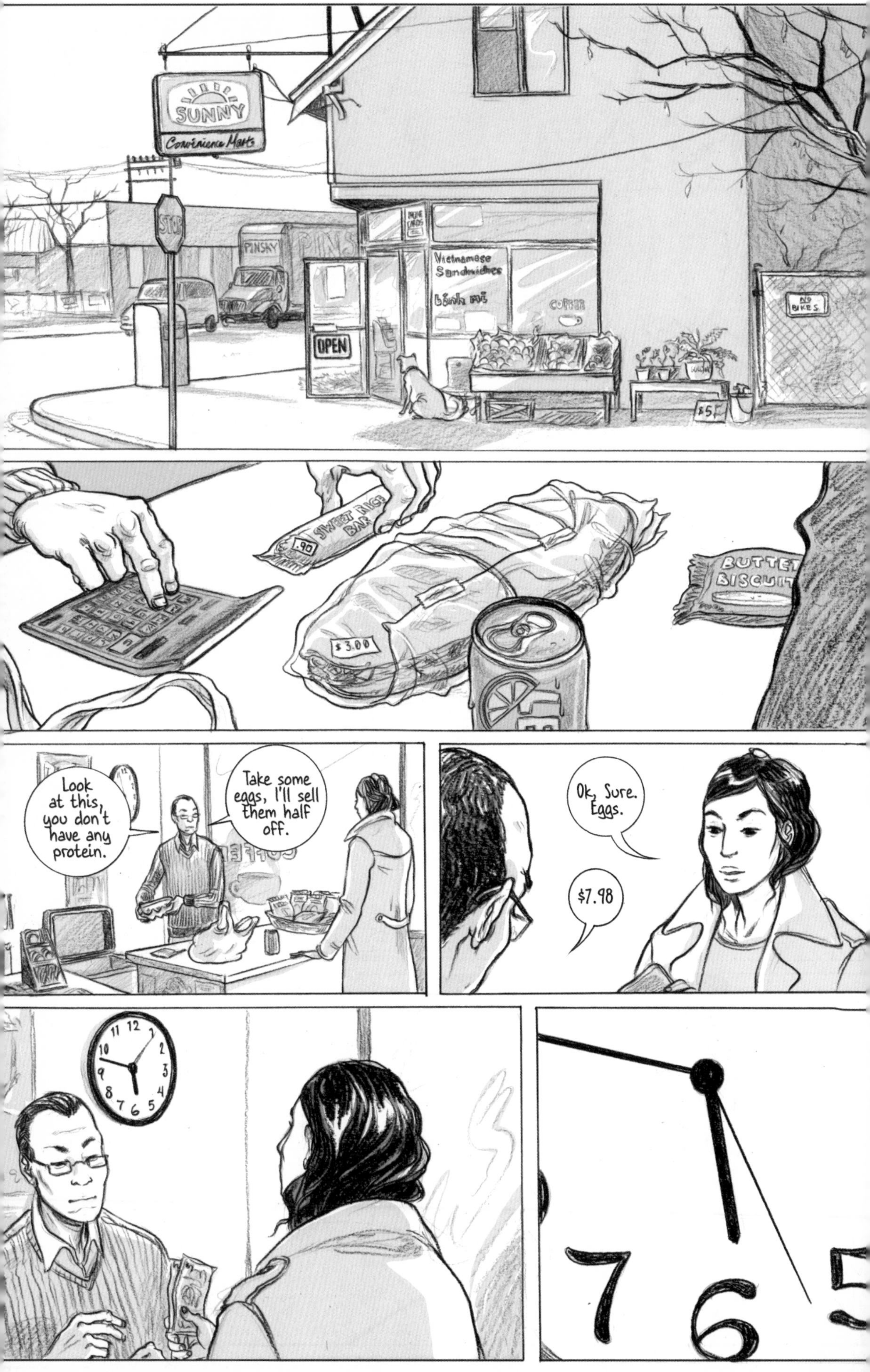
SUNNY
Convenience Marts
STOP
OPEN
Vietnamese Sandwiches
bánh mì
COFFEE
NO BIKES
$5
SWEET RICE BAR
.90
$3.00
BUTTER BISCUIT
Look at this, you don't have any protein.
Take some eggs, I'll sell them half off.
Ok, Sure. Eggs.
$7.98

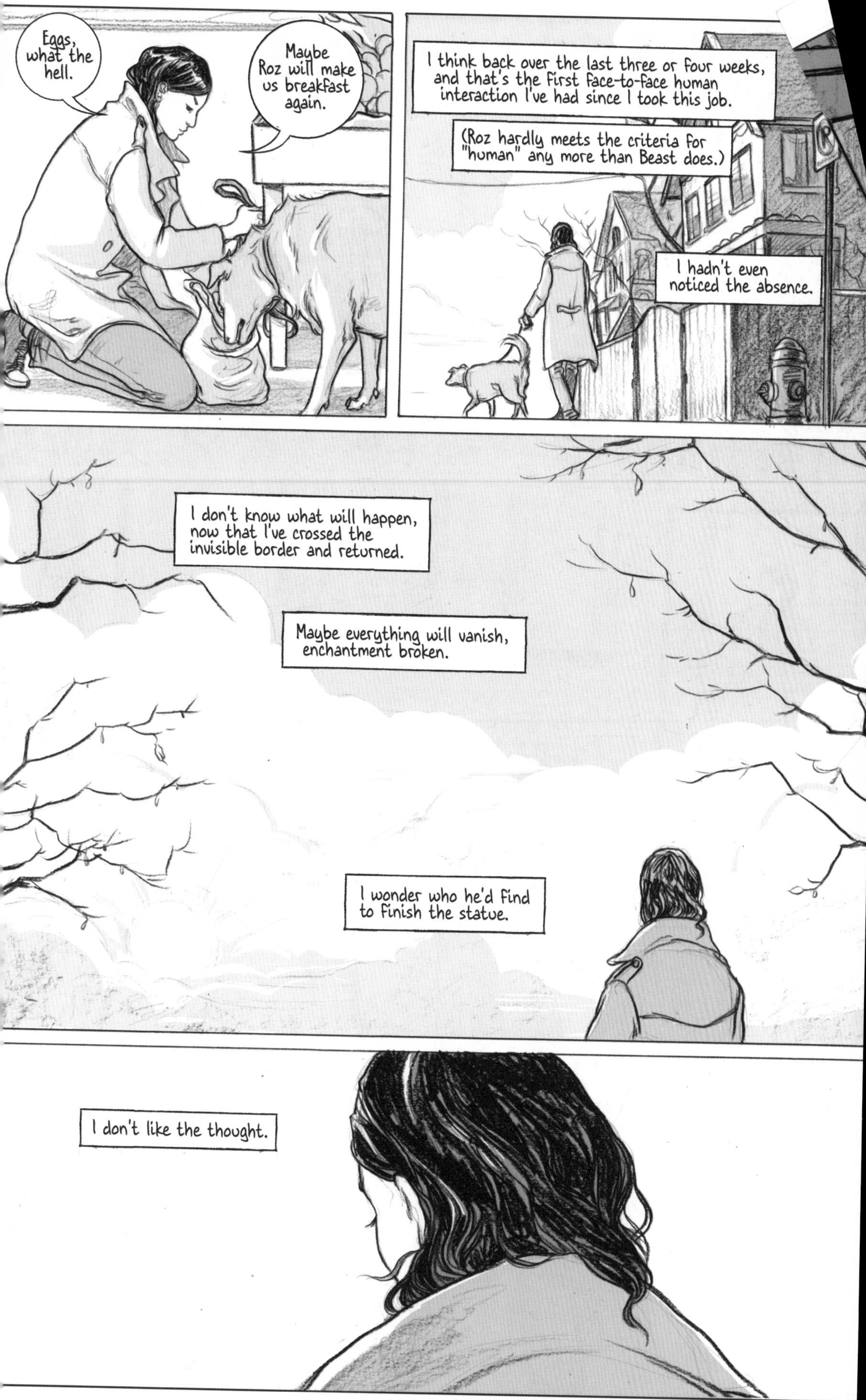
Eggs, what the hell.
Maybe Roz will make us breakfast again.
I think back over the last three or four weeks, and that's the first face-to-face human interaction I've had since I took this job.
(Roz hardly meets the criteria for "human" any more than Beast does.)
I hadn't even noticed the absence.
I don't know what will happen, now that I've crossed the invisible border and returned.
Maybe everything will vanish, enchantment broken.
I wonder who he'd find to finish the statue.
I don't like the thought.

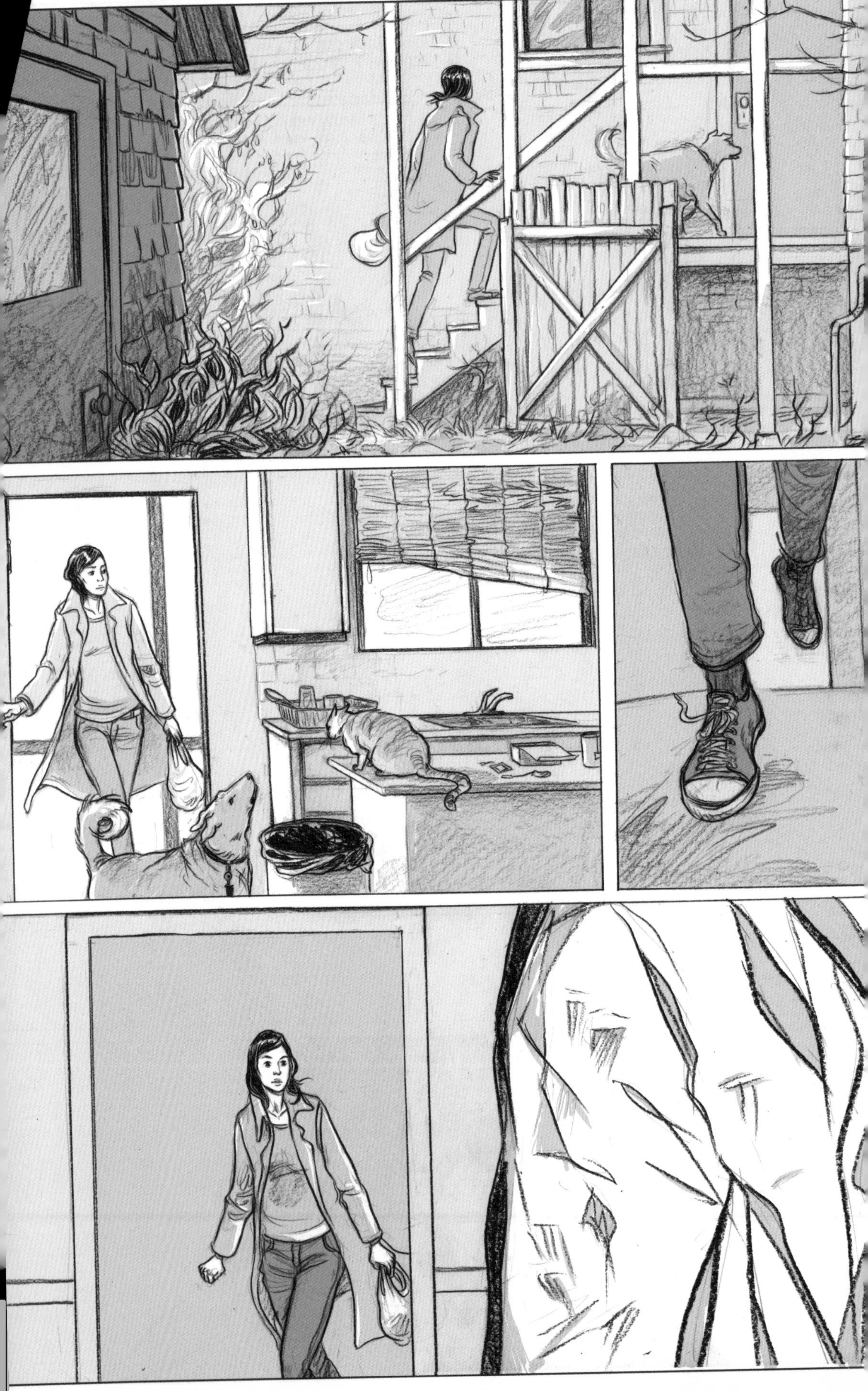

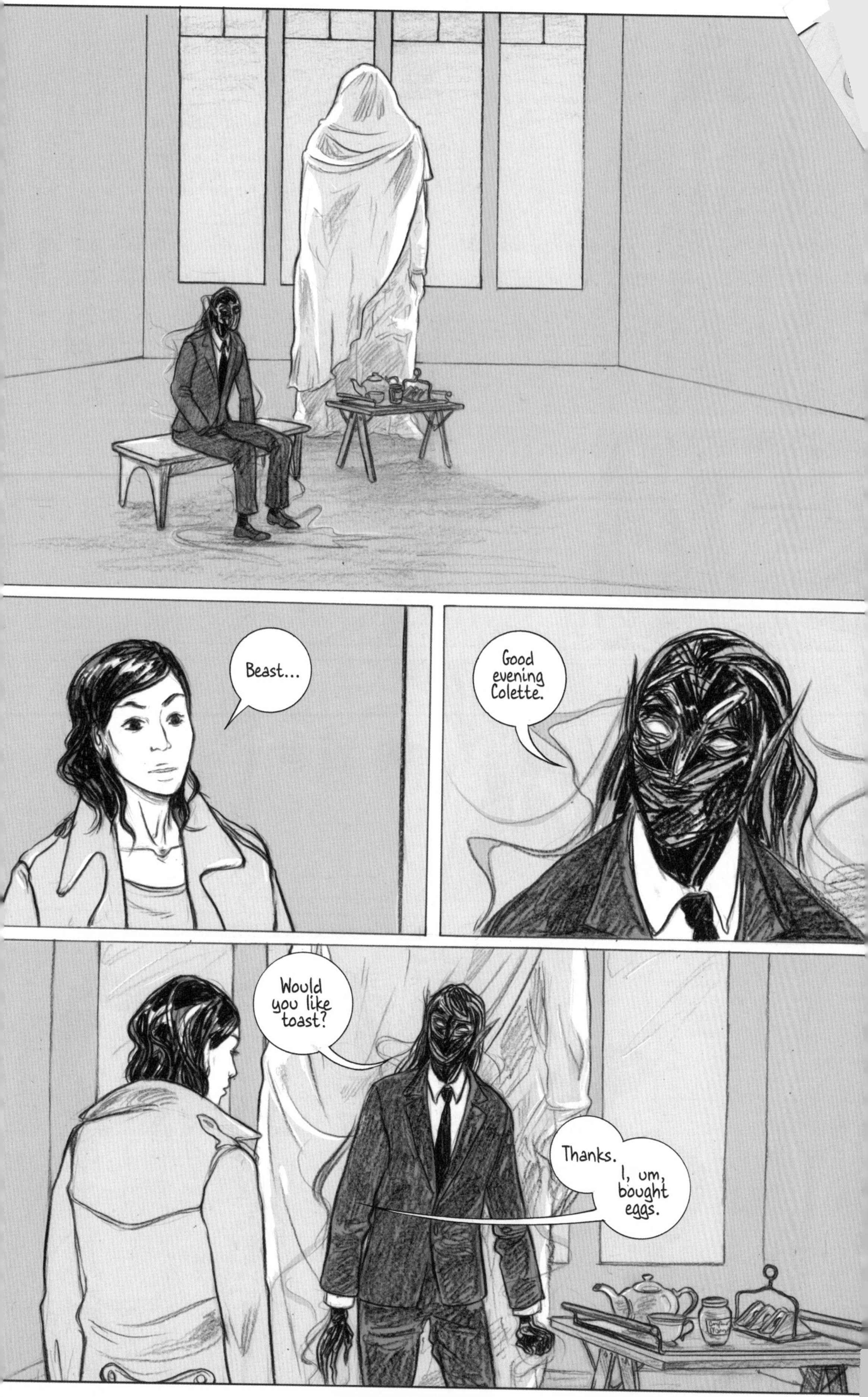
Beast...
Good evening Colette.
Would you like toast?
Thanks.
I, um, bought eggs.

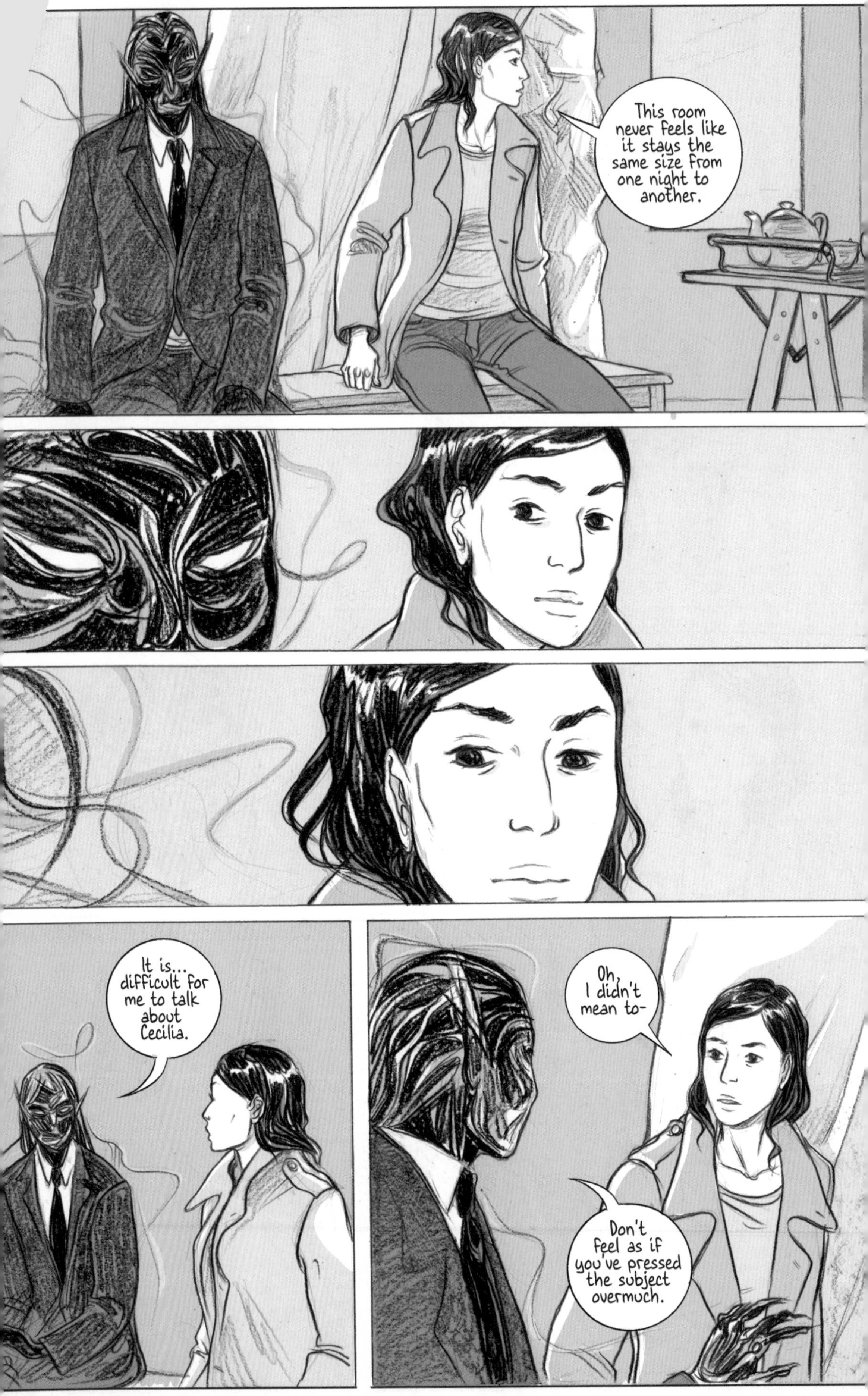
This room never feels like it stays the same size from one night to another.
It is... difficult for me to talk about Cecilia.
Oh, I didn't mean to-
Don't feel as if you've pressed the subject overmuch.

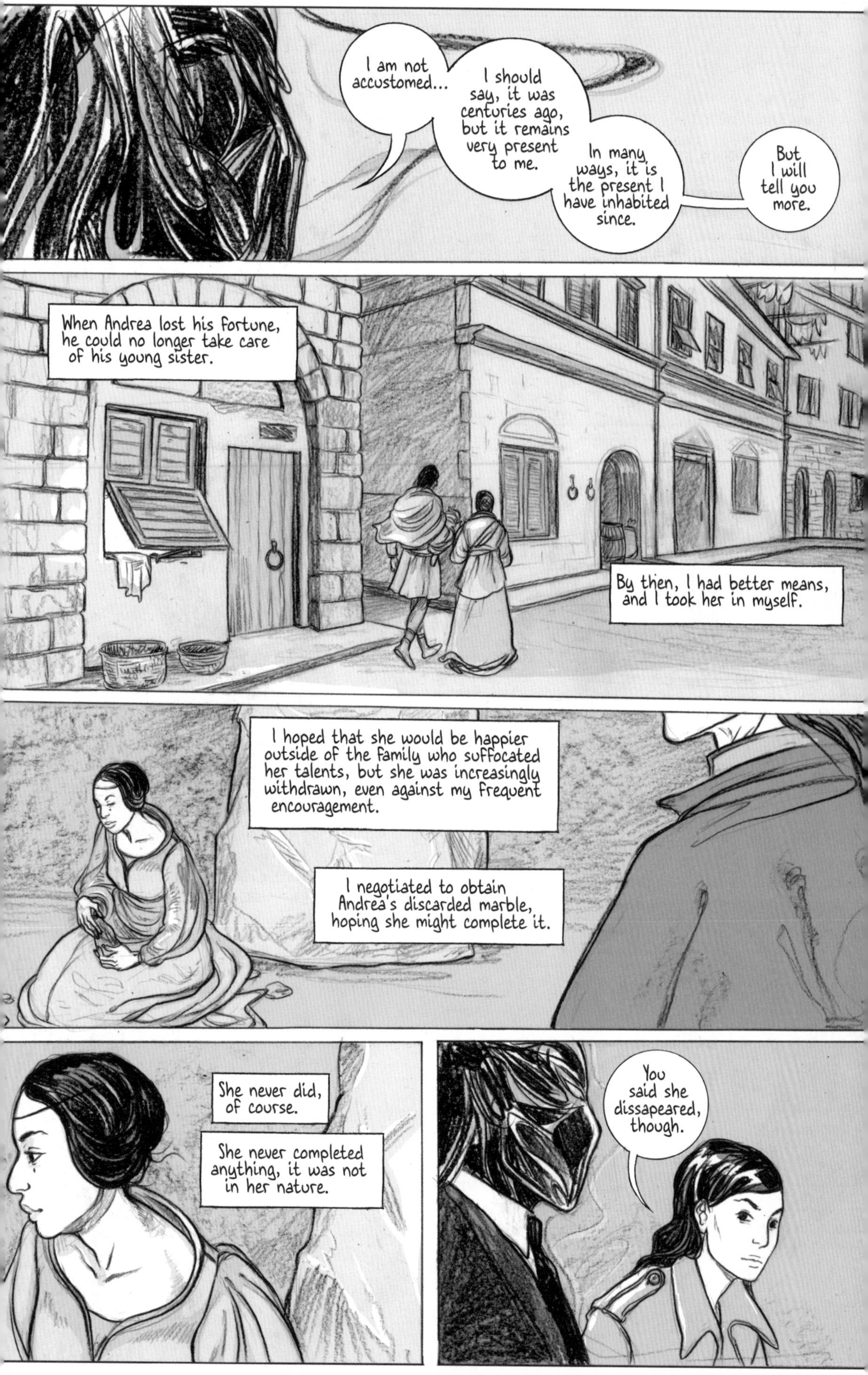
I am not accustomed...
I should say, it was centuries ago, but it remains very present to me.
In many ways, it is the present I have inhabited since.
But I will tell you more.
When Andrea lost his fortune, he could no longer take care of his young sister.
By then, I had better means, and I took her in myself.
I hoped that she would be happier outside of the family who suffocated her talents, but she was increasingly withdrawn, even against my frequent encouragement.
I negotiated to obtain Andrea's discarded marble, hoping she might complete it.
She never did, of course.
She never completed anything, it was not in her nature.
You said she dissapeared, though.

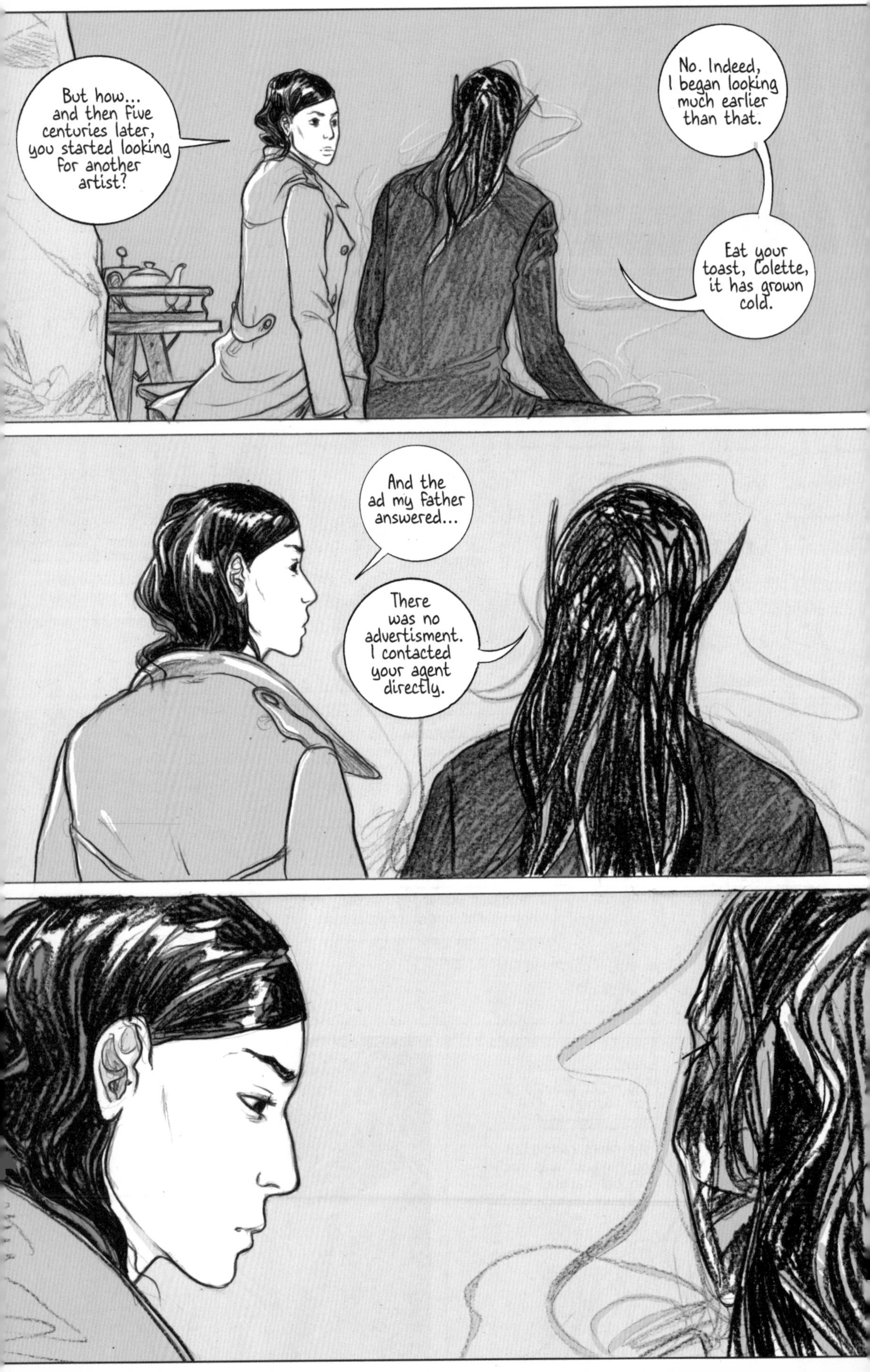
But how... and then five centuries later, you started looking for another artist?
No. Indeed, I began looking much earlier than that.
Eat your toast, Colette, it has grown cold.
And the ad my father answered...
There was no advertisment. I contacted your agent directly.

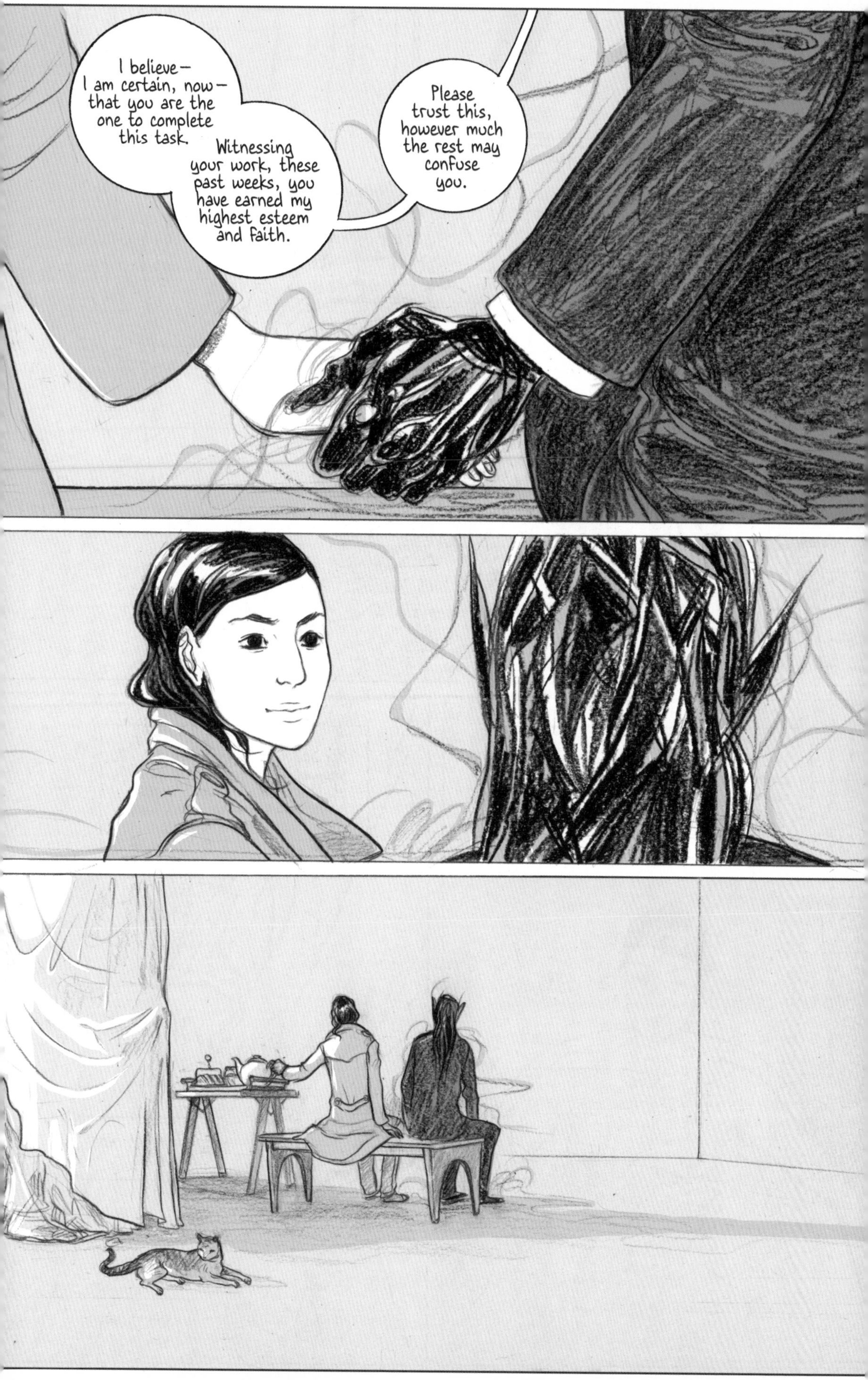
I believe—
I am certain, now—
that you are the
one to complete
this task.
Witnessing
your work, these
past weeks, you
have earned my
highest esteem
and faith.
Please
trust this,
however much
the rest may
confuse
you.

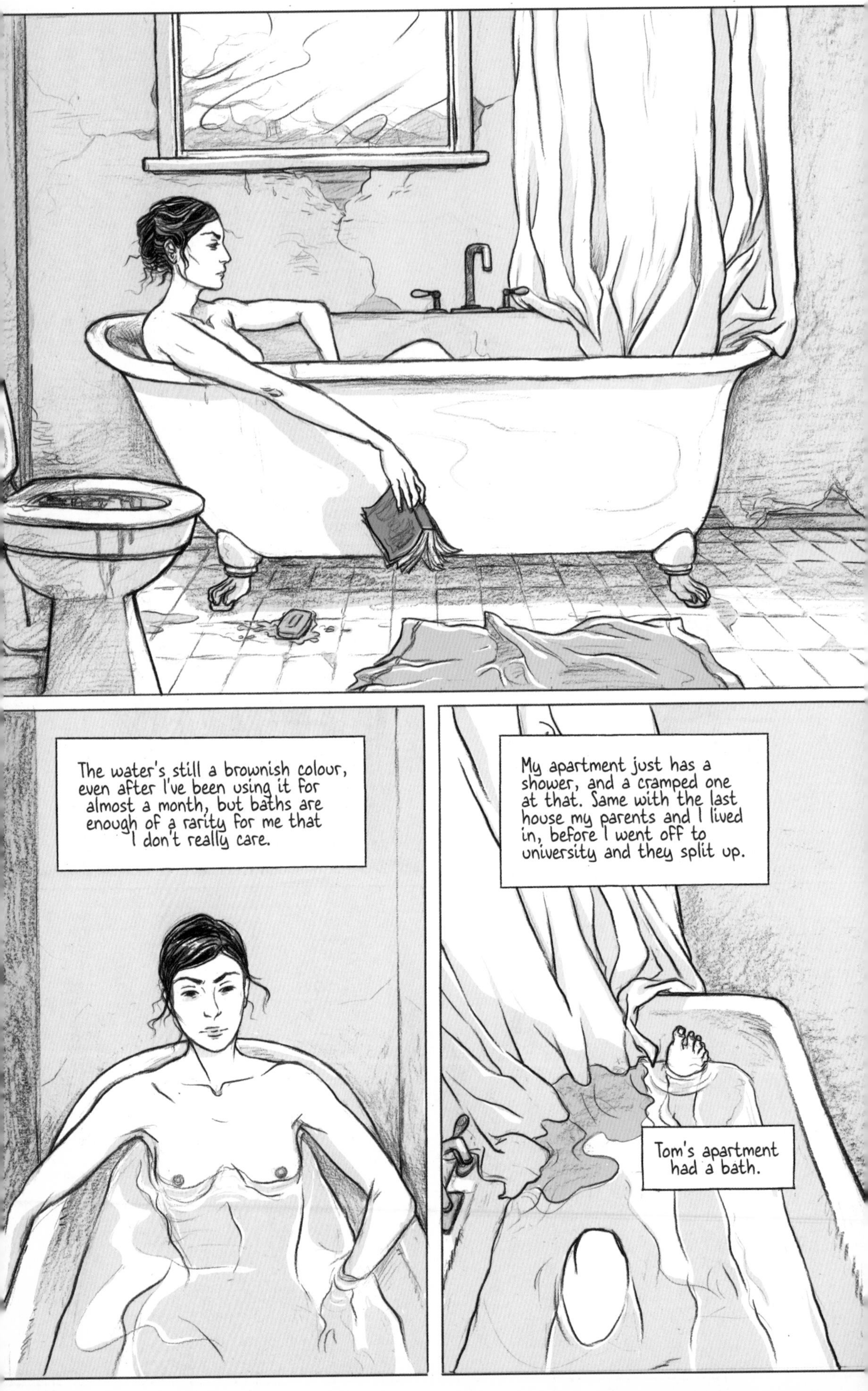
The water's still a brownish colour, even after I've been using it for almost a month, but baths are enough of a rarity for me that I don't really care.
My apartment just has a shower, and a cramped one at that. Same with the last house my parents and I lived in, before I went off to university and they split up.
Tom's apartment had a bath.

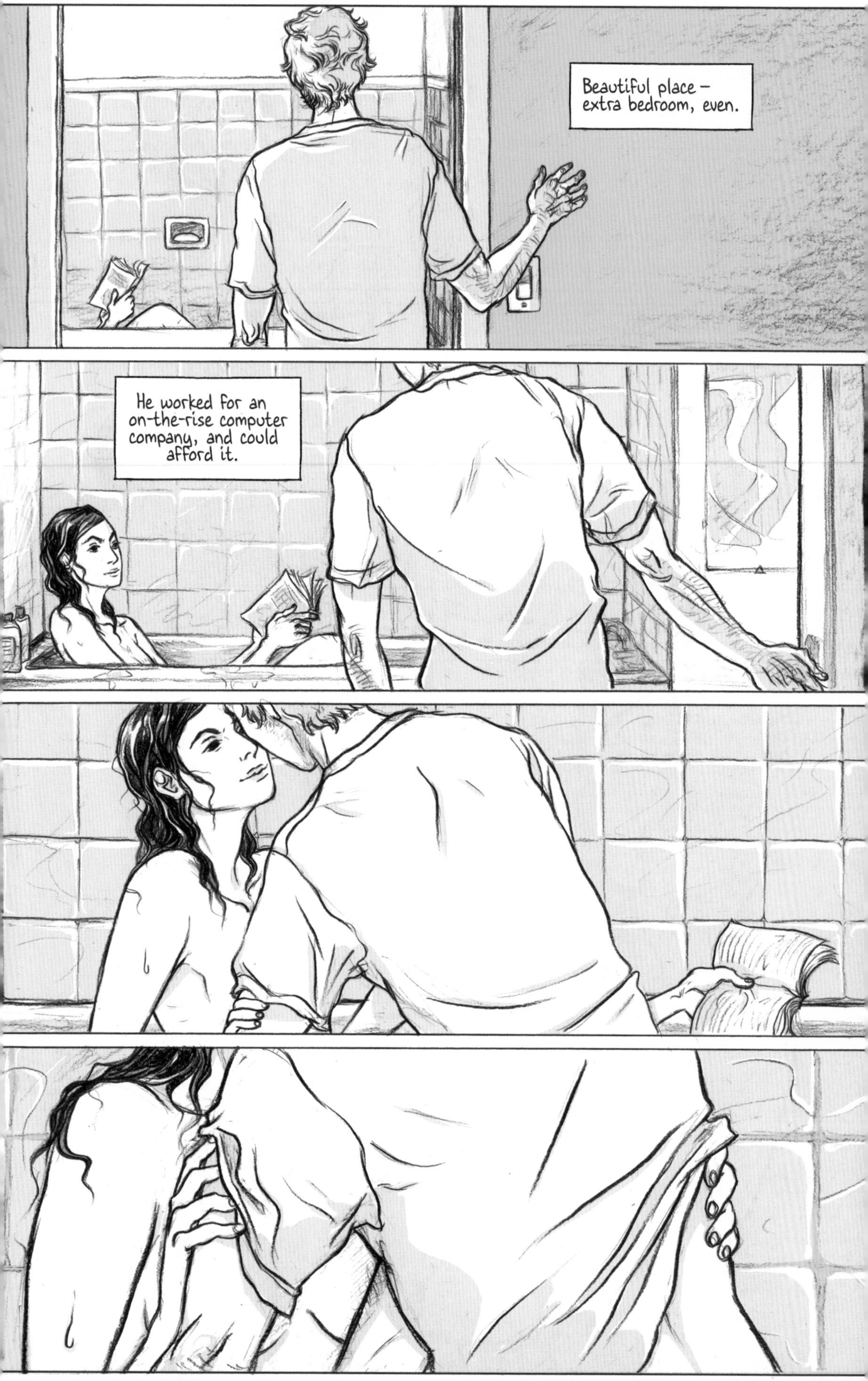
Beautiful place — extra bedroom, even.
He worked for an on-the-rise computer company, and could afford it.

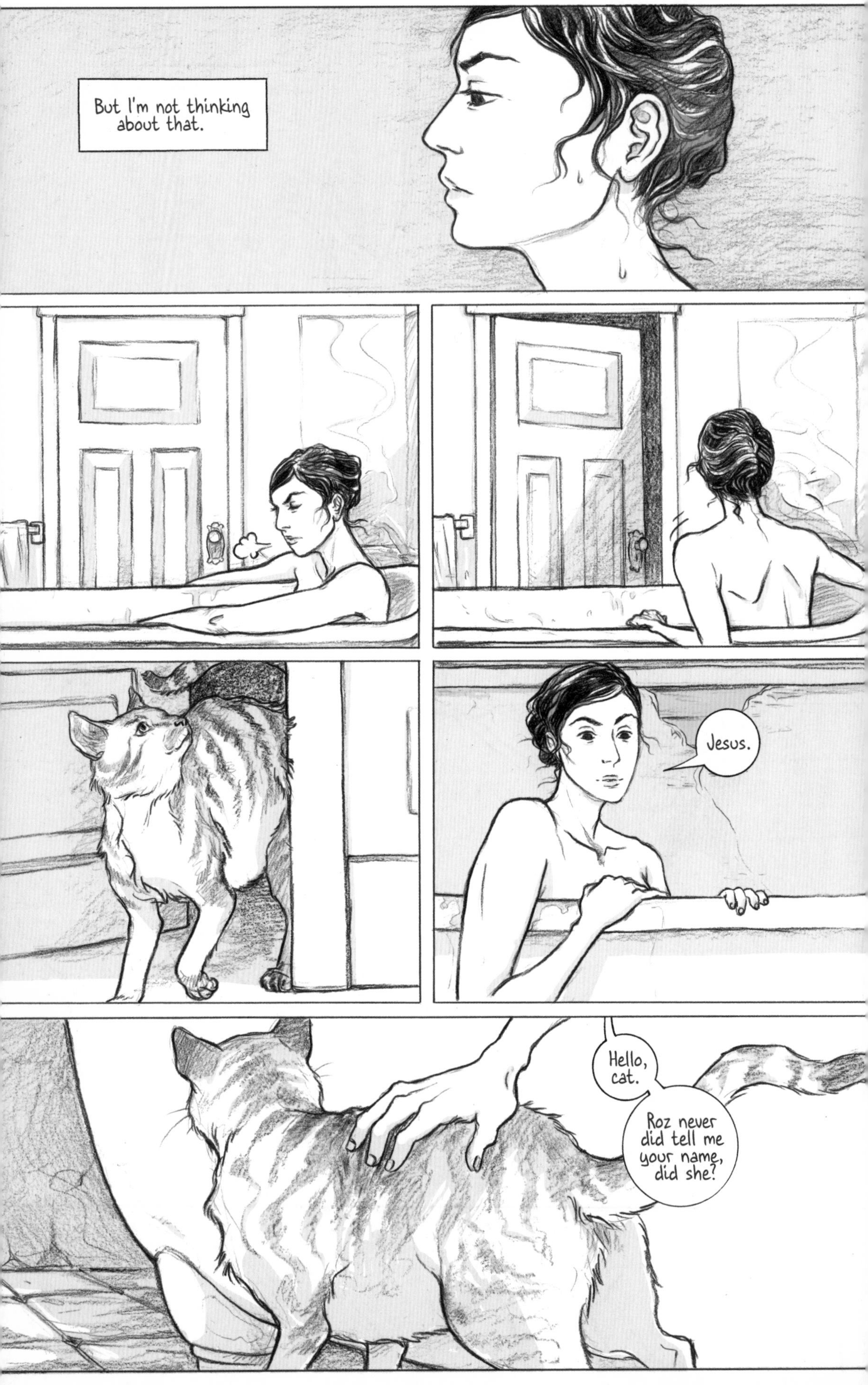
But I'm not thinking about that.
Jesus.
Hello, cat.
Roz never did tell me your name, did she?

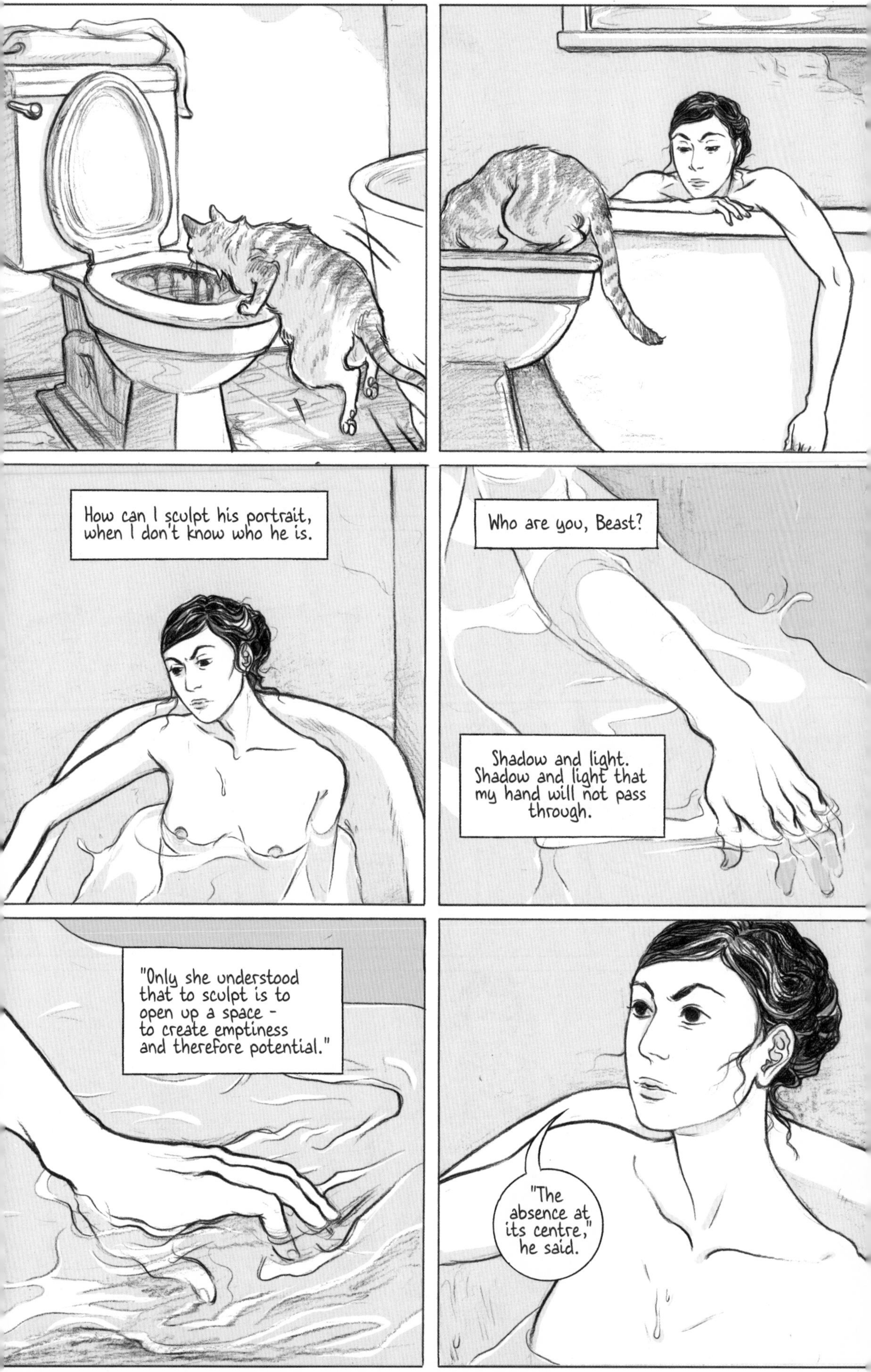
How can I sculpt his portrait, when I don't know who he is.
Who are you, Beast?
Shadow and light. Shadow and light that my hand will not pass through.
"Only she understood that to sculpt is to open up a space - to create emptiness and therefore potential."
"The absence at its centre," he said.

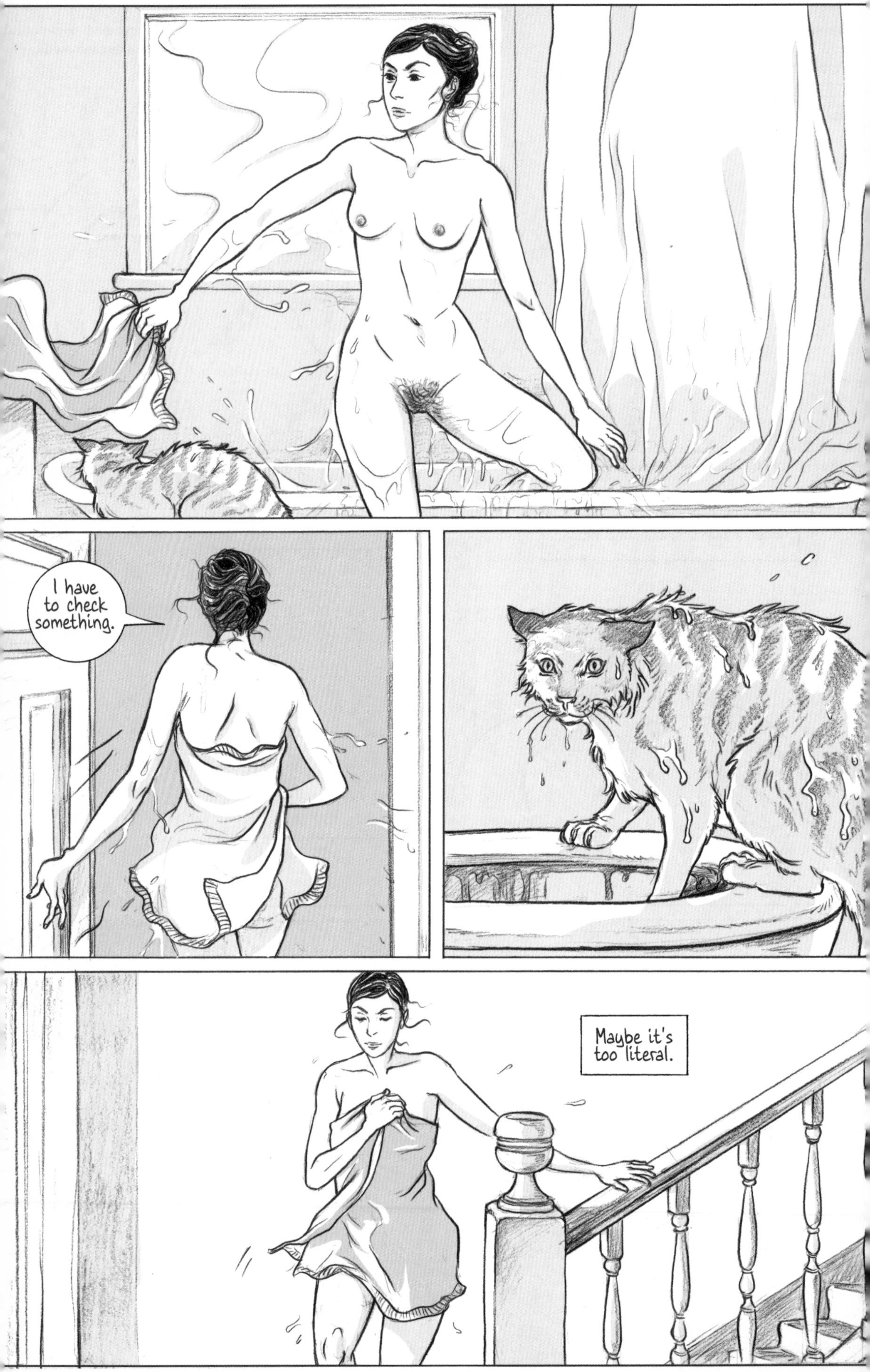
I have to check something.
Maybe it's too literal.

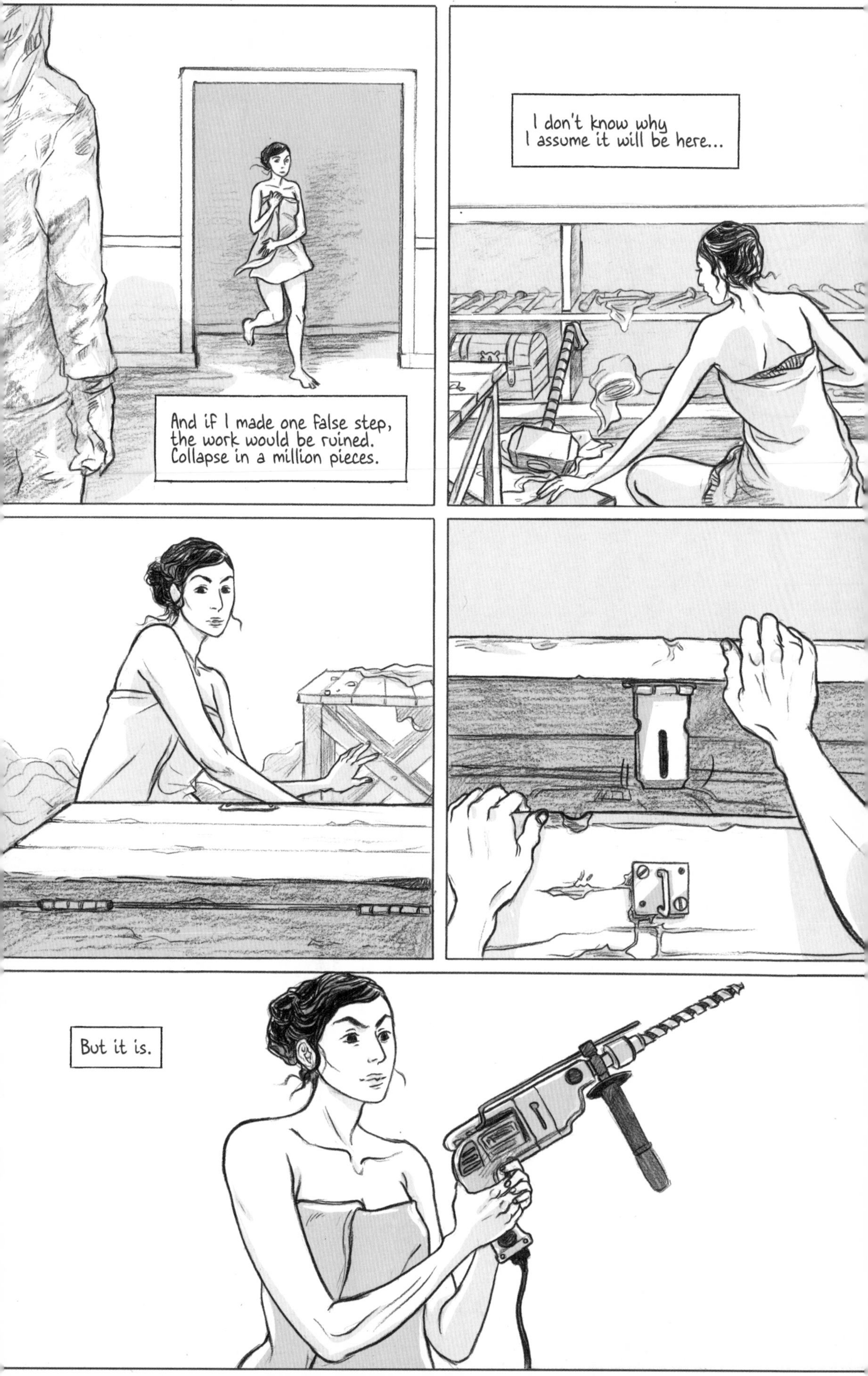
And if I made one false step, the work would be ruined. Collapse in a million pieces.
I don't know why I assume it will be here...
But it is.

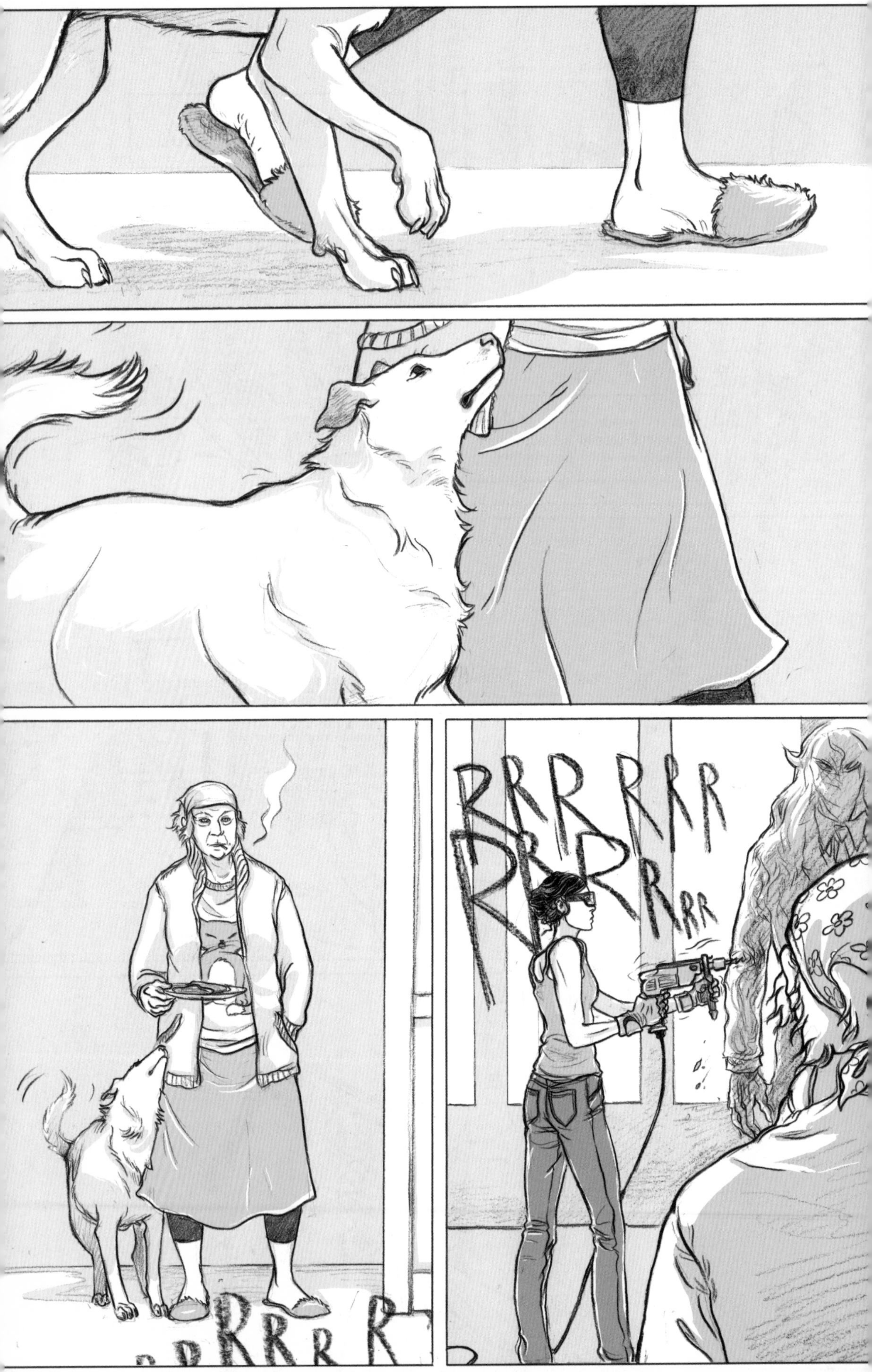

RRRRRR
RRRRRRR
RRRRR

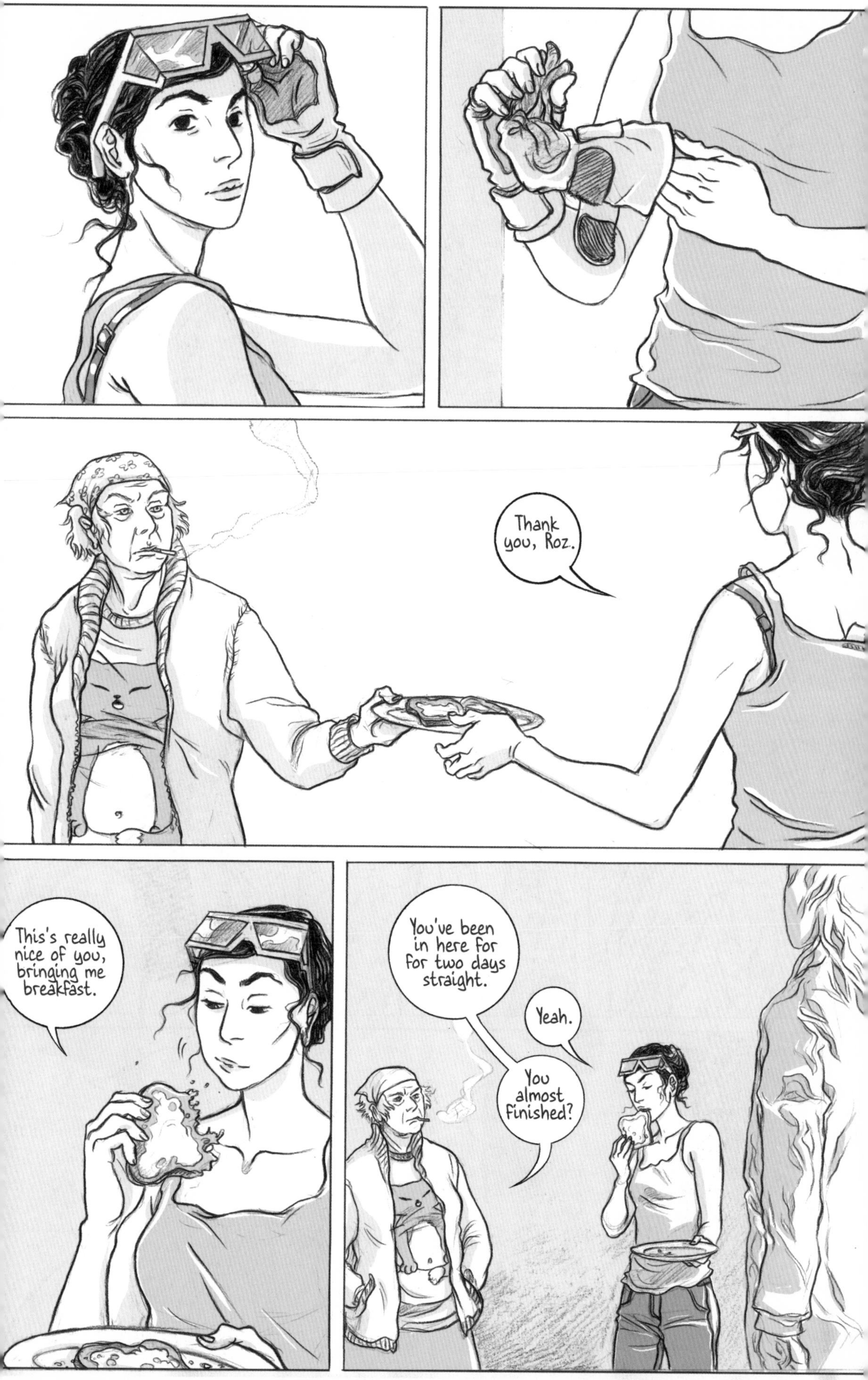
Thank you, Roz.
This's really nice of you, bringing me breakfast.
You've been in here for for two days straight.
Yeah.
You almost finished?

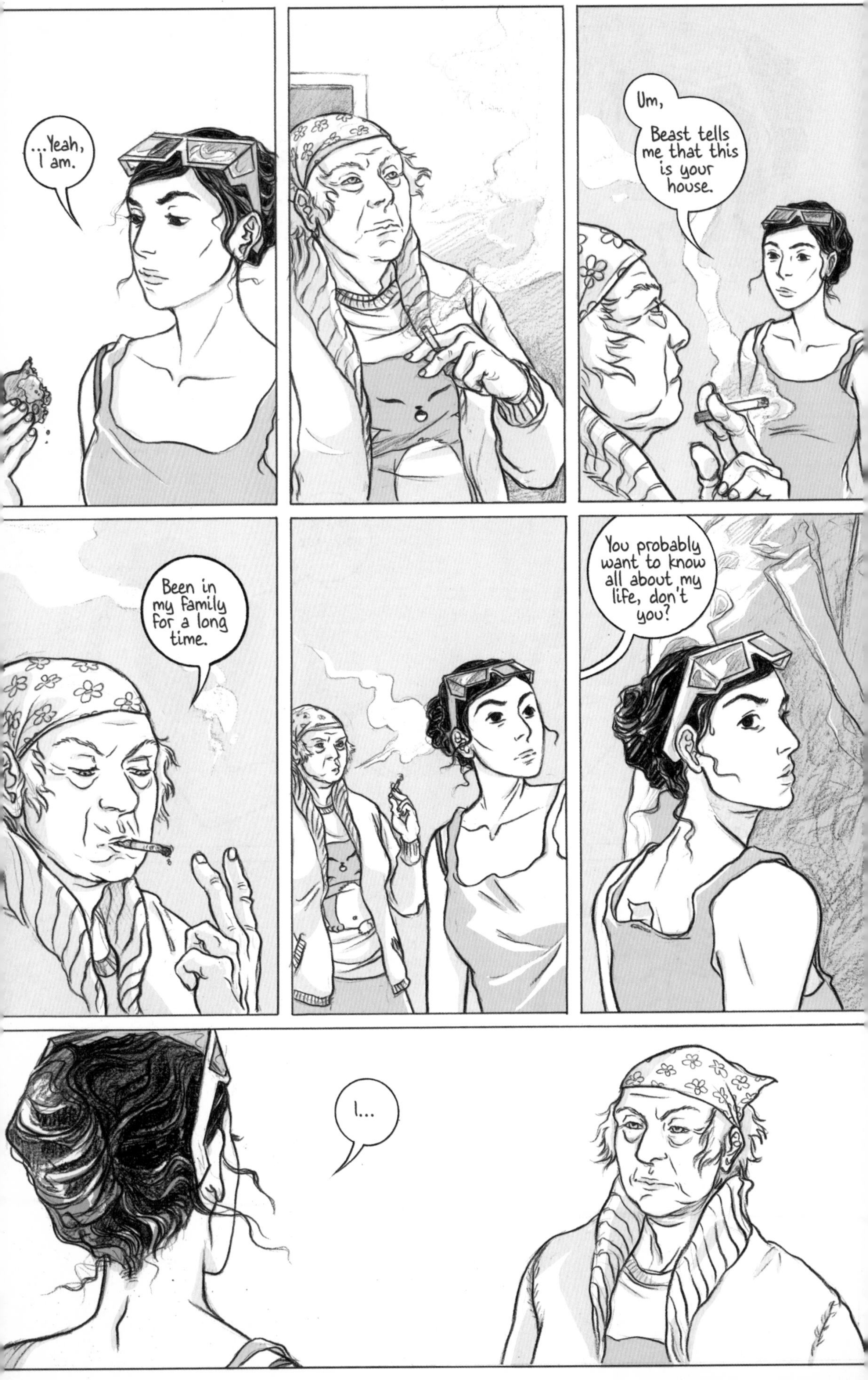

...Yeah, I am.
Um,
Beast tells me that this is your house.
Been in my family for a long time.
You probably want to know all about my life, don't you?
I...

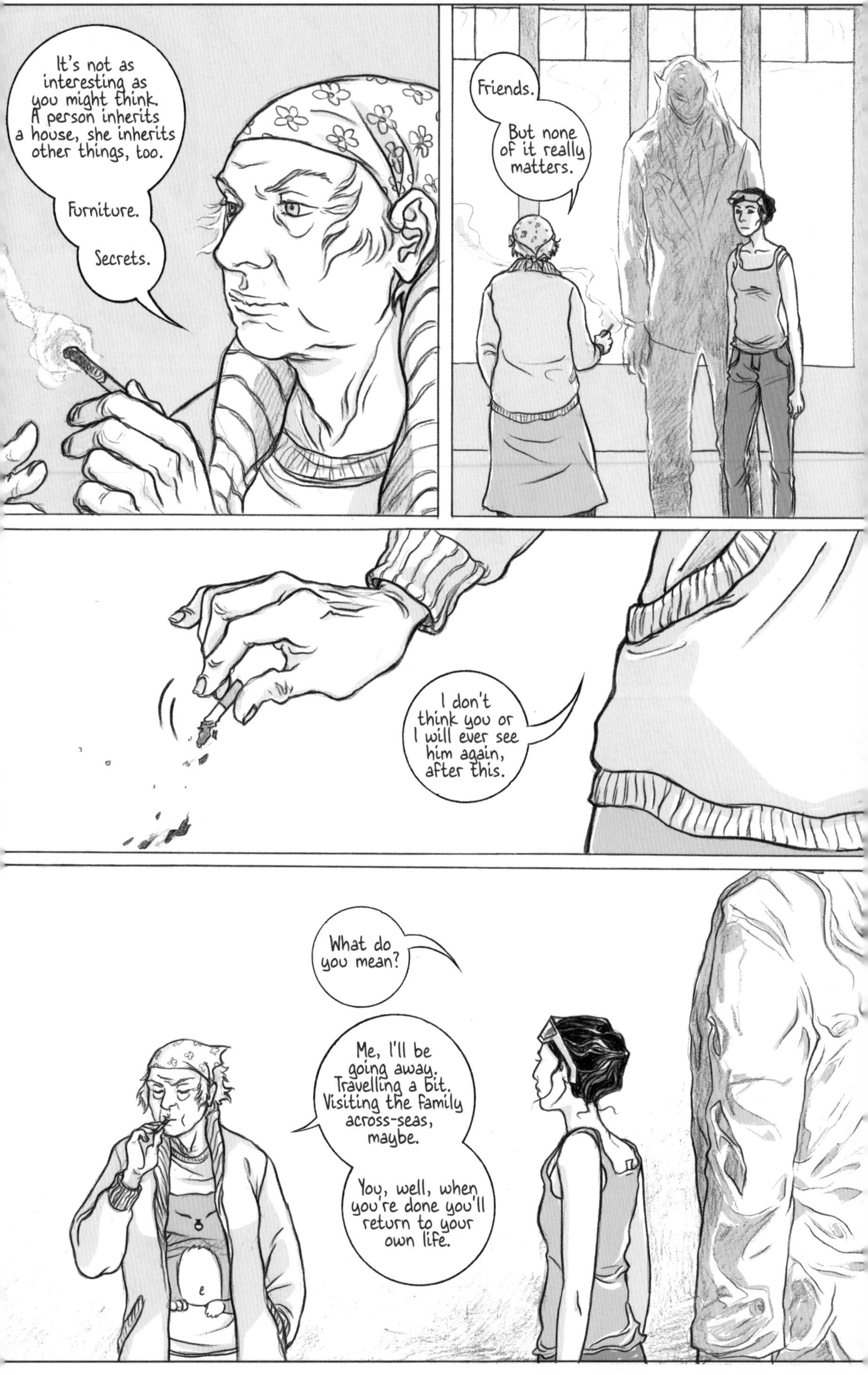
It's not as interesting as you might think. A person inherits a house, she inherits other things, too.
Furniture.
Secrets.
Friends.
But none of it really matters.
I don't think you or I will ever see him again, after this.
What do you mean?
Me, I'll be going away. Travelling a bit. Visiting the family across-seas, maybe.
You, well, when you're done you'll return to your own life.

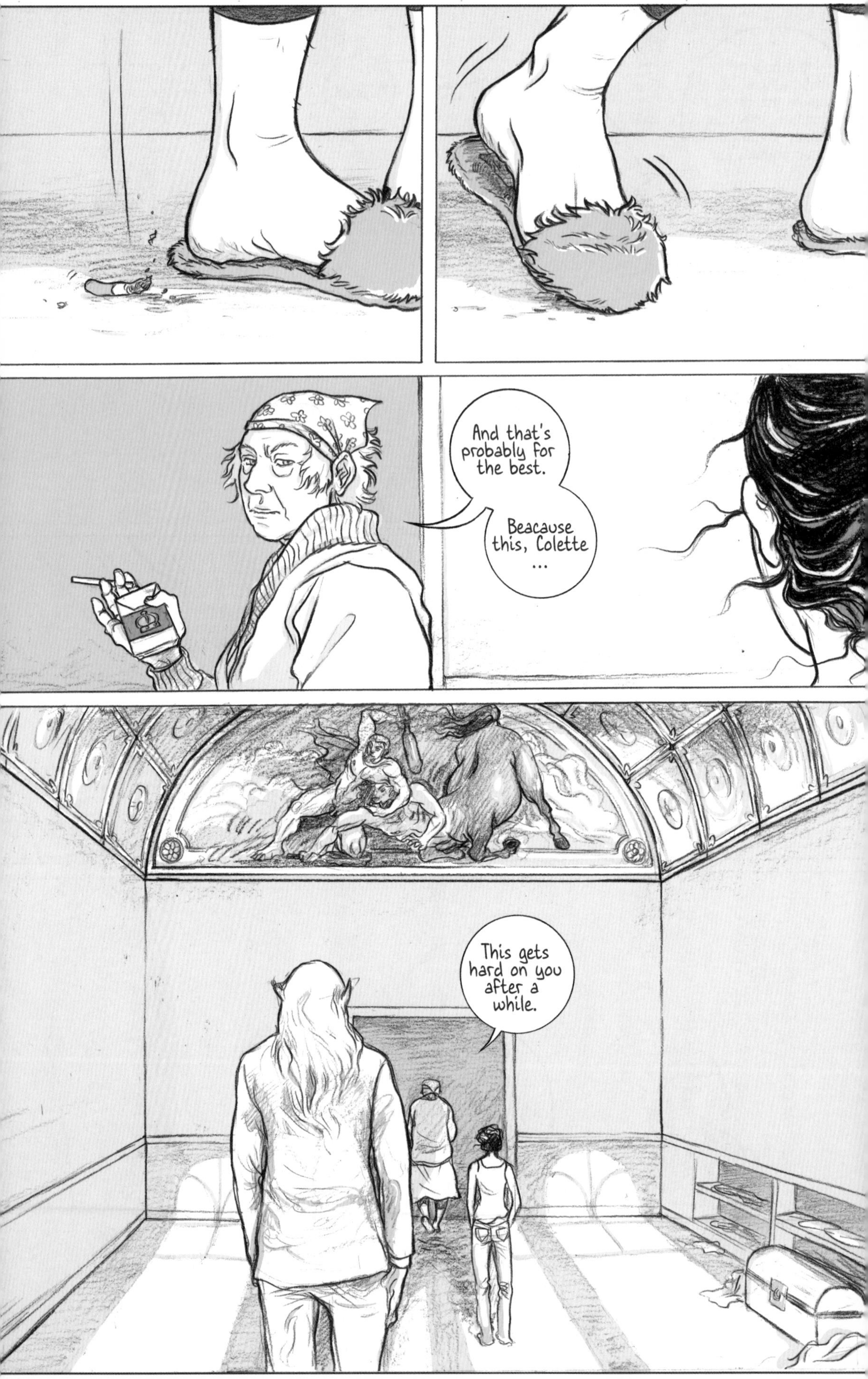
And that's probably for the best.
Beacause this, Colette ...
This gets hard on you after a while.

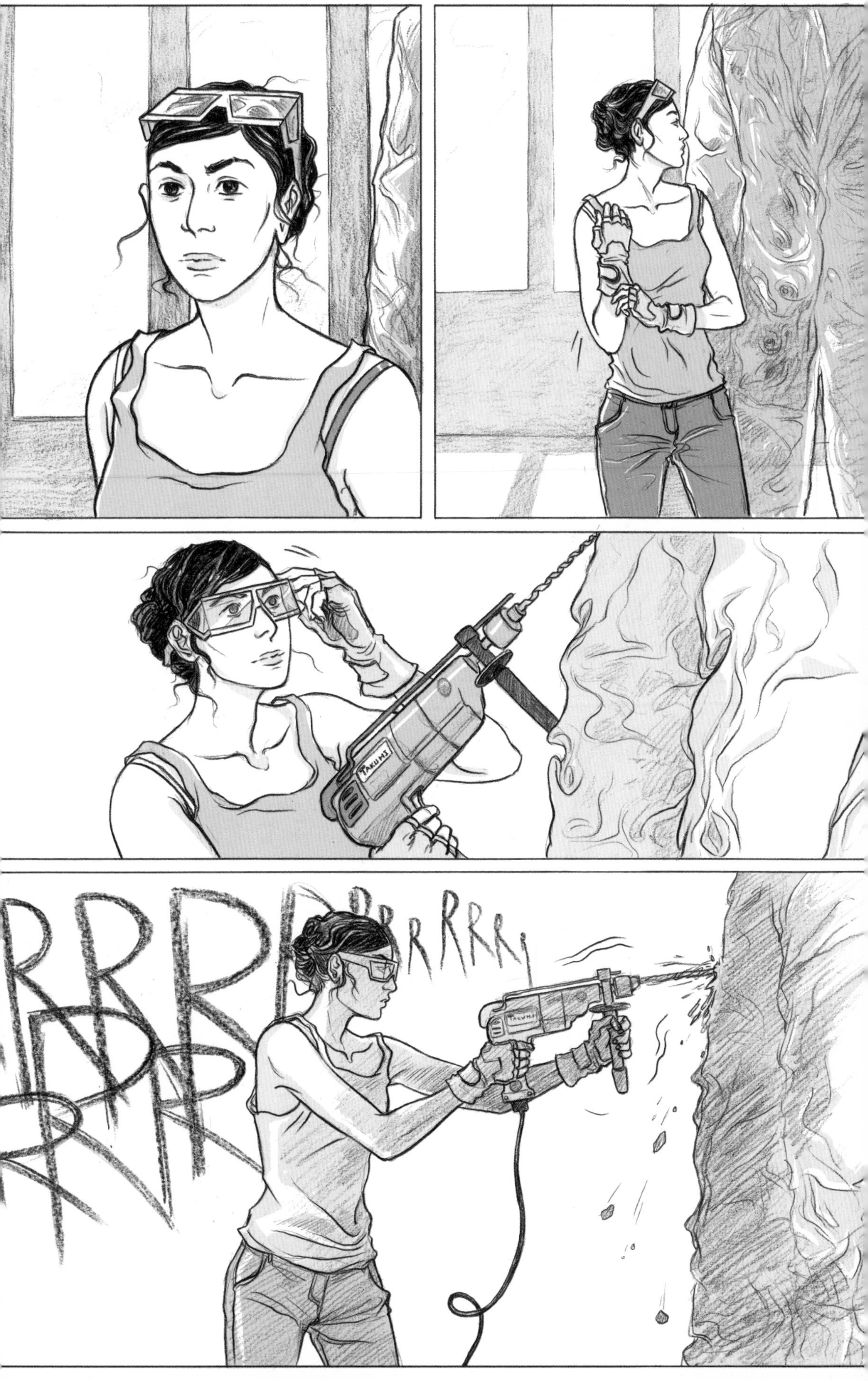
TAKUMI
RRRRRRRRR
TAKUMI

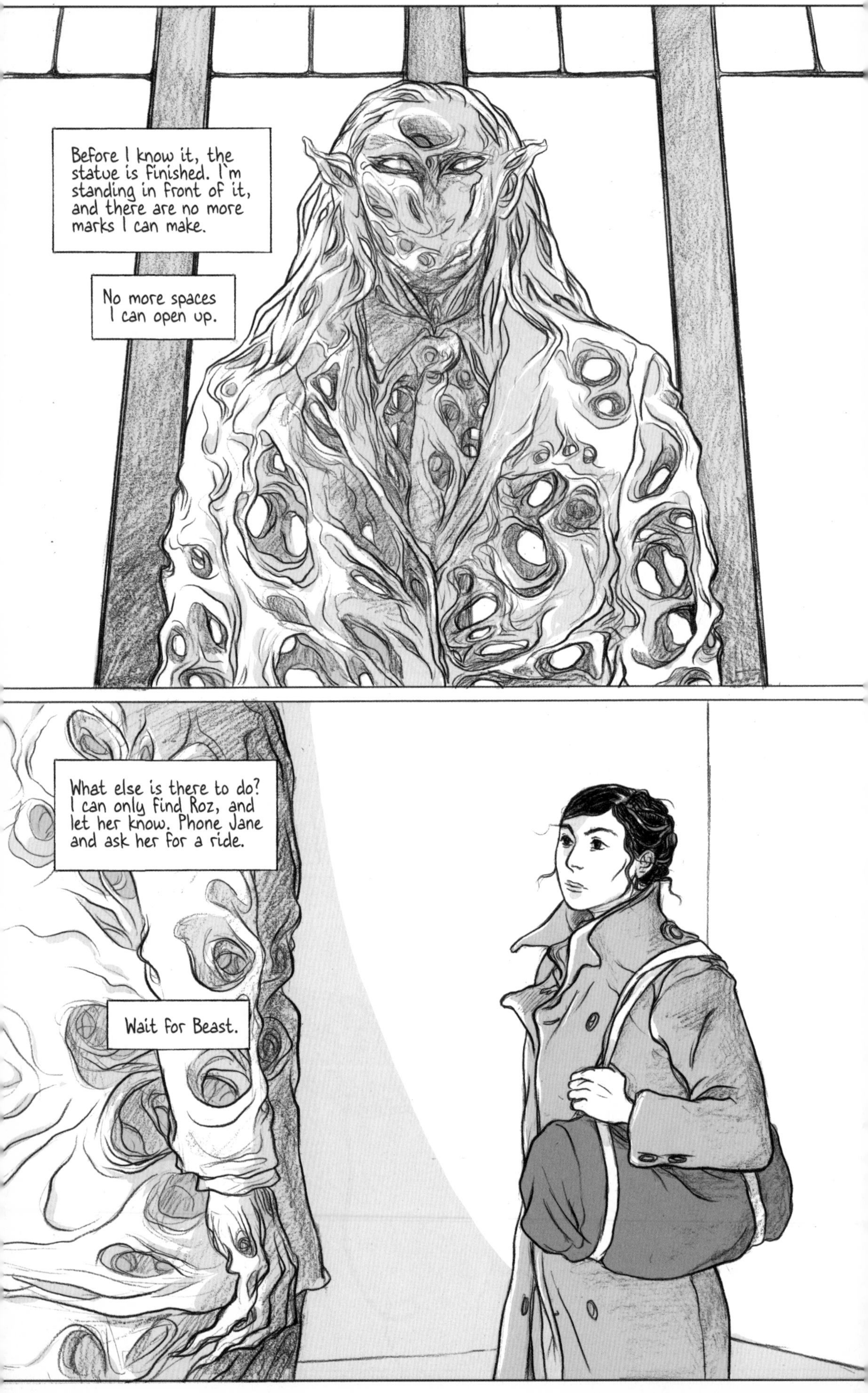
Before I know it, the statue is finished. I'm standing in front of it, and there are no more marks I can make.
No more spaces I can open up.
What else is there to do? I can only find Roz, and let her know. Phone Jane and ask her for a ride.
Wait for Beast.

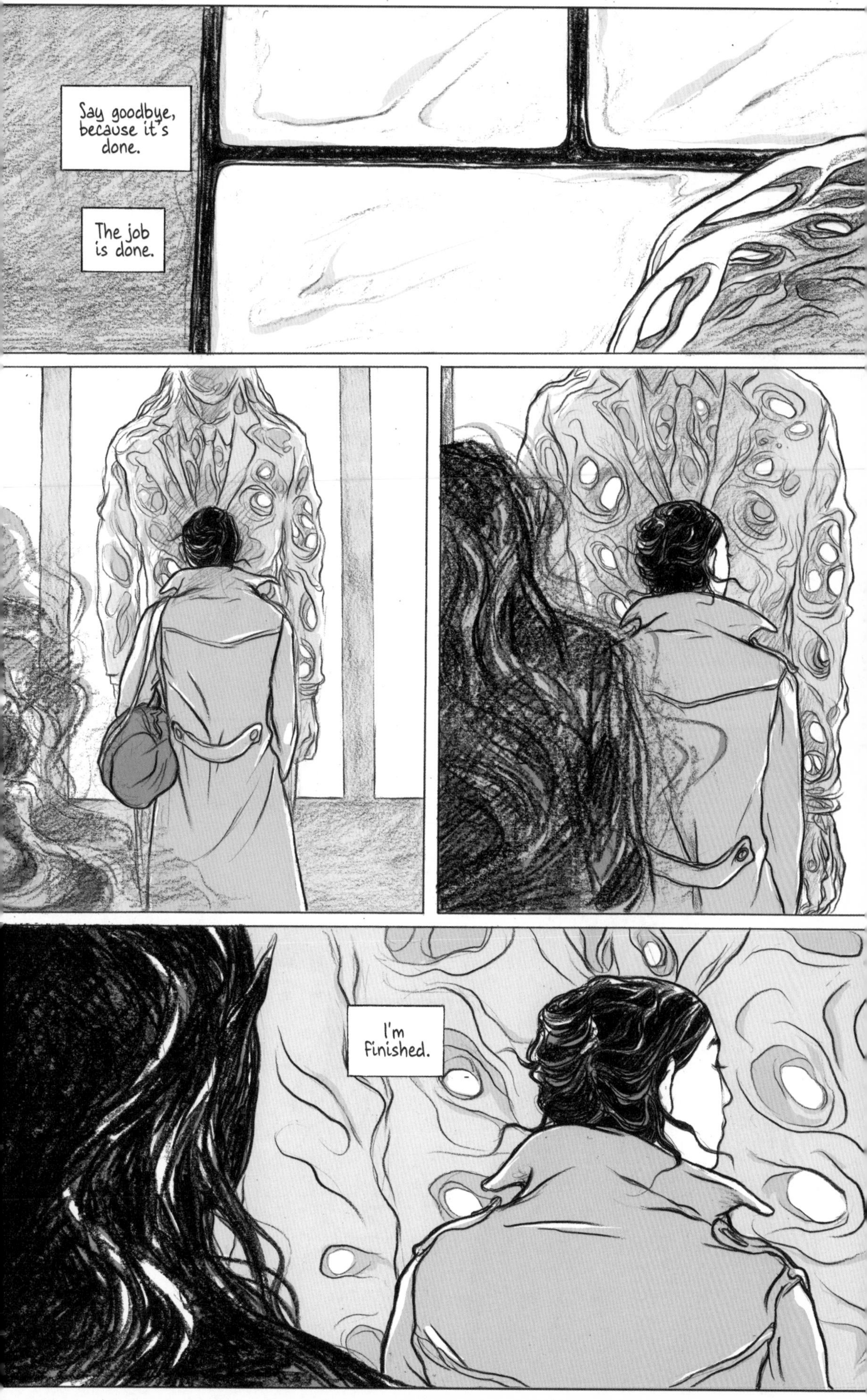
Say goodbye, because it's done.
The job is done.
I'm finished.

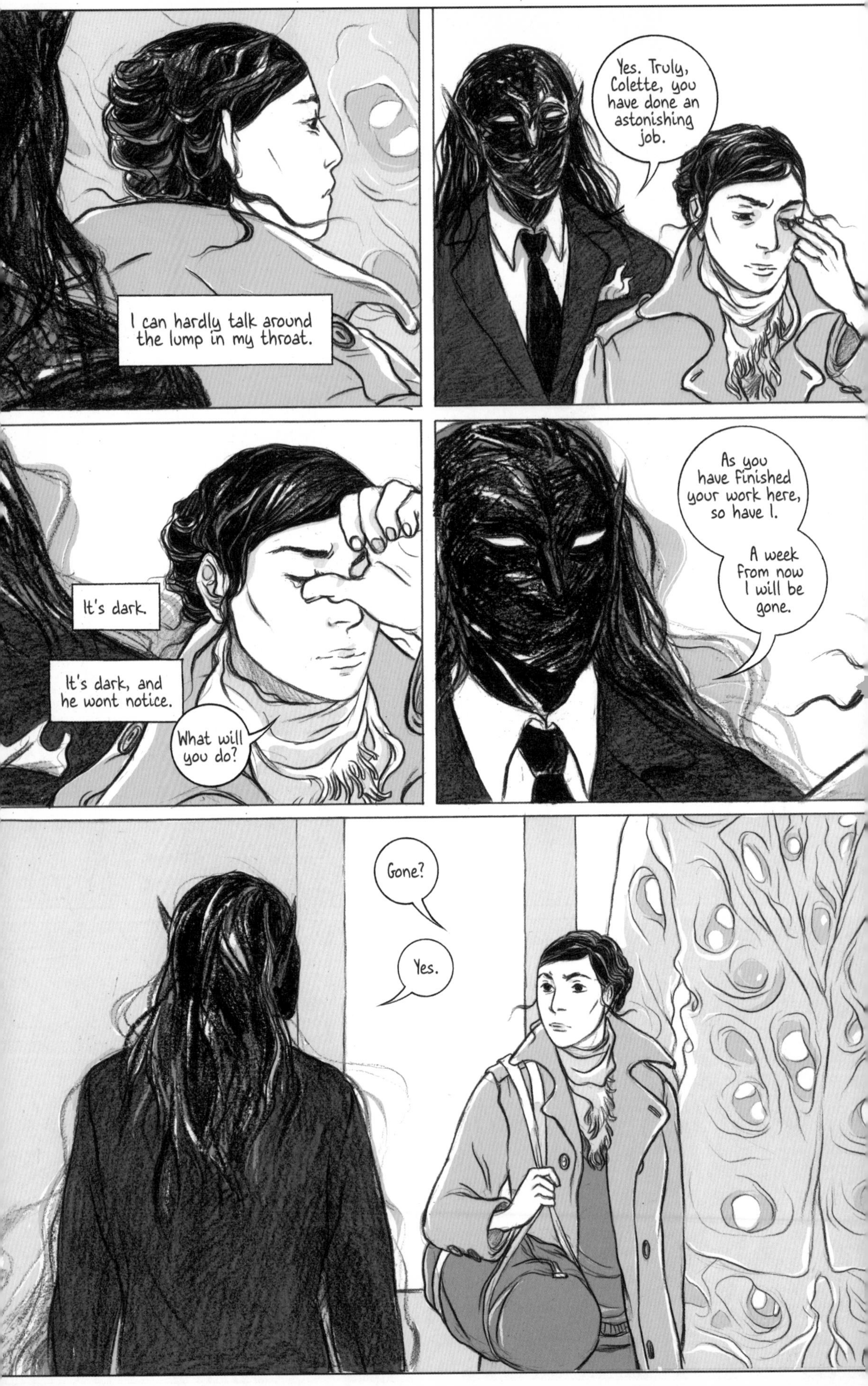
I can hardly talk around the lump in my throat.
Yes. Truly, Colette, you have done an astonishing job.
It's dark.
It's dark, and he wont notice.
What will you do?
As you have finished your work here, so have I.
A week from now I will be gone.
Gone?
Yes.

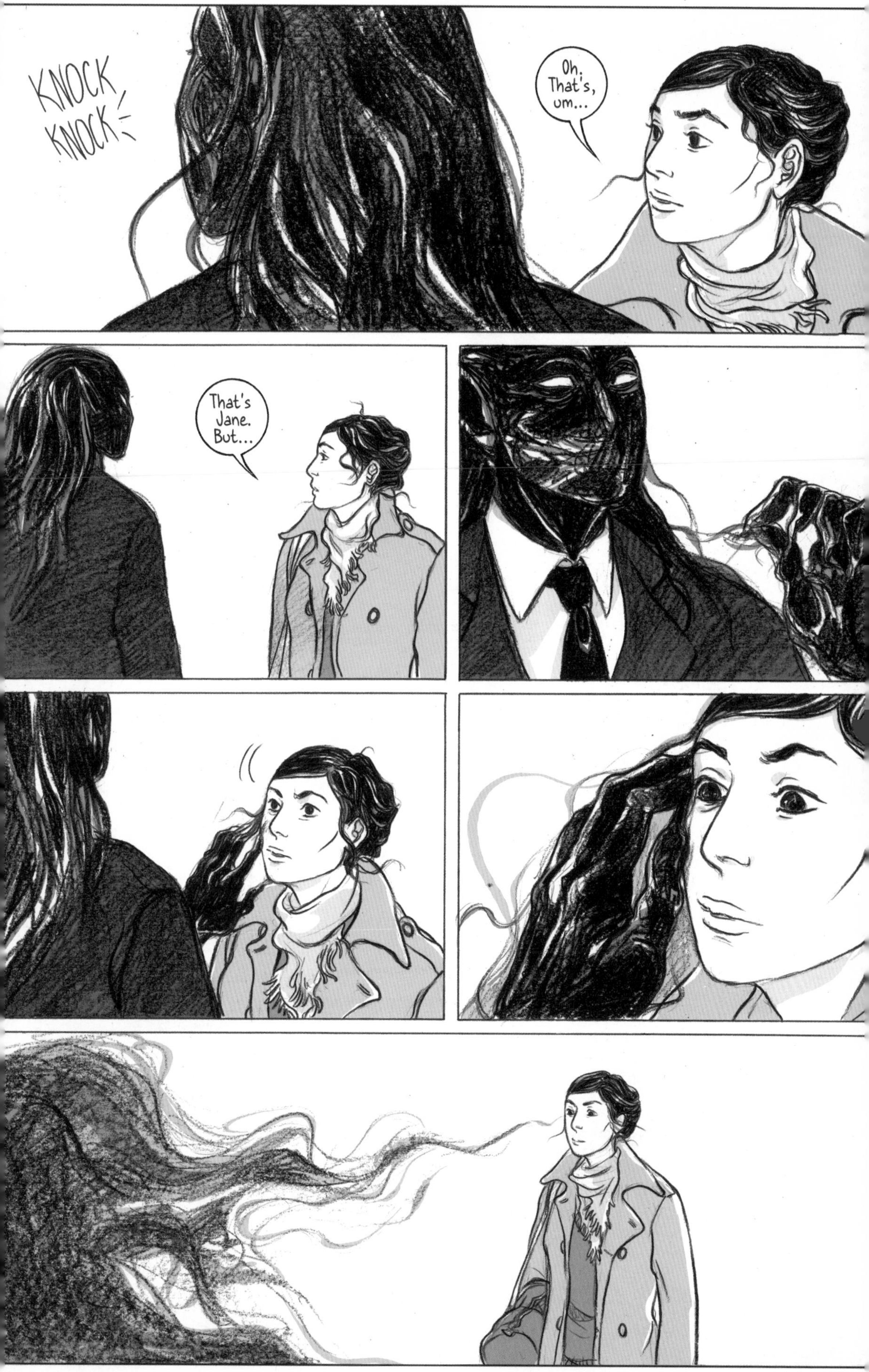
KNOCK KNOCK
Oh. That's, um...
That's Jane. But...

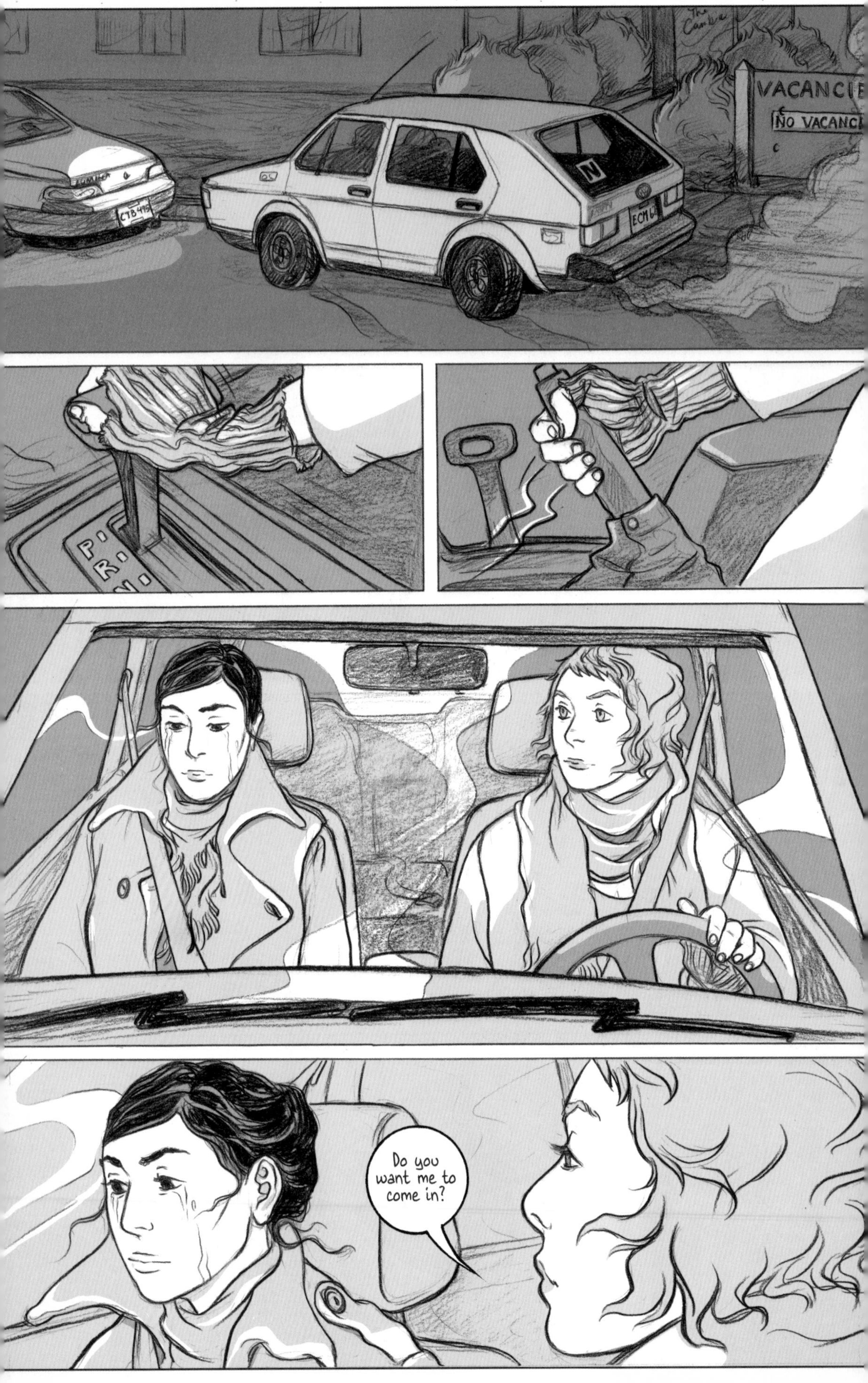
VACANCIE
NO VACANC
Do you want me to come in?

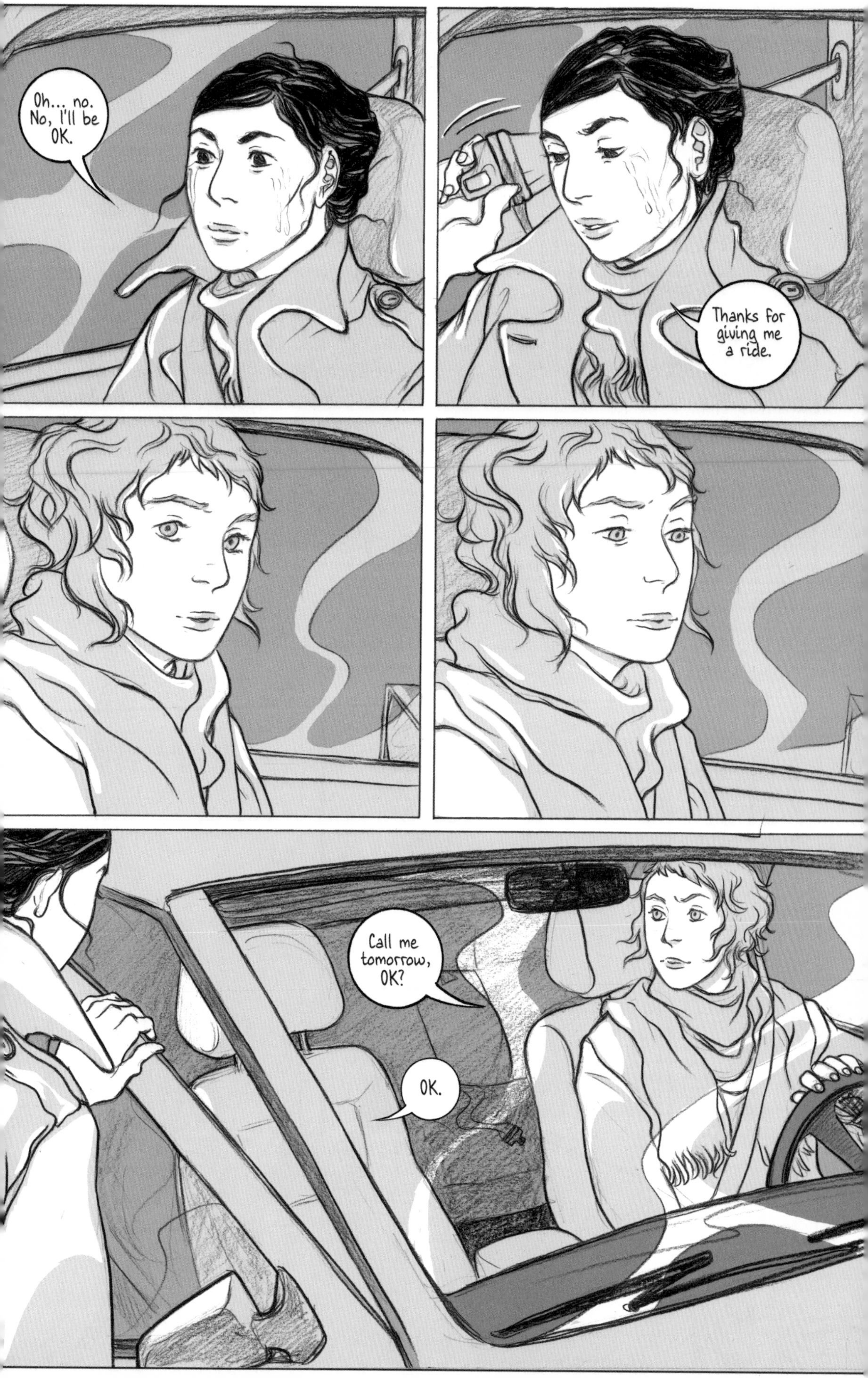
Oh... no. No, I'll be OK.
Thanks for giving me a ride.
Call me tomorrow, OK?
OK.

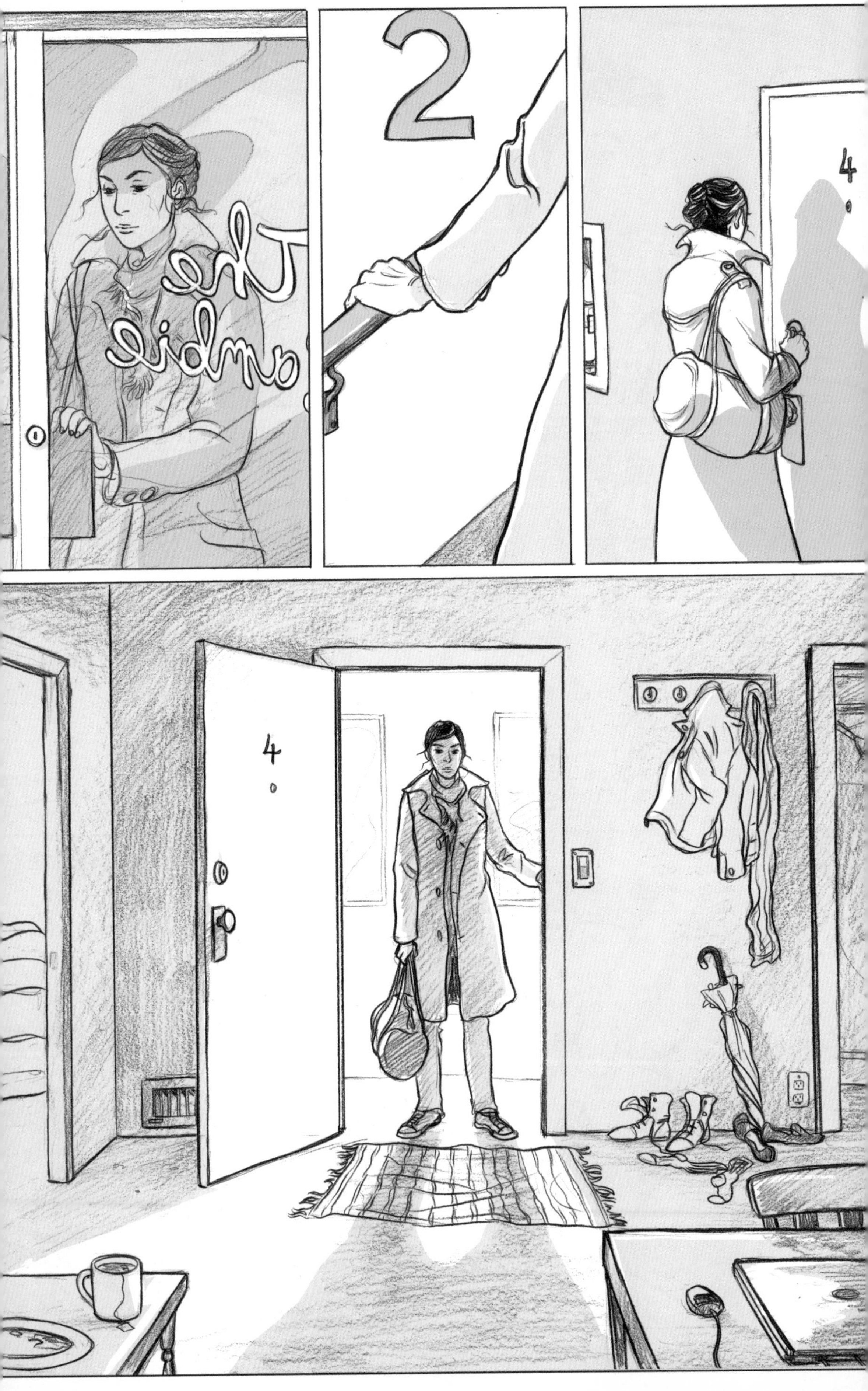
2
4
4

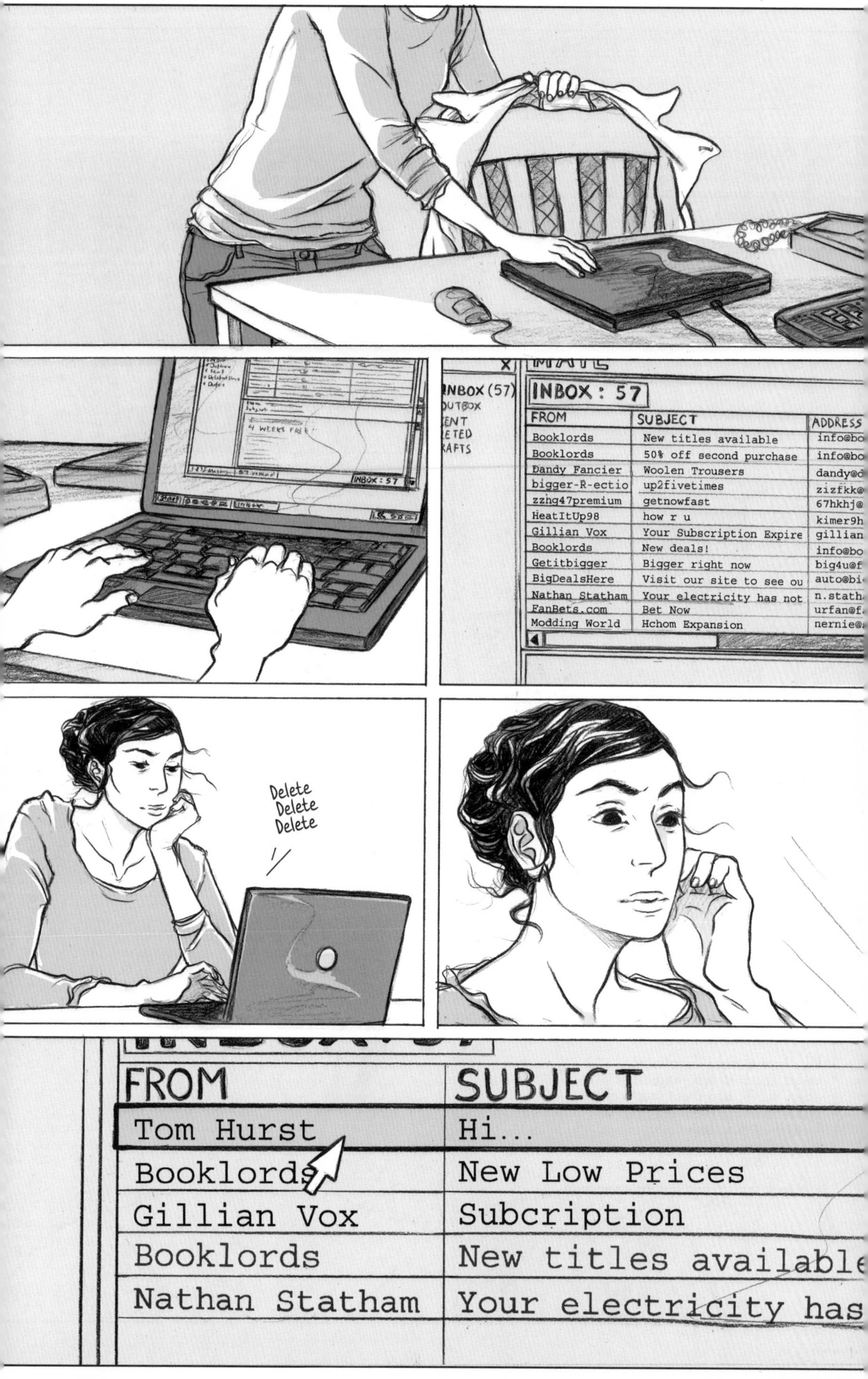

INBOX : 57
INBOX : 57
FROM
SUBJECT
ADDRESS
Booklords
New titles available
Booklords
50% off second purchase
Dandy Fancier
Woolen Trousers
bigger-R-ectio
up2fivetimes
zzhg47premium
getnowfast
HeatItUp98
how r u
Gillian Vox
Your Subscription Expire
Booklords
New deals!
Getitbigger
Bigger right now
BigDealsHere
Visit our site to see ou
Nathan Statham
Your electricity has not
FanBets.com
Bet Now
Modding World
Hchom Expansion
Delete
Delete
Delete
FROM
SUBJECT
Tom Hurst
Hi...
Booklords
New Low Prices
Gillian Vox
Subcription
Booklords
New titles availabl
Nathan Statham
Your electricity has

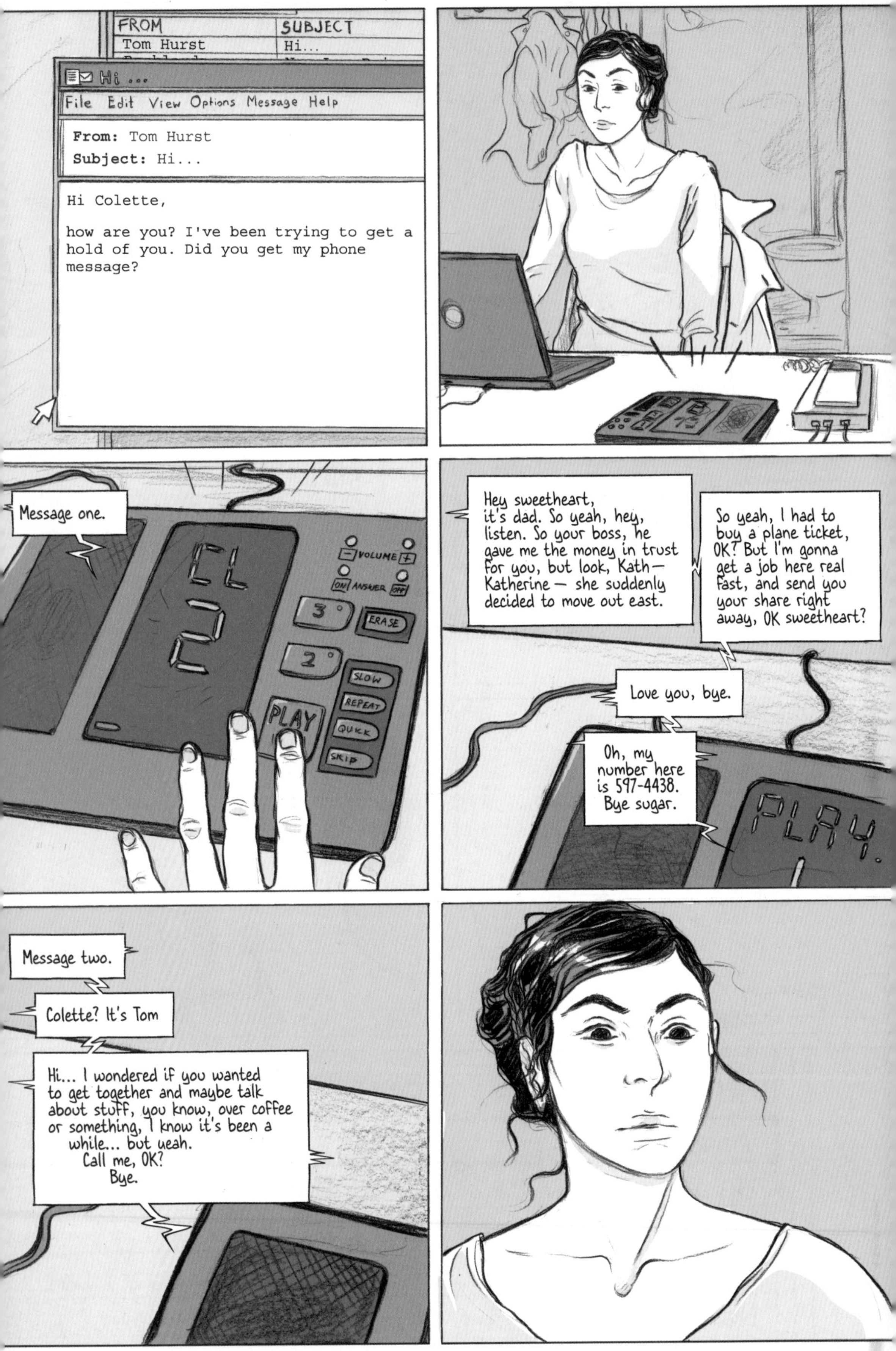
FROM
SUBJECT
Tom Hurst
Hi...
Hi ...
File Edit View Options Message Help
From: Tom Hurst
Subject: Hi...
Hi Colette,
how are you? I've been trying to get a hold of you. Did you get my phone message?
Message one.
CL 2
VOLUME
ON ANSWER OFF
ERASE
SLOW
REPEAT
QUICK
SKIP
PLAY
Hey sweetheart, it's dad. So yeah, hey, listen. So your boss, he gave me the money in trust for you, but look, Kath— Katherine — she suddenly decided to move out east.
So yeah, I had to buy a plane ticket, OK? But I'm gonna get a job here real fast, and send you your share right away, OK sweetheart?
Love you, bye.
Oh, my number here is 597-4438. Bye sugar.
PLAY.
Message two.
Colette? It's Tom
Hi... I wondered if you wanted to get together and maybe talk about stuff, you know, over coffee or something, I know it's been a while... but yeah. Call me, OK? Bye.

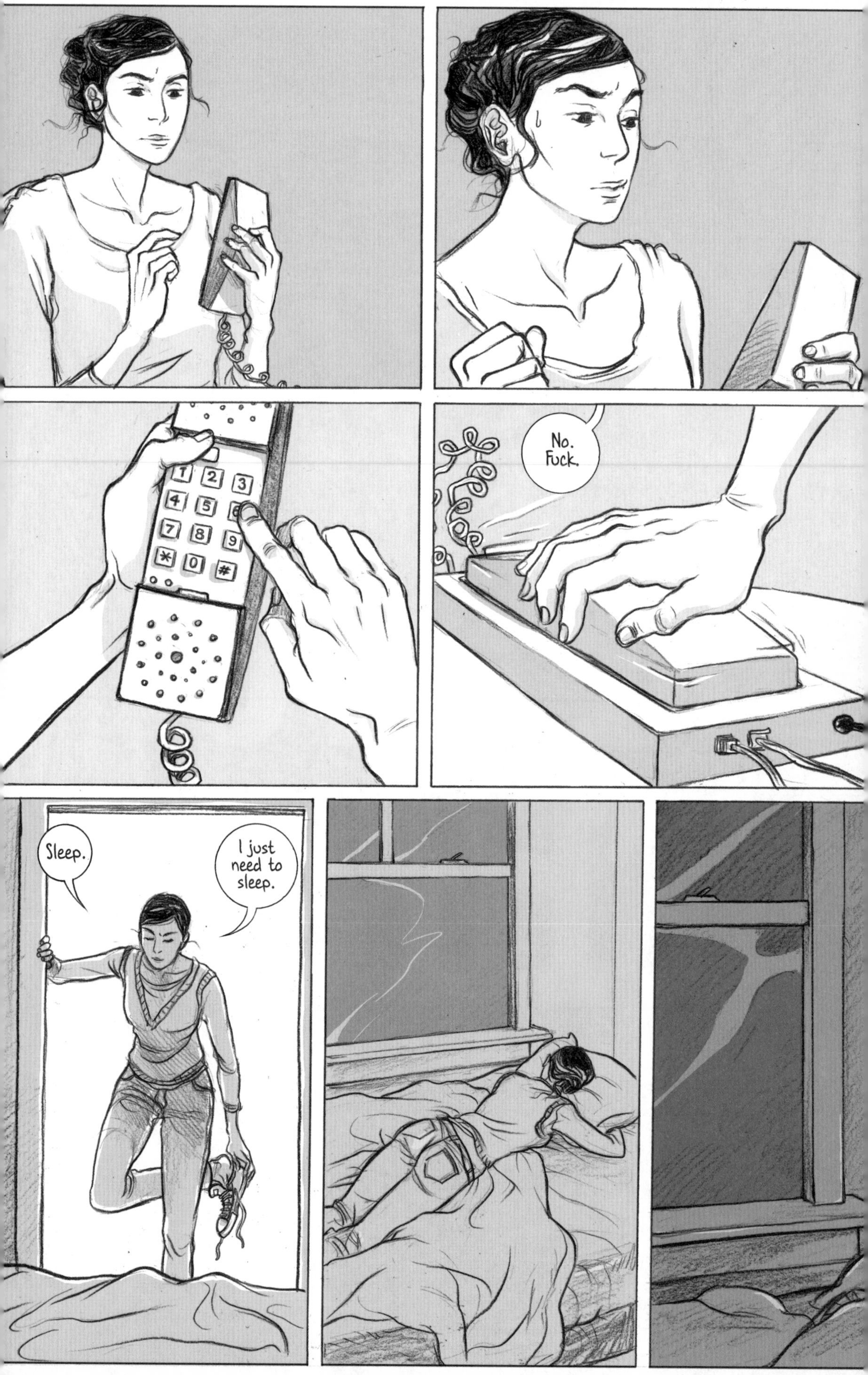
No. Fuck.
Sleep.
I just need to sleep.

Part Three

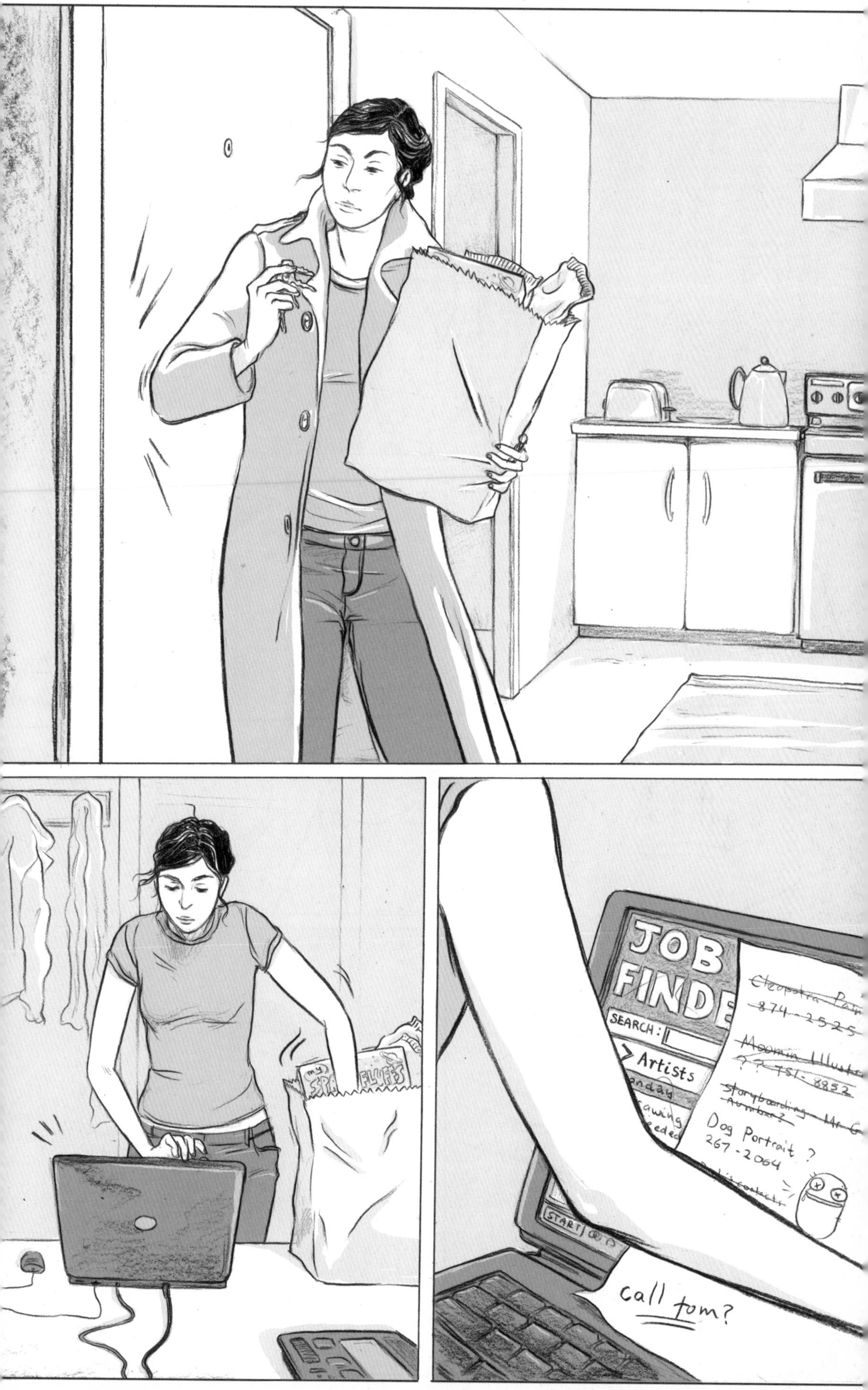
JOB FINDE
SEARCH:
Artists
Dog Portrait ?
267-2064
call tom?

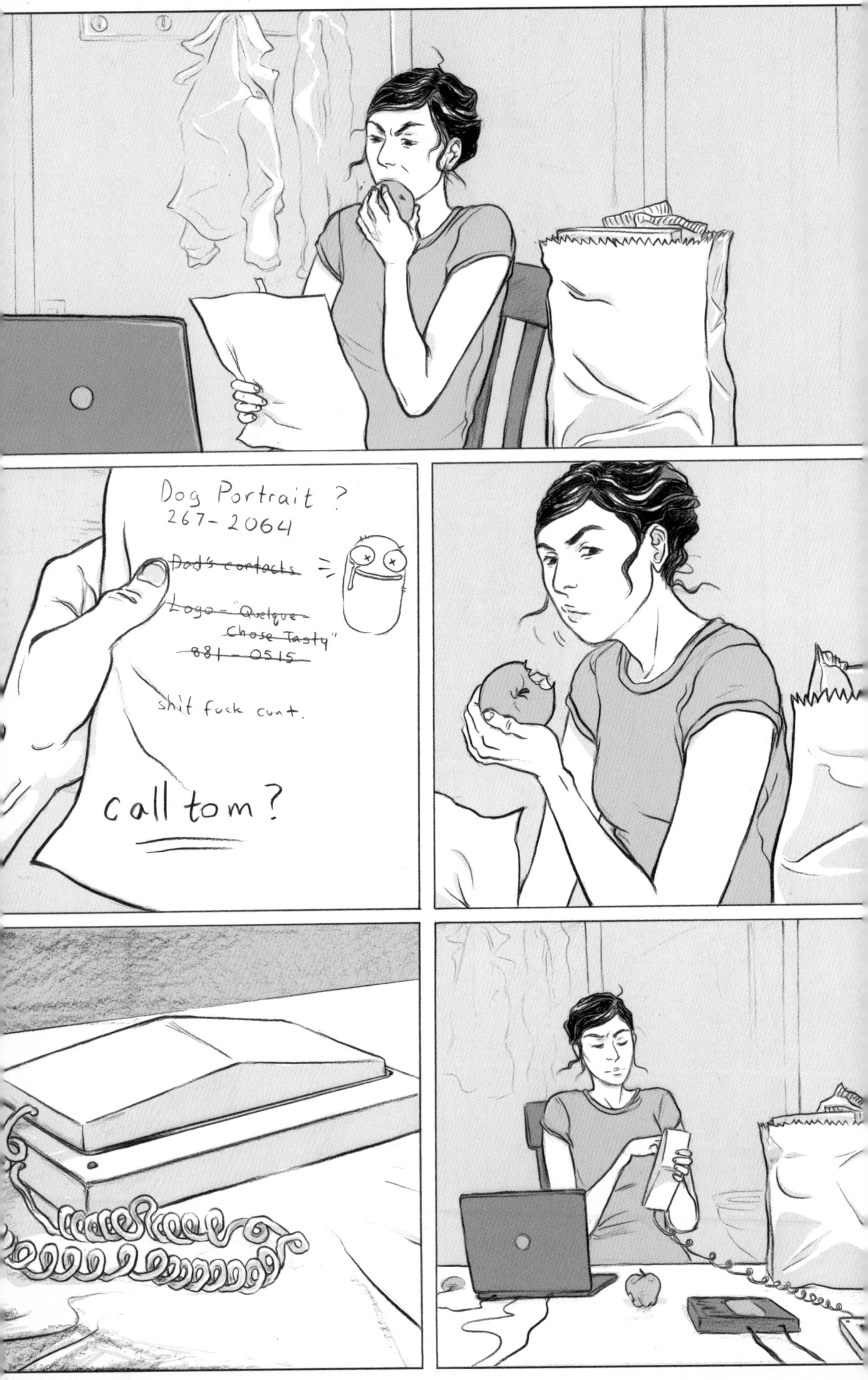
Dog Portrait ?
267-2064
Dad's contacts
Logo - "Quelque-
Chose Tasty"
881-0515
shit fuck cunt.
call tom?

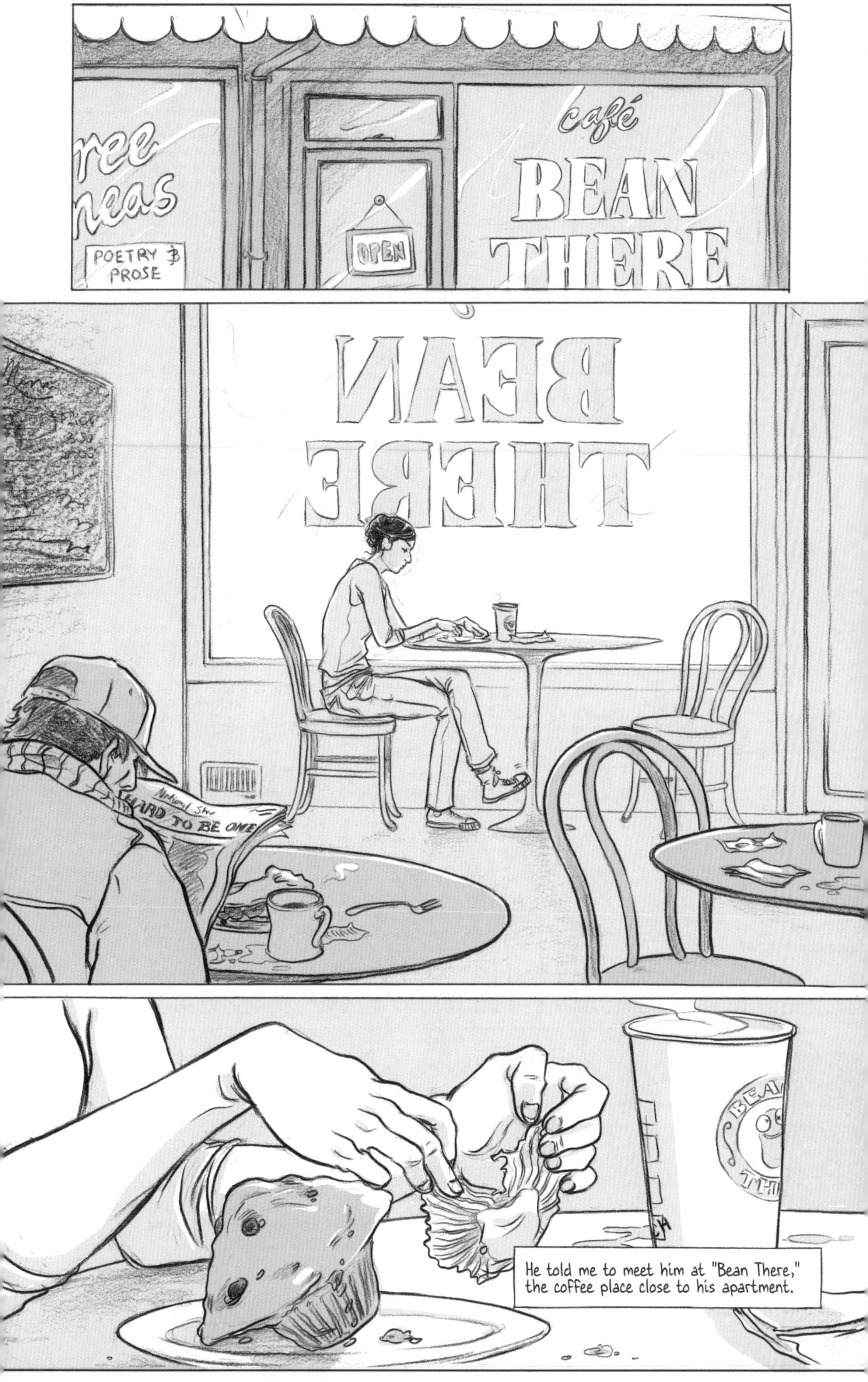
POETRY & PROSE
OPEN
café
BEAN
THERE
HARD TO BE ONE
He told me to meet him at "Bean There," the coffee place close to his apartment.

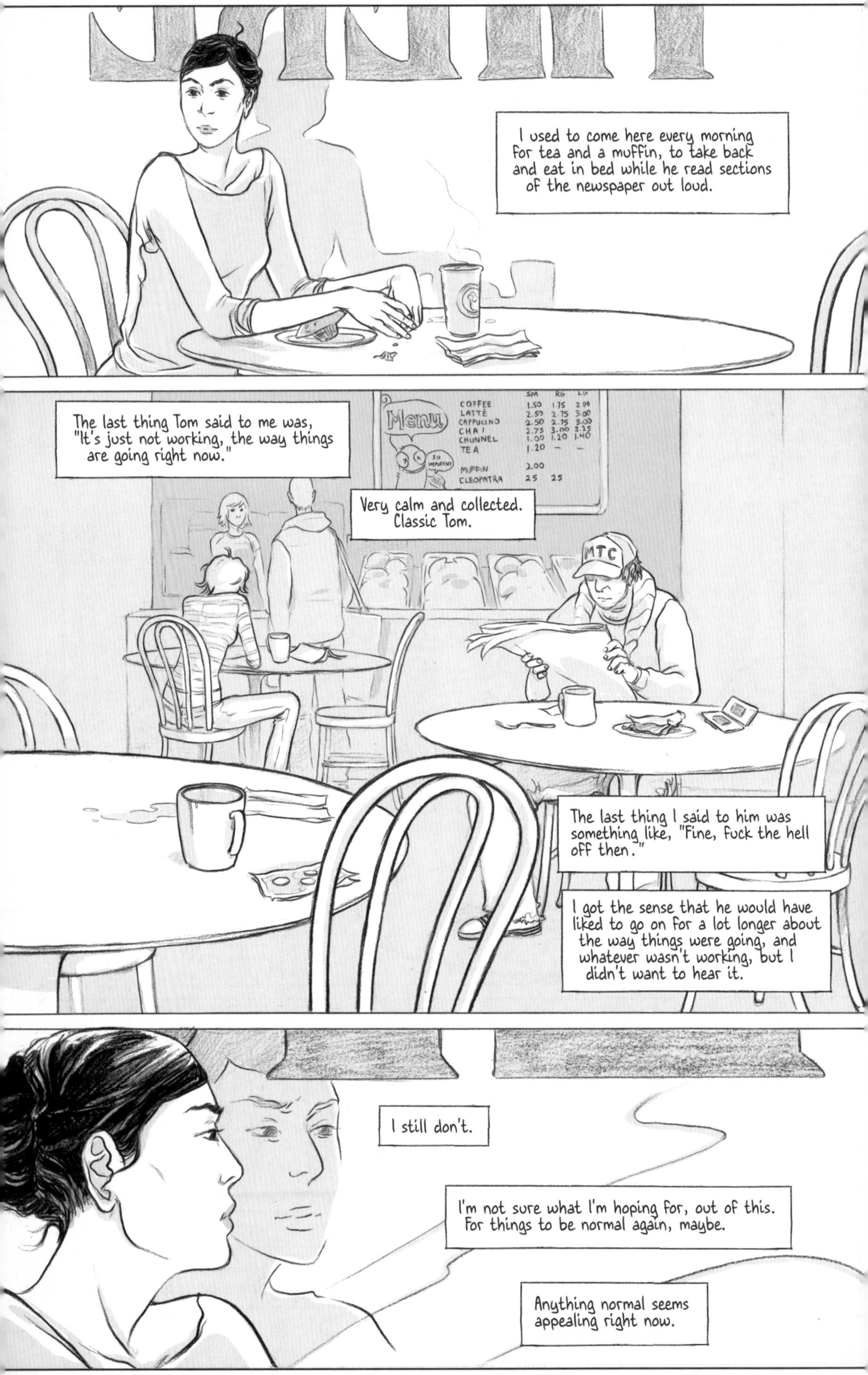
I used to come here every morning for tea and a muffin, to take back and eat in bed while he read sections of the newspaper out loud.
Menu
SM RG LG
COFFEE 1.50 1.75 2.00
LATTÉ 2.50 2.75 3.00
CAPPUCINO 2.50 2.75 3.00
CHAI 2.75 3.00 3.25
CHUNNEL 1.00 1.20 1.40
TEA 1.20 — —
MUFFIN 2.00
CLEOPATRA 25 25
The last thing Tom said to me was, "It's just not working, the way things are going right now."
Very calm and collected. Classic Tom.
MTC
The last thing I said to him was something like, "Fine, fuck the hell off then."
I got the sense that he would have liked to go on for a lot longer about the way things were going, and whatever wasn't working, but I didn't want to hear it.
I still don't.
I'm not sure what I'm hoping for, out of this. For things to be normal again, maybe.
Anything normal seems appealing right now.

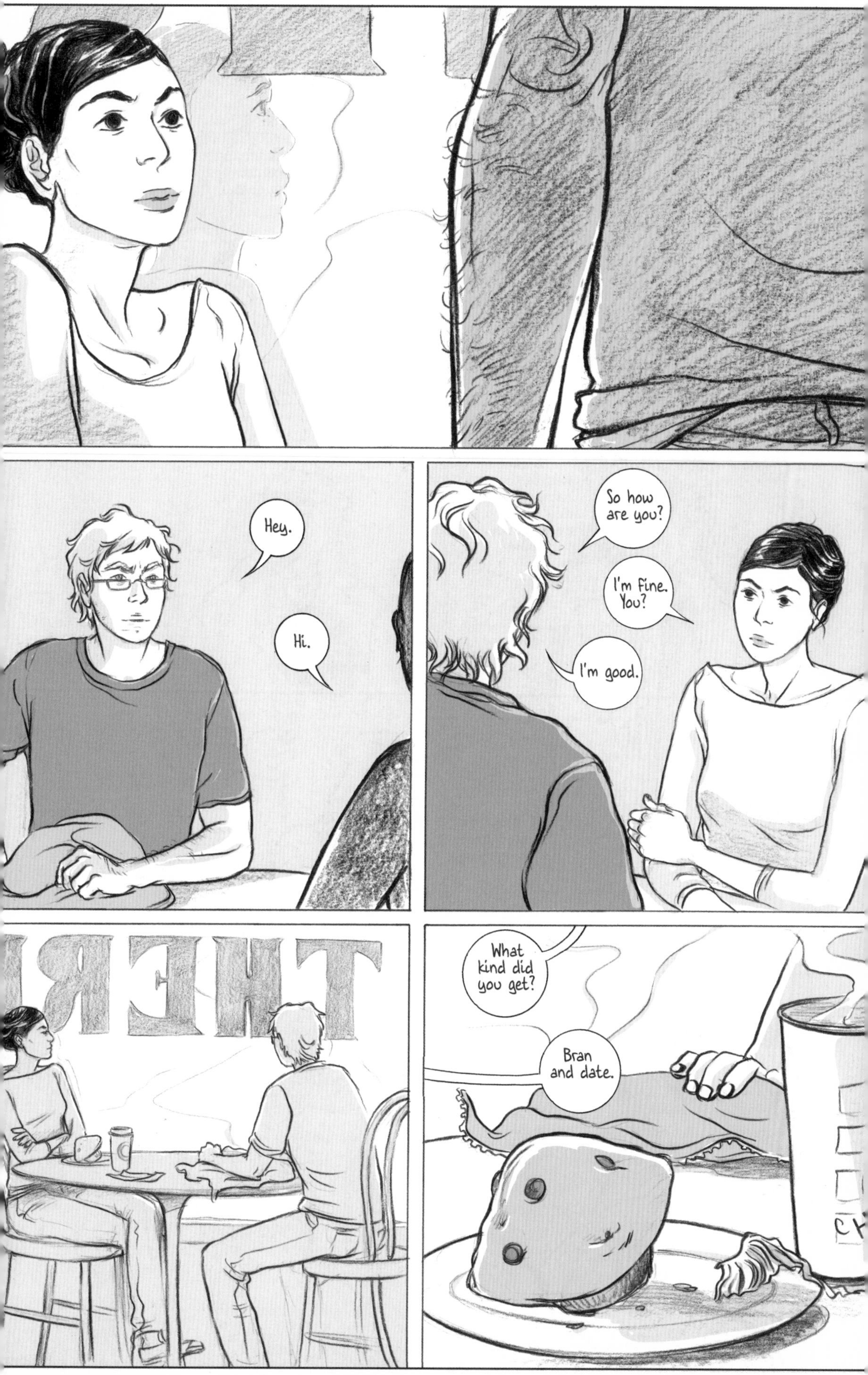
Hey.
Hi.
So how are you?
I'm fine. You?
I'm good.
What kind did you get?
Bran and date.

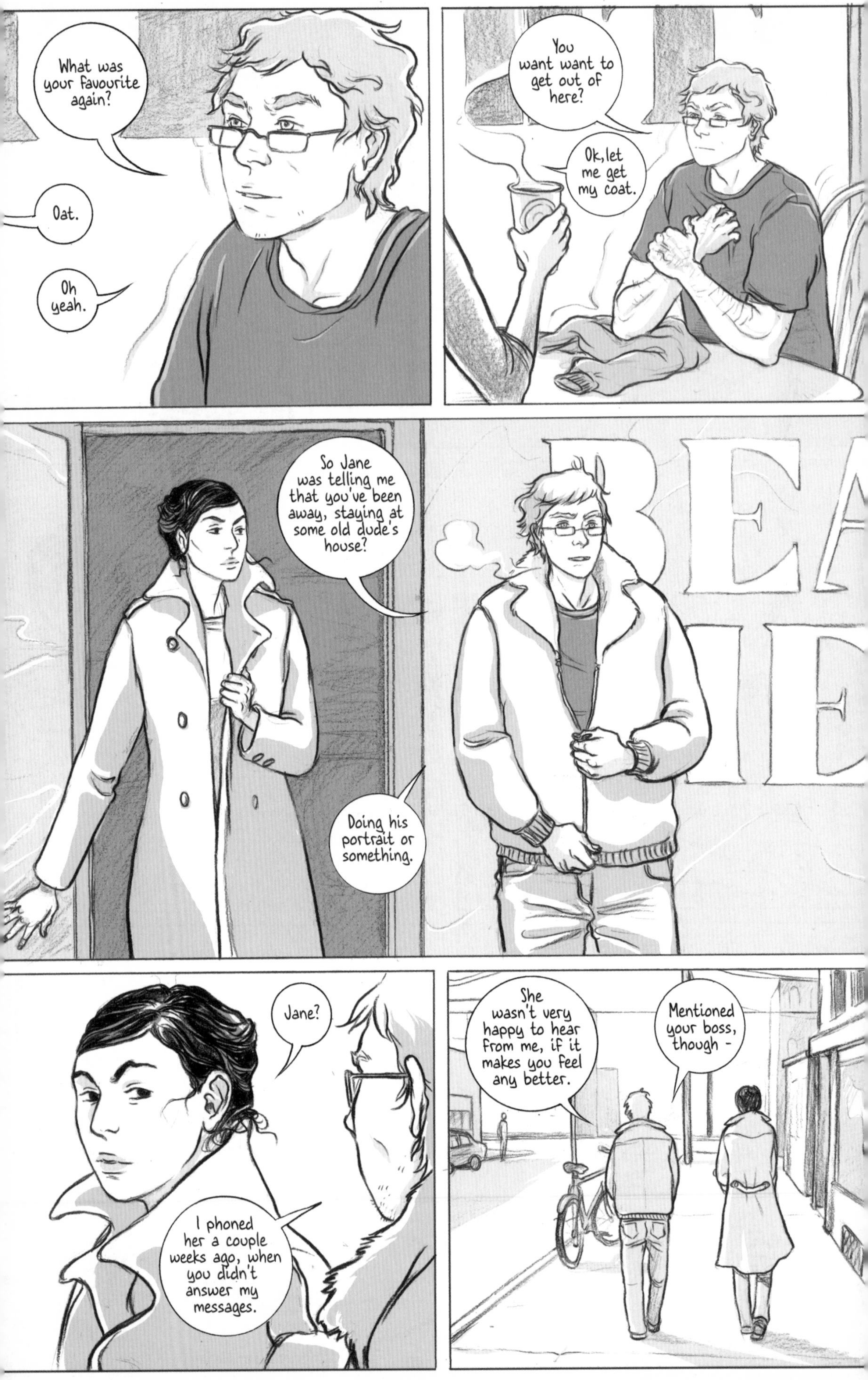
What was your favourite again?
Oat.
Oh yeah.
You want want to get out of here?
Ok, let me get my coat.
So Jane was telling me that you've been away, staying at some old dude's house?
Doing his portrait or something.
Jane?
I phoned her a couple weeks ago, when you didn't answer my messages.
She wasn't very happy to hear from me, if it makes you feel any better.
Mentioned your boss, though -

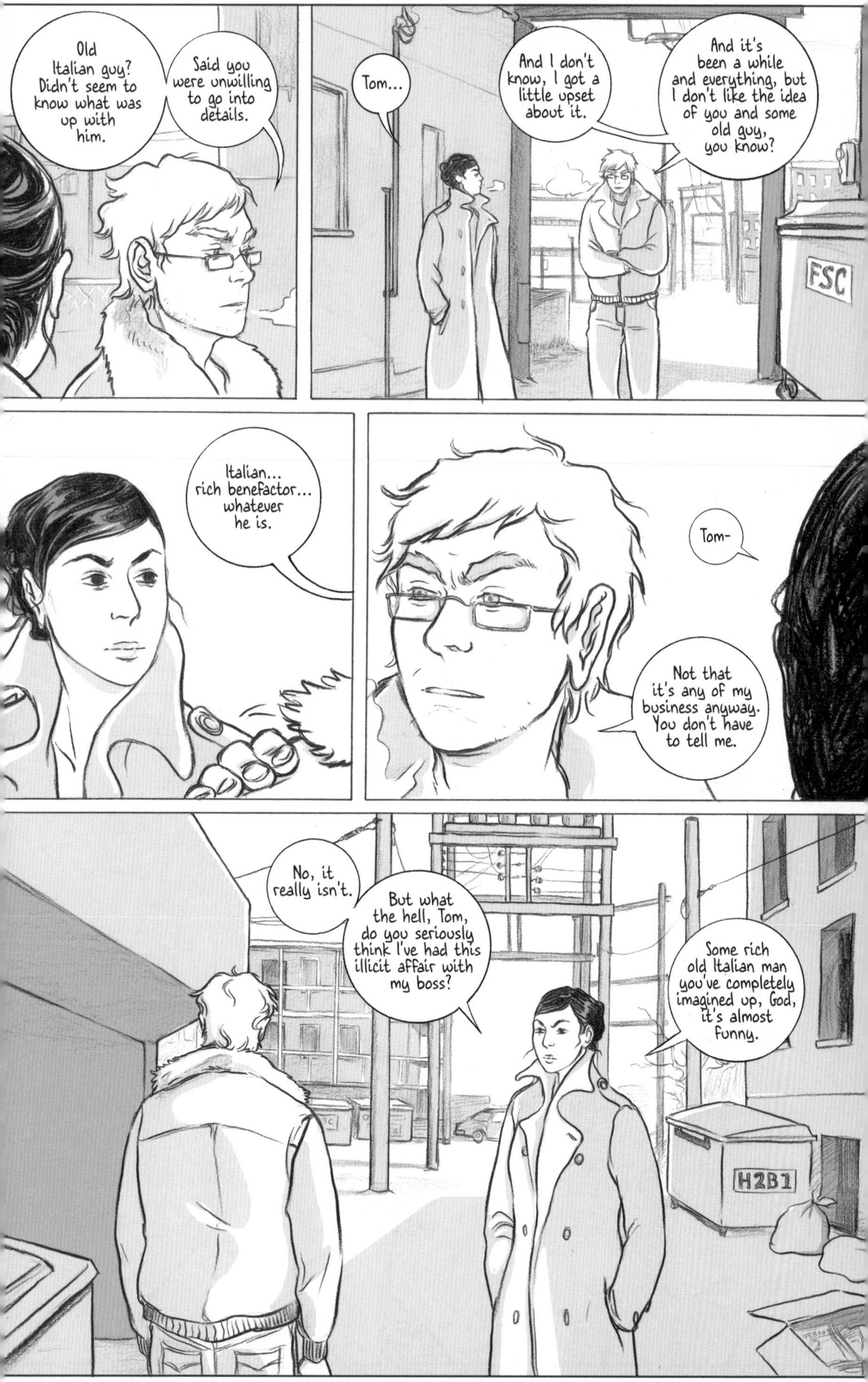
Old Italian guy? Didn't seem to know what was up with him.
Said you were unwilling to go into details.
Tom...
And I don't know, I got a little upset about it.
And it's been a while and everything, but I don't like the idea of you and some old guy, you know?
FSC
Italian... rich benefactor... whatever he is.
Tom-
Not that it's any of my business anyway. You don't have to tell me.
No, it really isn't.
But what the hell, Tom, do you seriously think I've had this illicit affair with my boss?
Some rich old Italian man you've completely imagined up, God, it's almost funny.
H2B1

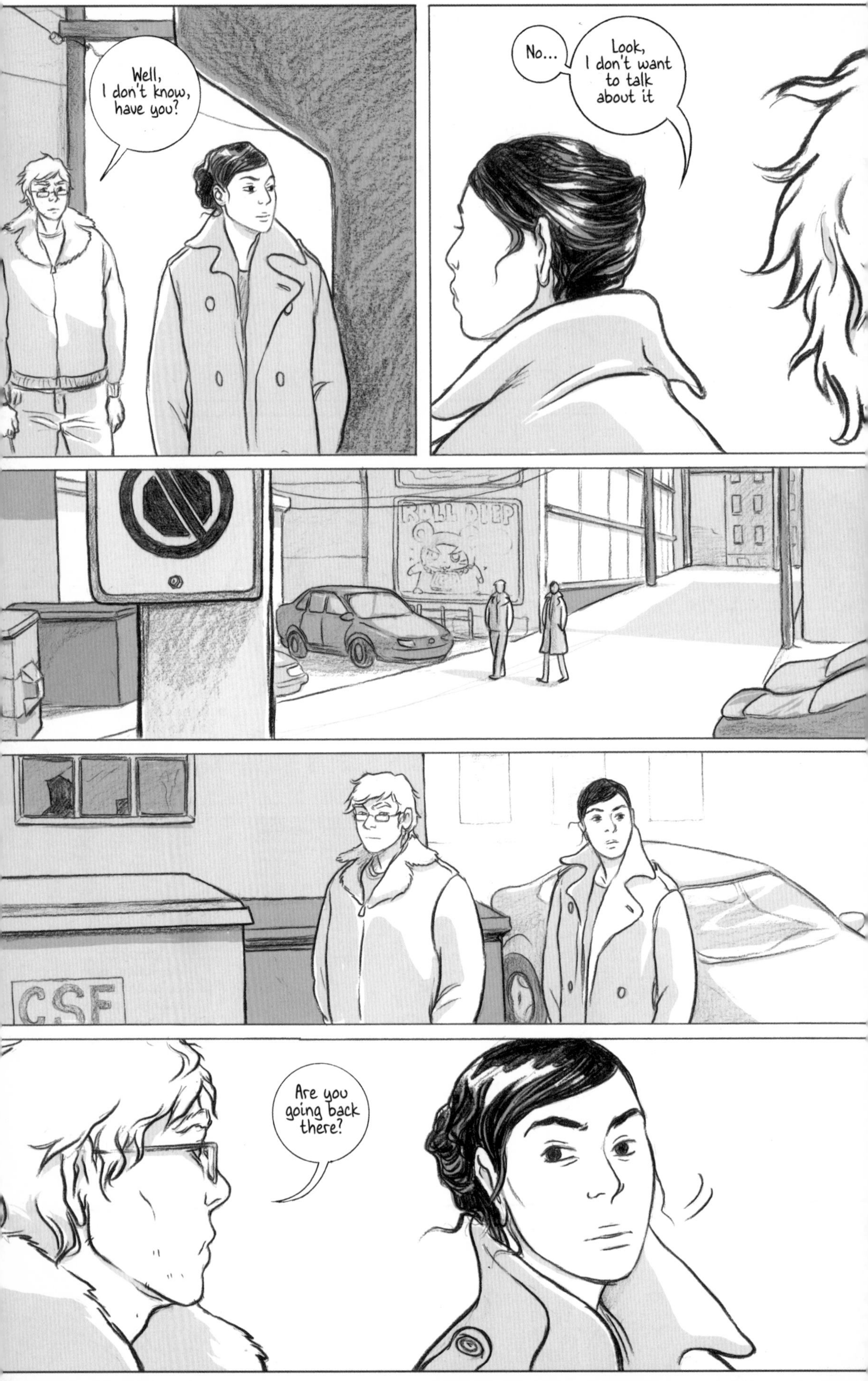
Well, I don't know, have you?
No...
Look, I don't want to talk about it
CSF
Are you going back there?

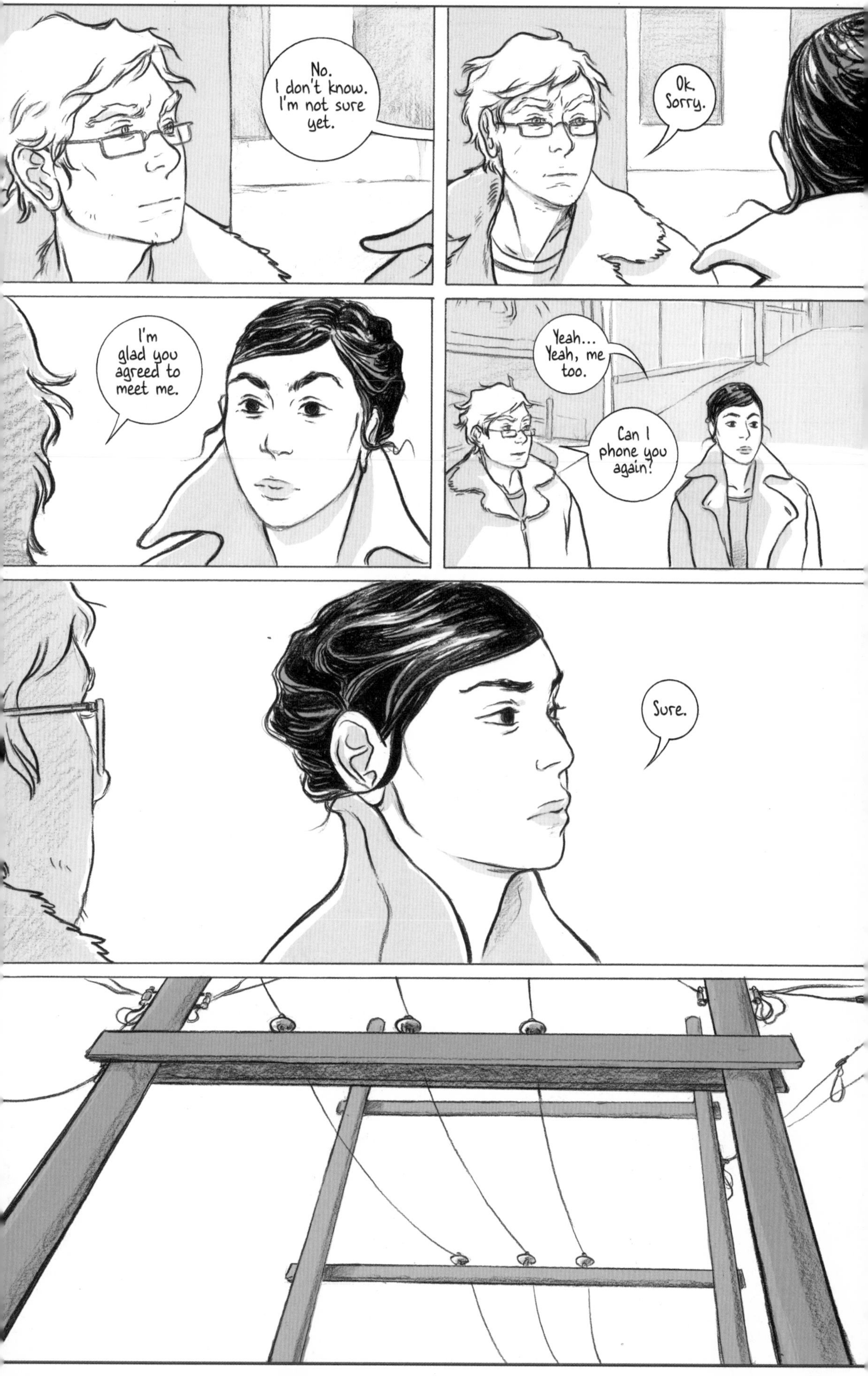
No. I don't know. I'm not sure yet.
Ok. Sorry.
I'm glad you agreed to meet me.
Yeah... Yeah, me too.
Can I phone you again?
Sure.

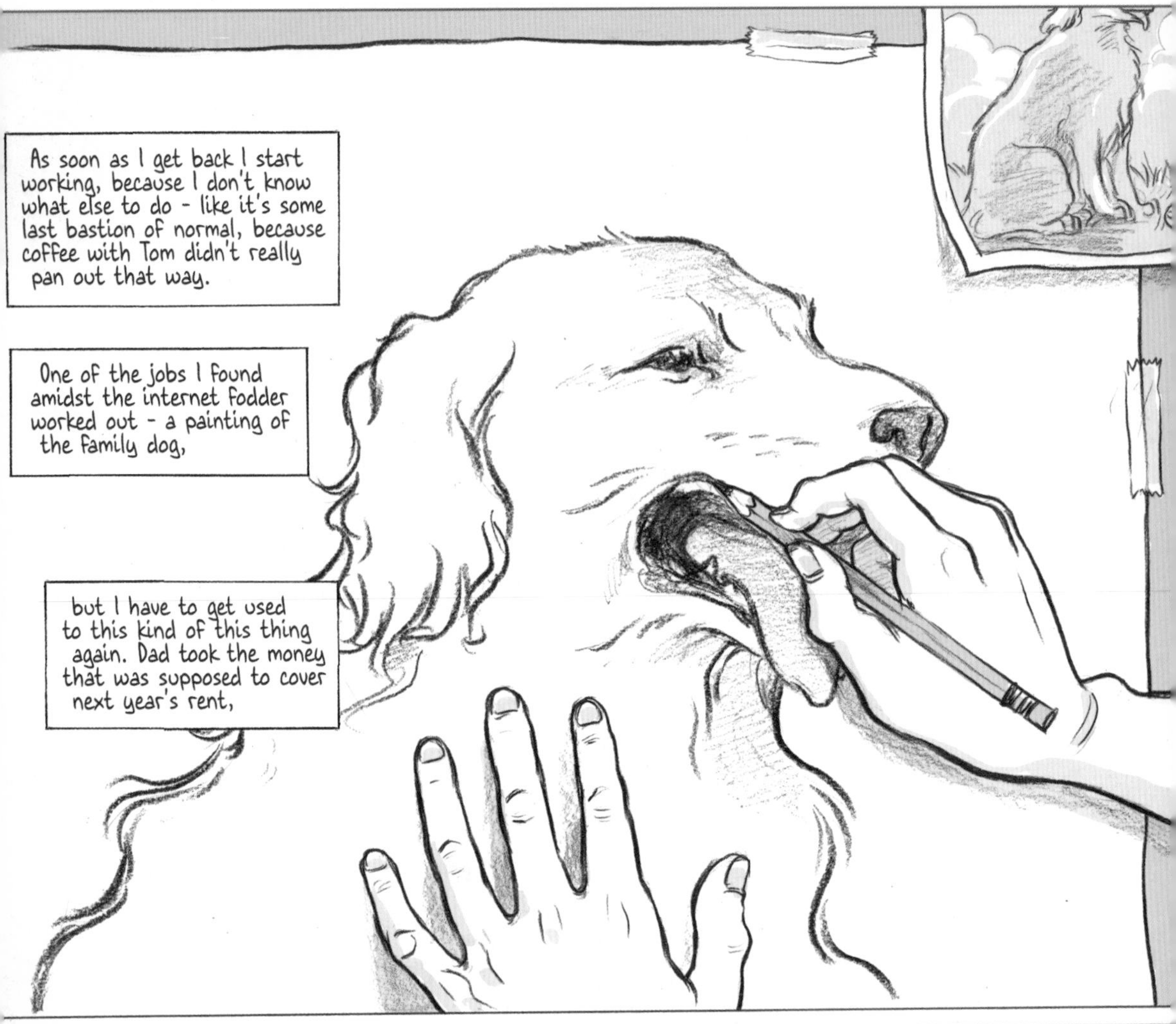
As soon as I get back I start working, because I don't know what else to do - like it's some last bastion of normal, because coffee with Tom didn't really pan out that way.
One of the jobs I found amidst the internet fodder worked out - a painting of the family dog,
but I have to get used to this kind of this thing again. Dad took the money that was supposed to cover next year's rent,

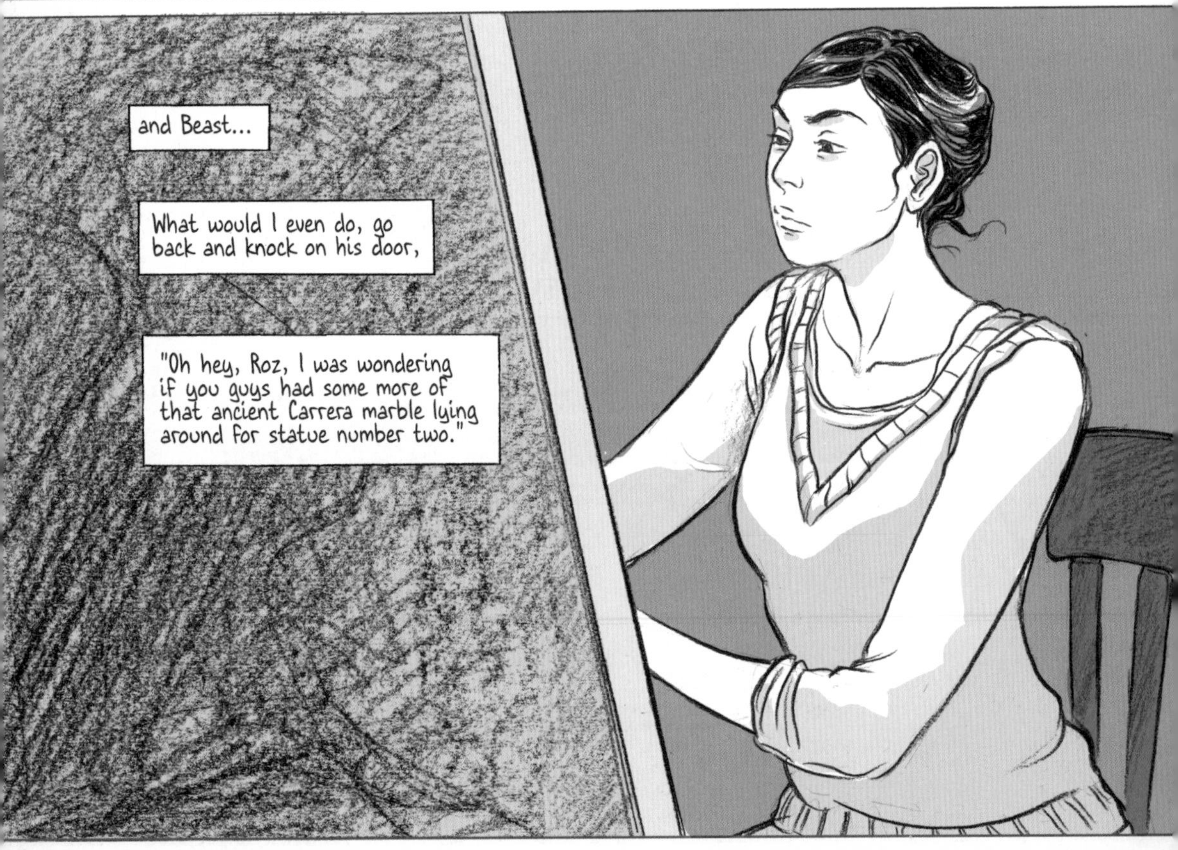
and Beast...
What would I even do, go back and knock on his door,
"Oh hey, Roz, I was wondering if you guys had some more of that ancient Carrera marble lying around for statue number two."

Part of me knows that maybe if I went back and spoke to Beast, I could do something about the money my dad took. Get that sorted out.

It's probably even a little ridiculous that I won't return.

Can't.

Because the terror I felt that first day, when I saw Beast approach me from the dark of the hallway, has long since been replaced by another kind of fear, more persuasive and paralyzing.

And never underestimate the sheer, blunt strength of cowardice.

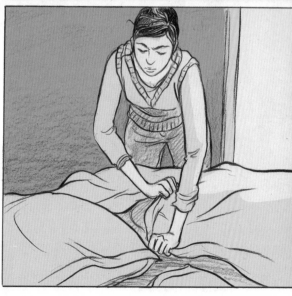

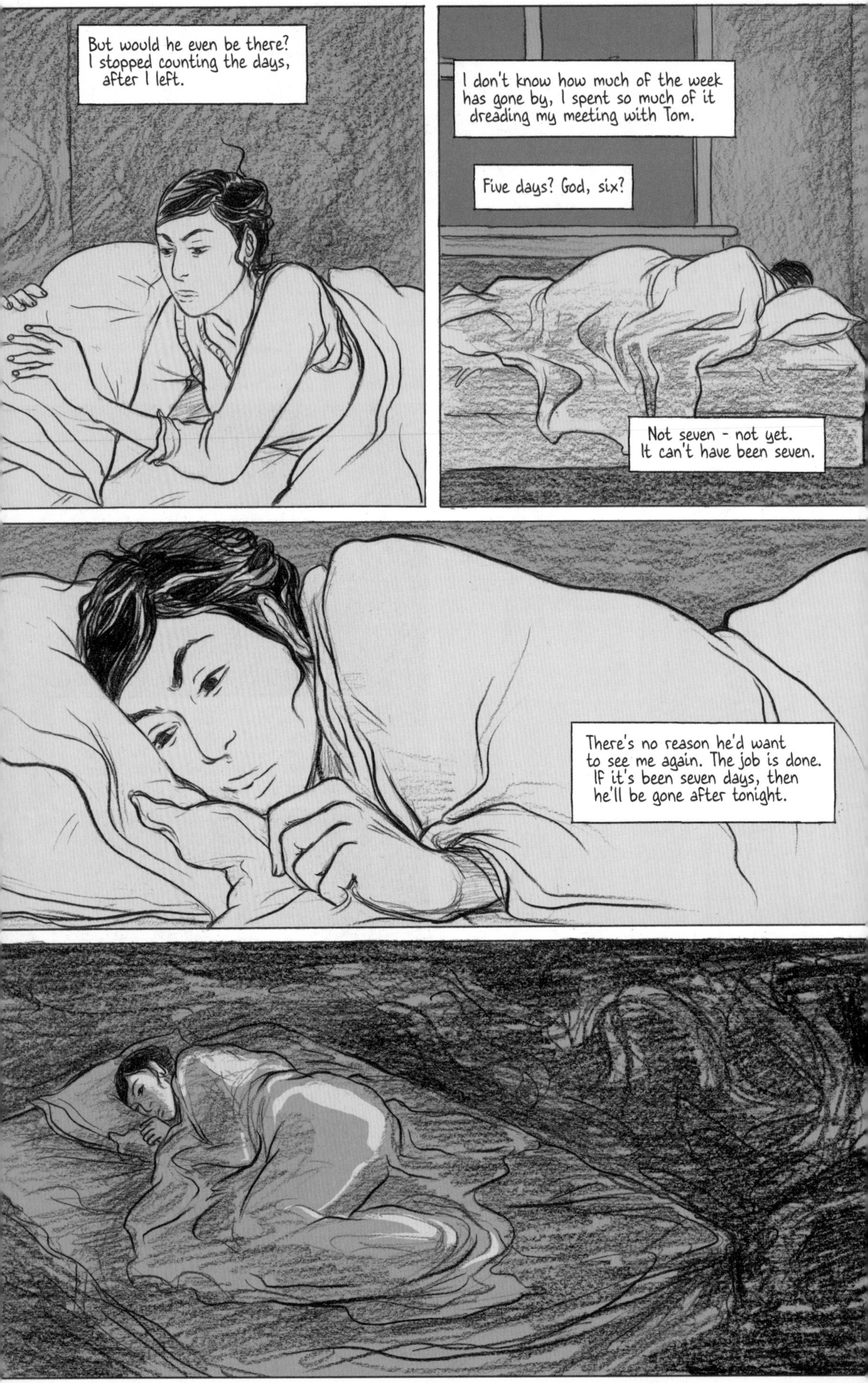
But would he even be there? I stopped counting the days, after I left.
I don't know how much of the week has gone by, I spent so much of it dreading my meeting with Tom.
Five days? God, six?
Not seven - not yet. It can't have been seven.
There's no reason he'd want to see me again. The job is done. If it's been seven days, then he'll be gone after tonight.

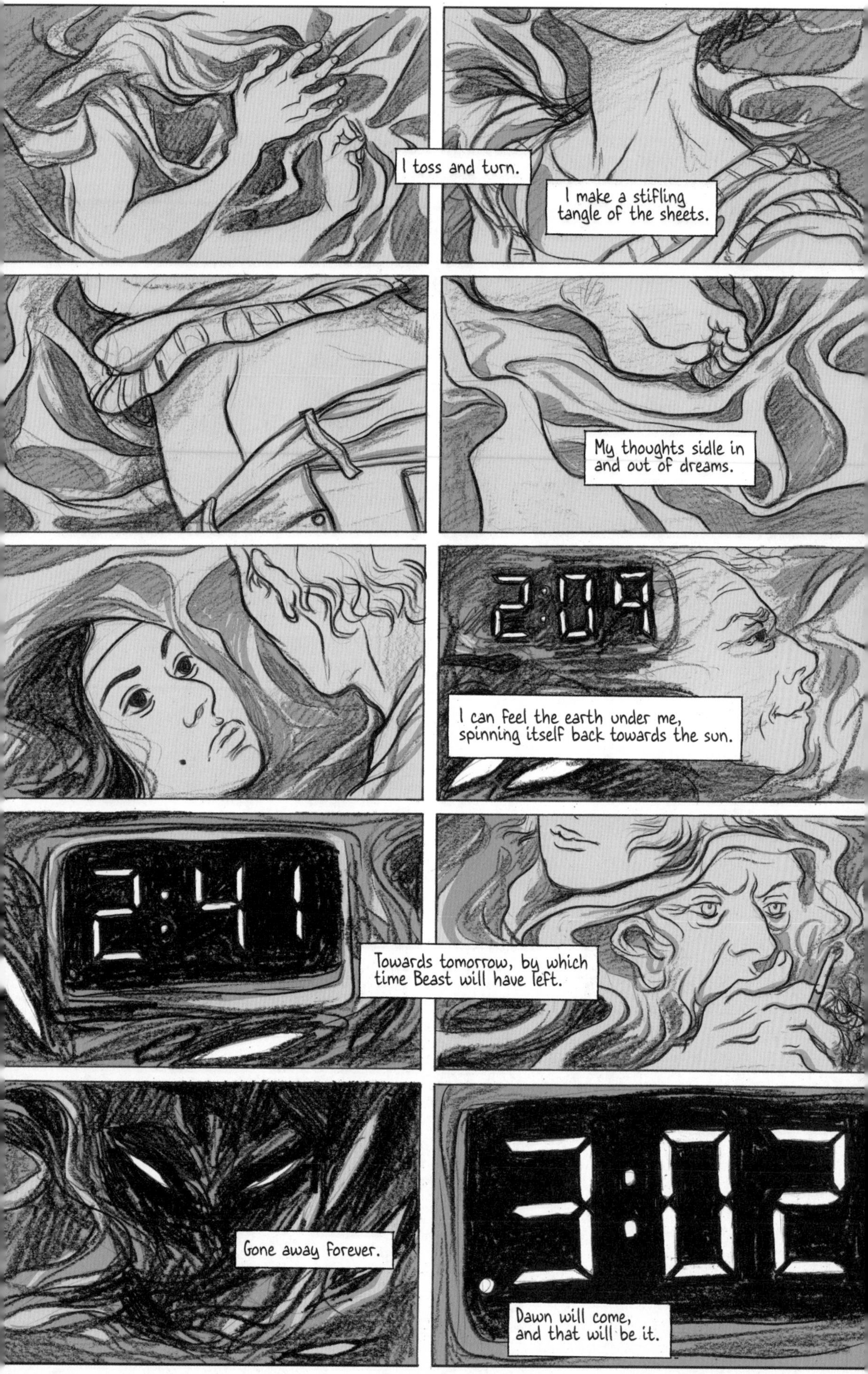
I toss and turn.
I make a stifling tangle of the sheets.
My thoughts sidle in and out of dreams.
2:09
I can feel the earth under me, spinning itself back towards the sun.
2:41
Towards tomorrow, by which time Beast will have left.
Gone away forever.
3:02
Dawn will come, and that will be it.

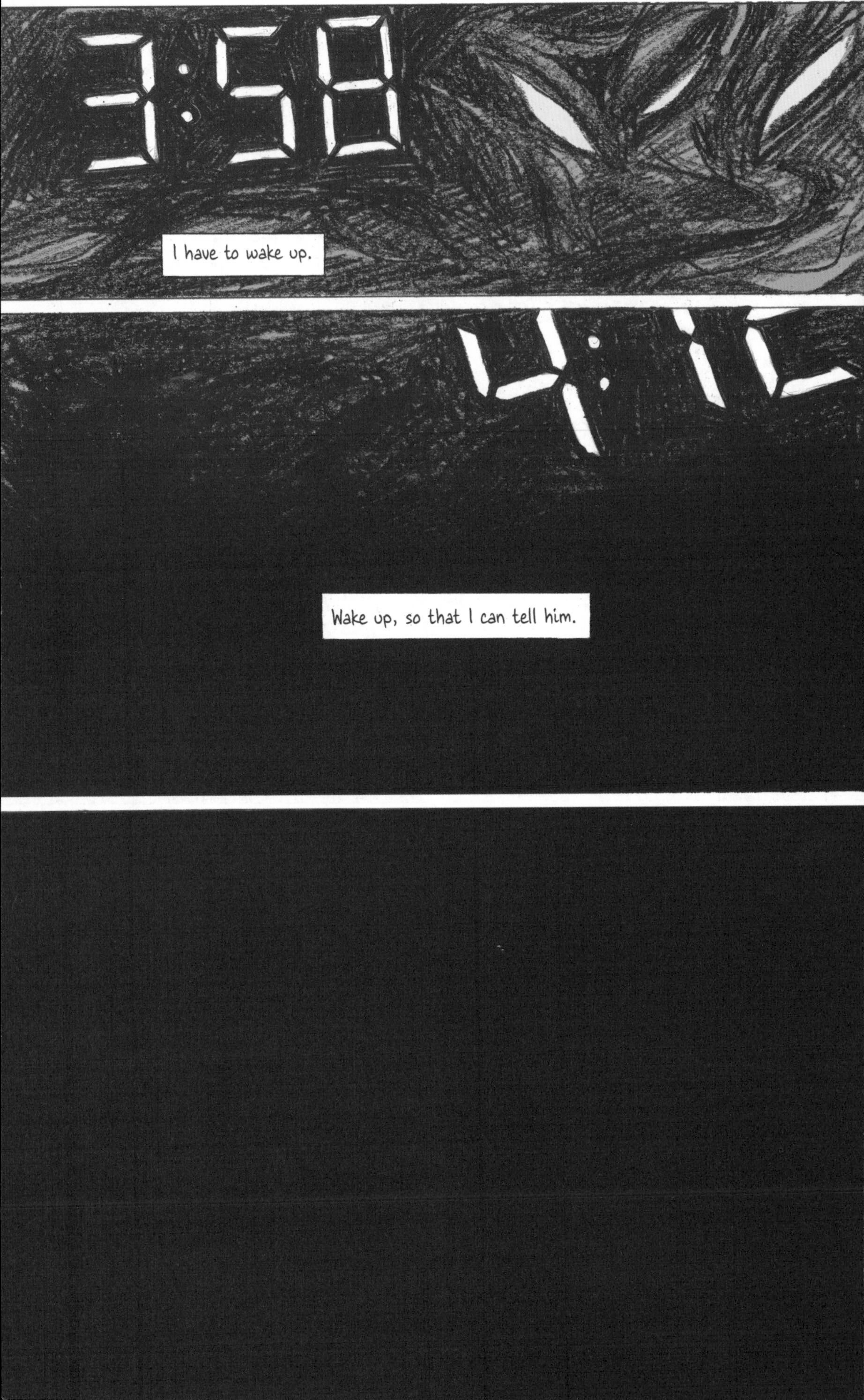
I have to wake up.
Wake up, so that I can tell him.

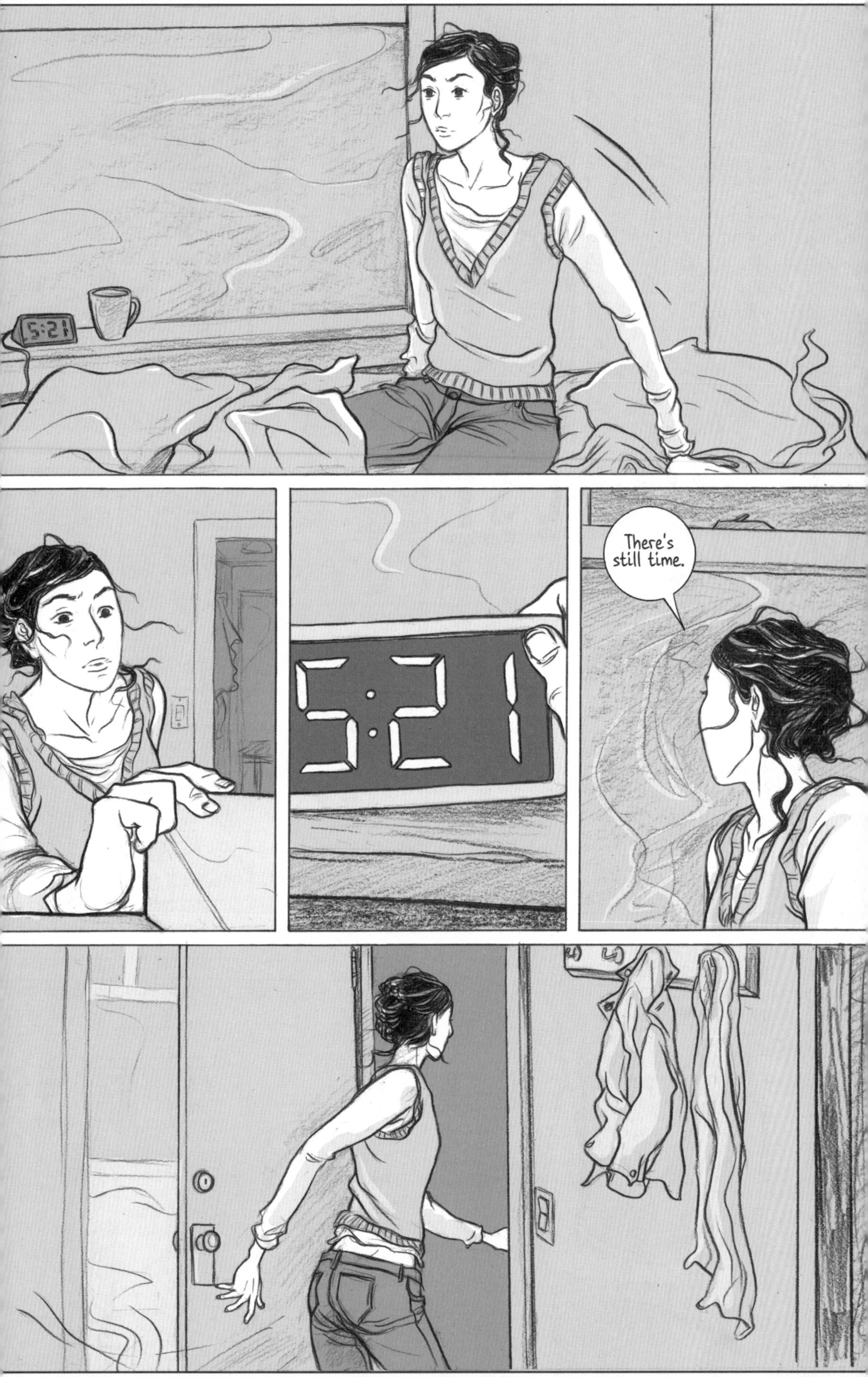
5:21
5:21
There's still time.

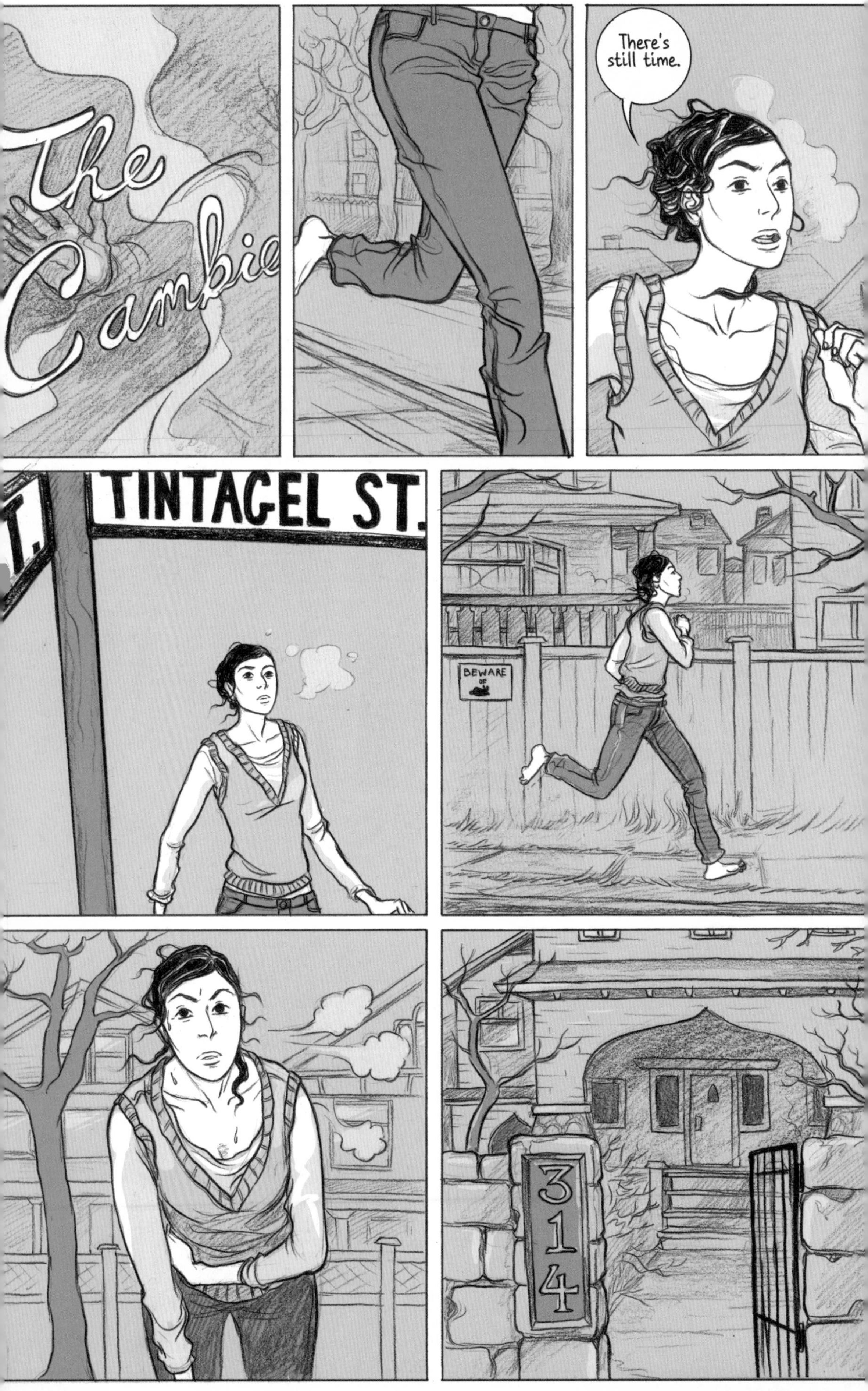
The Cambie
There's still time.
TINTAGEL ST.
BEWARE OF
314

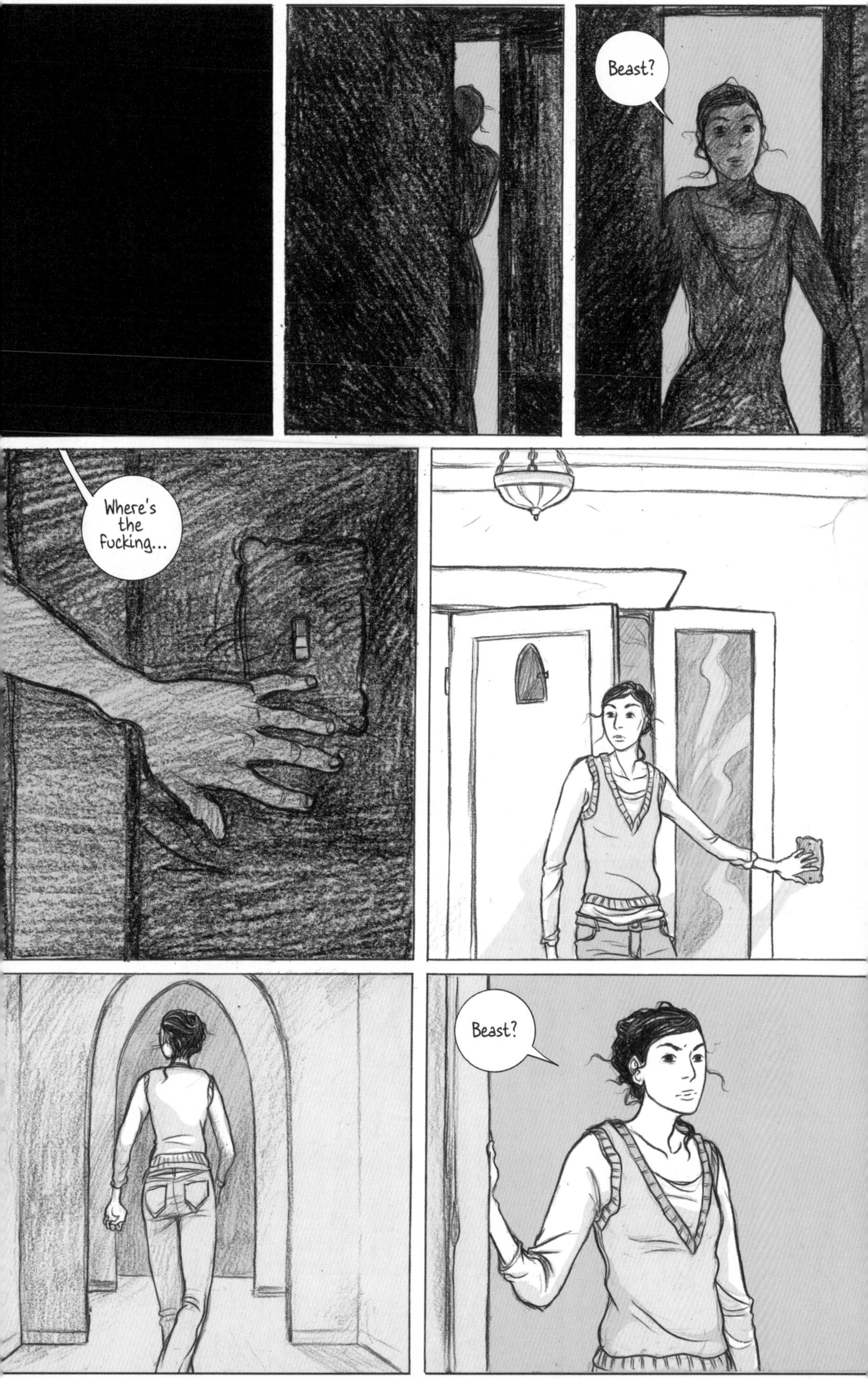
Beast?
Where's the fucking...
Beast?

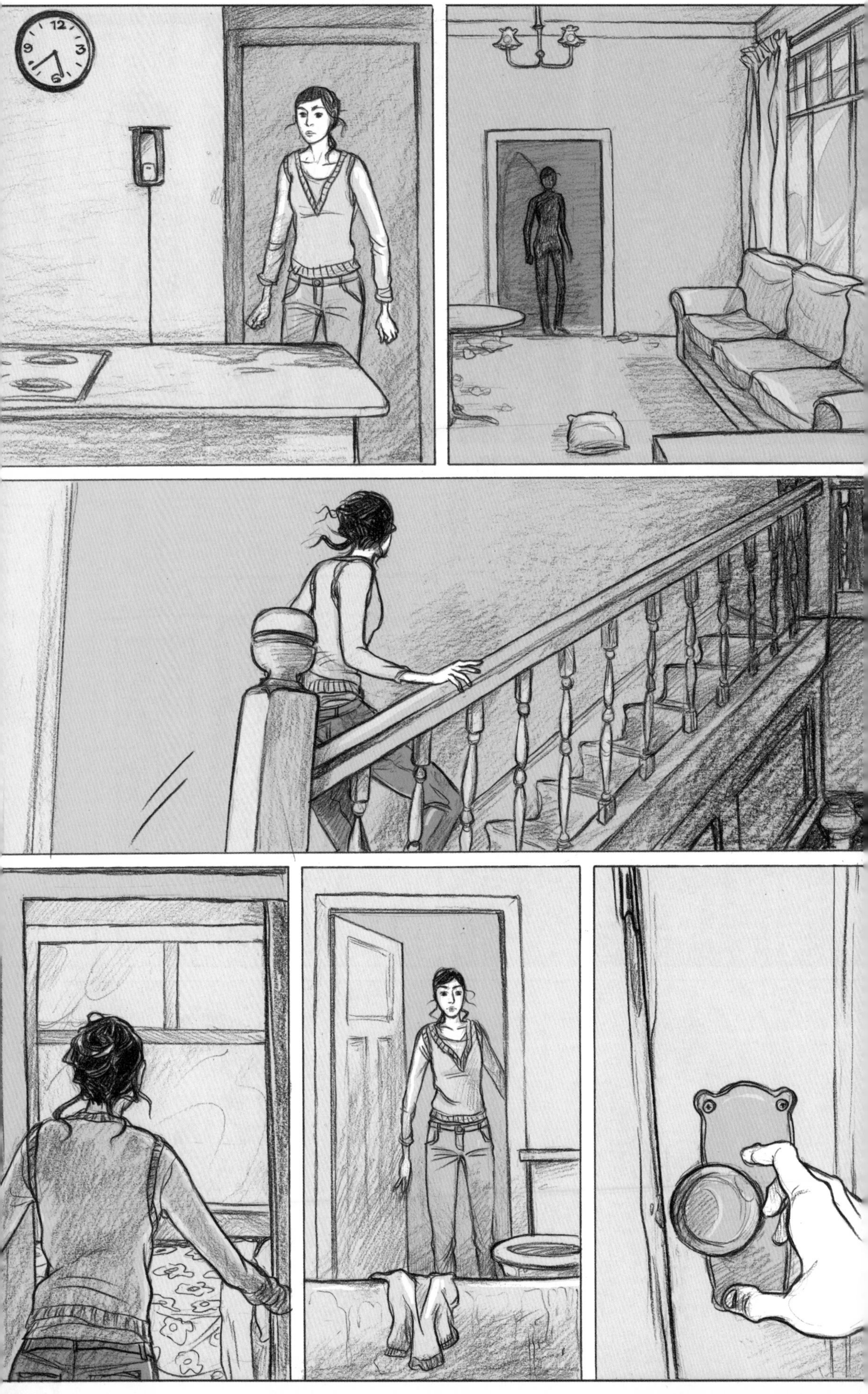

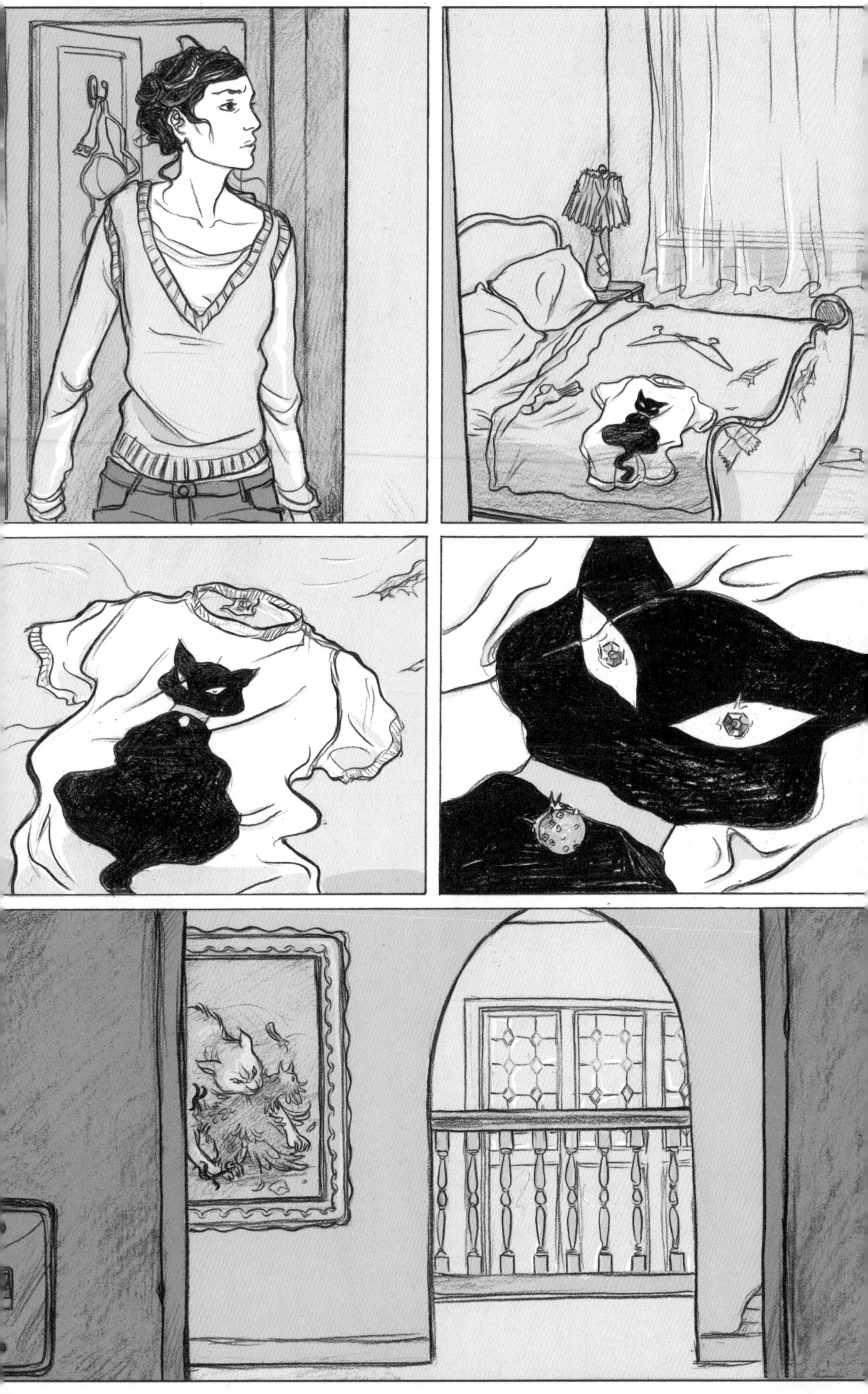

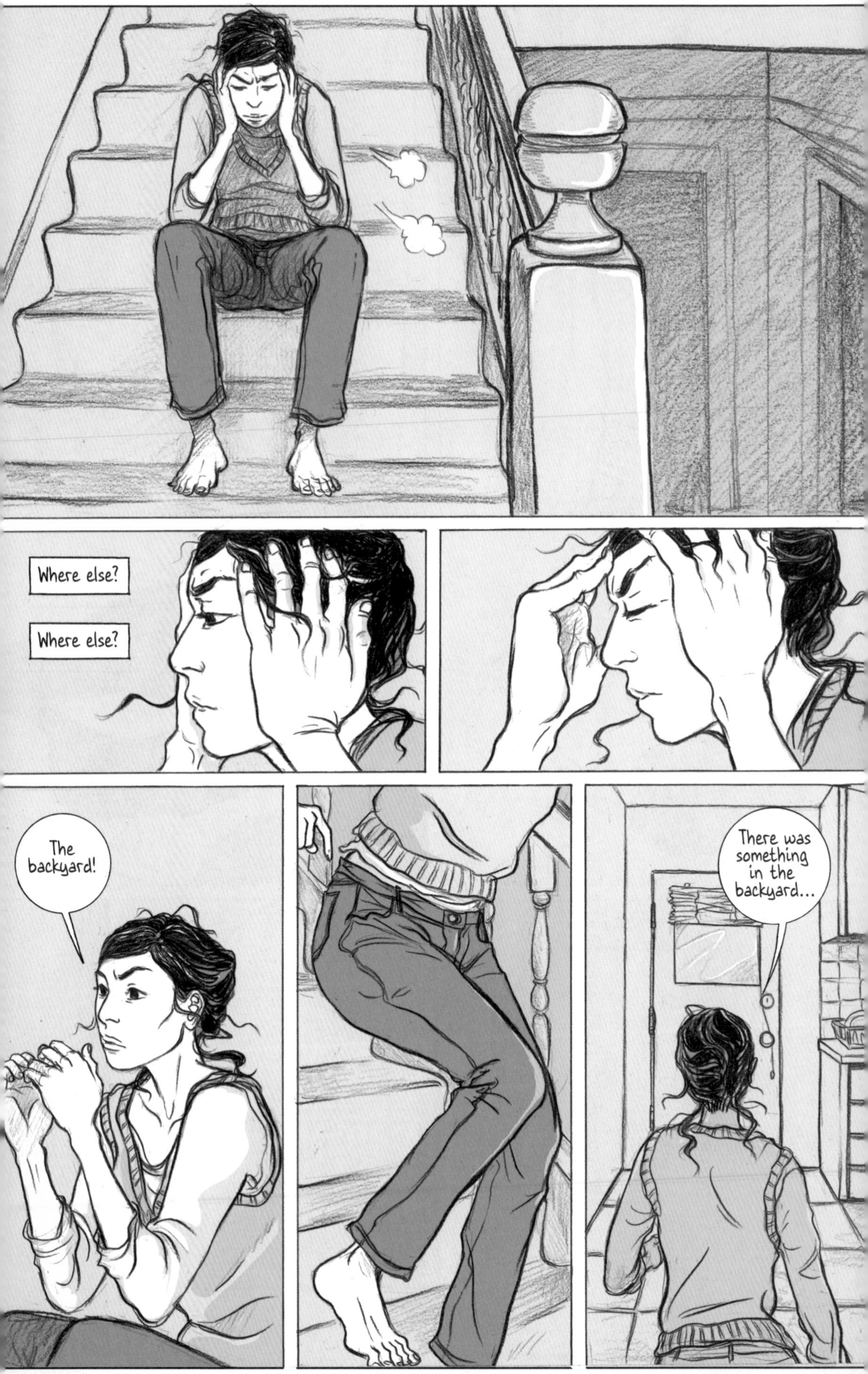
Where else?
Where else?
The backyard!
There was something in the backyard...

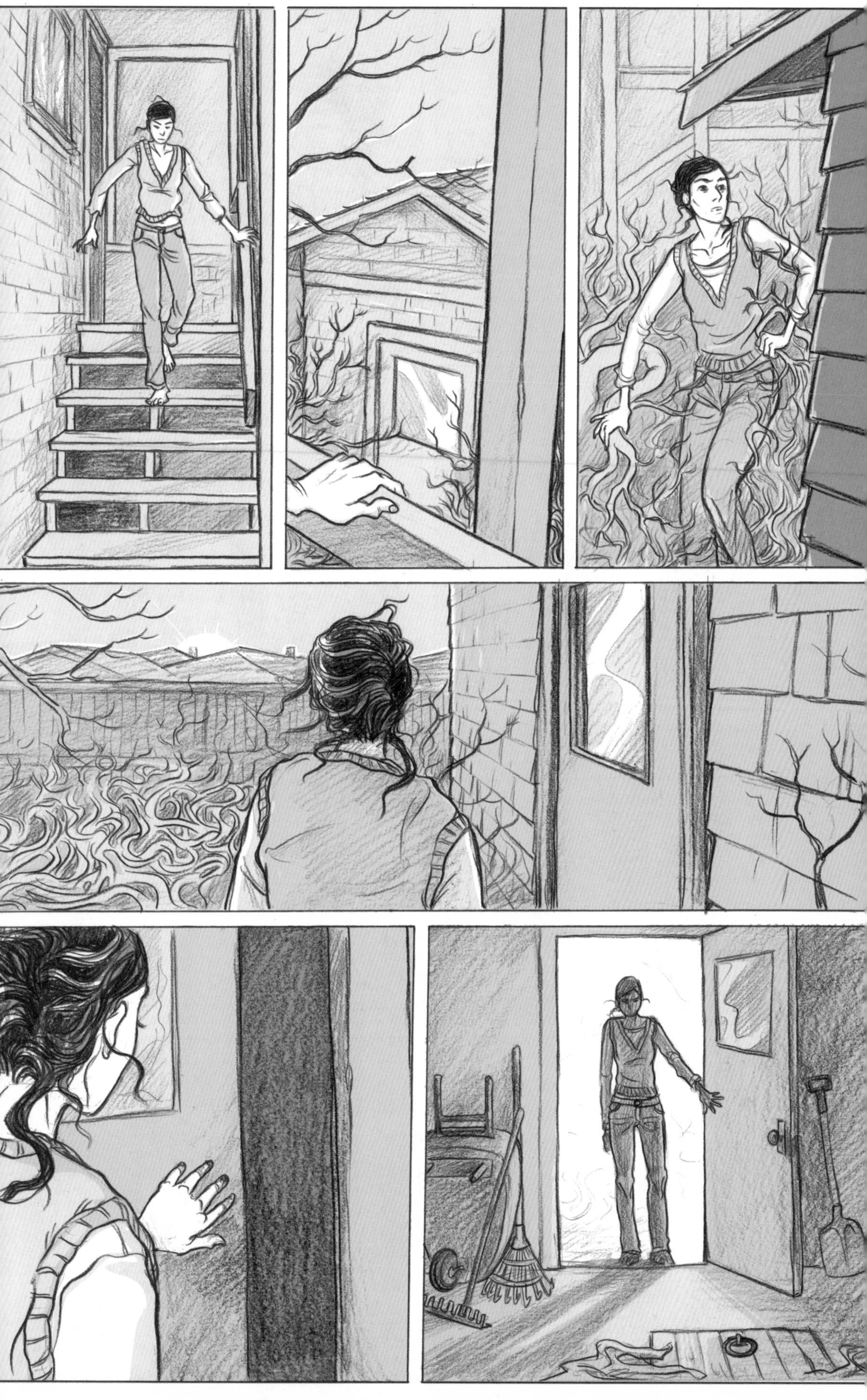

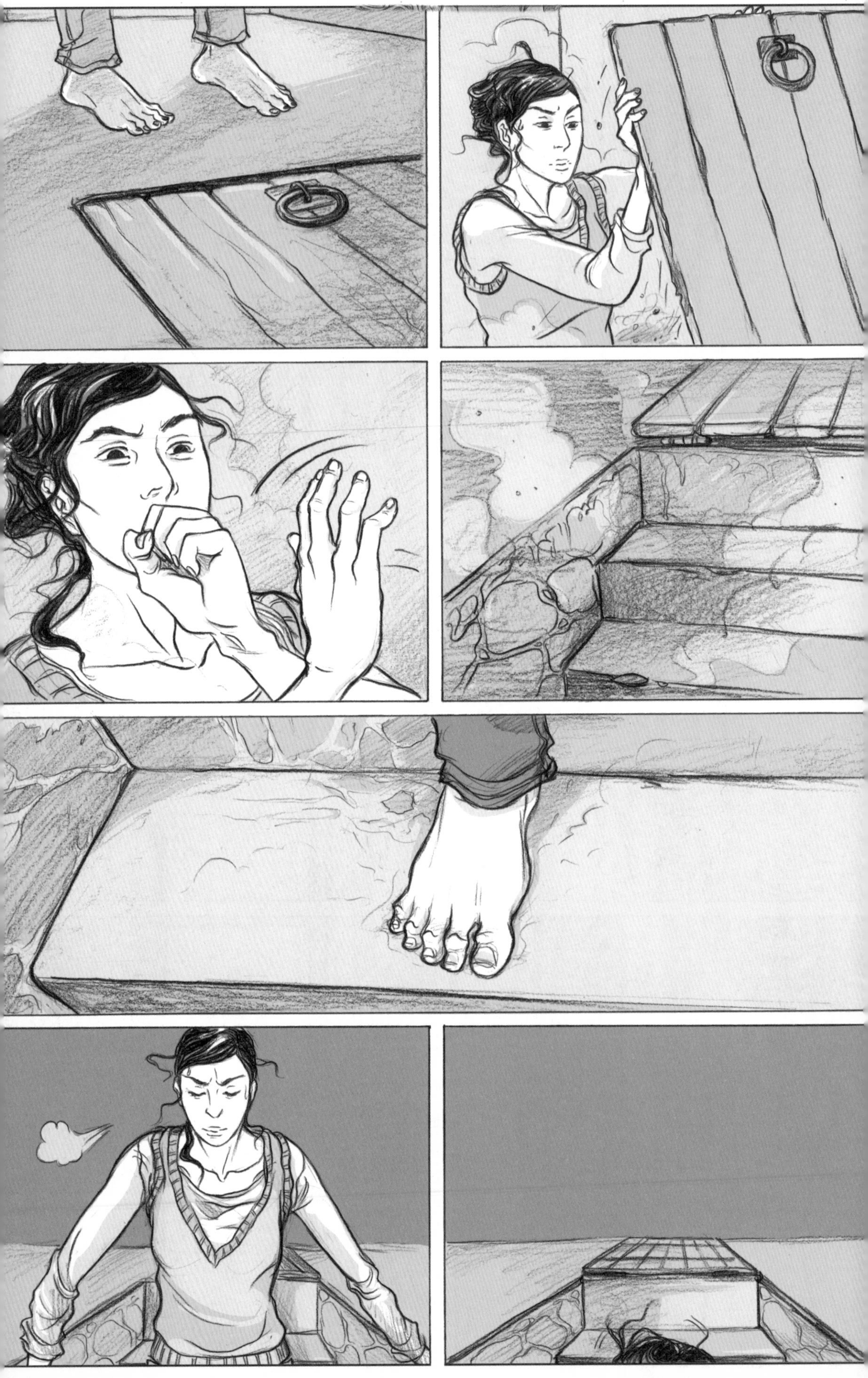

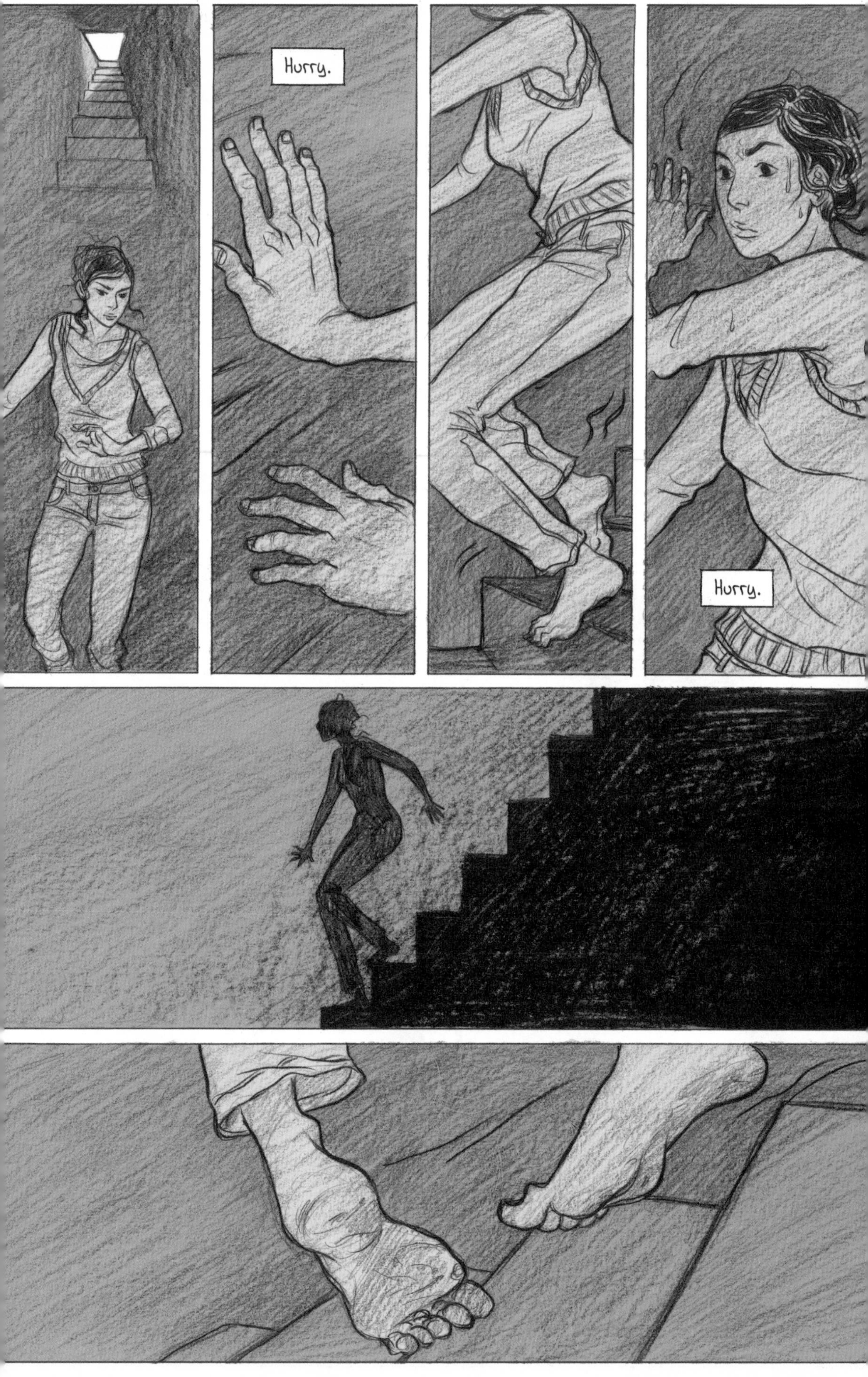
Hurry.
Hurry.

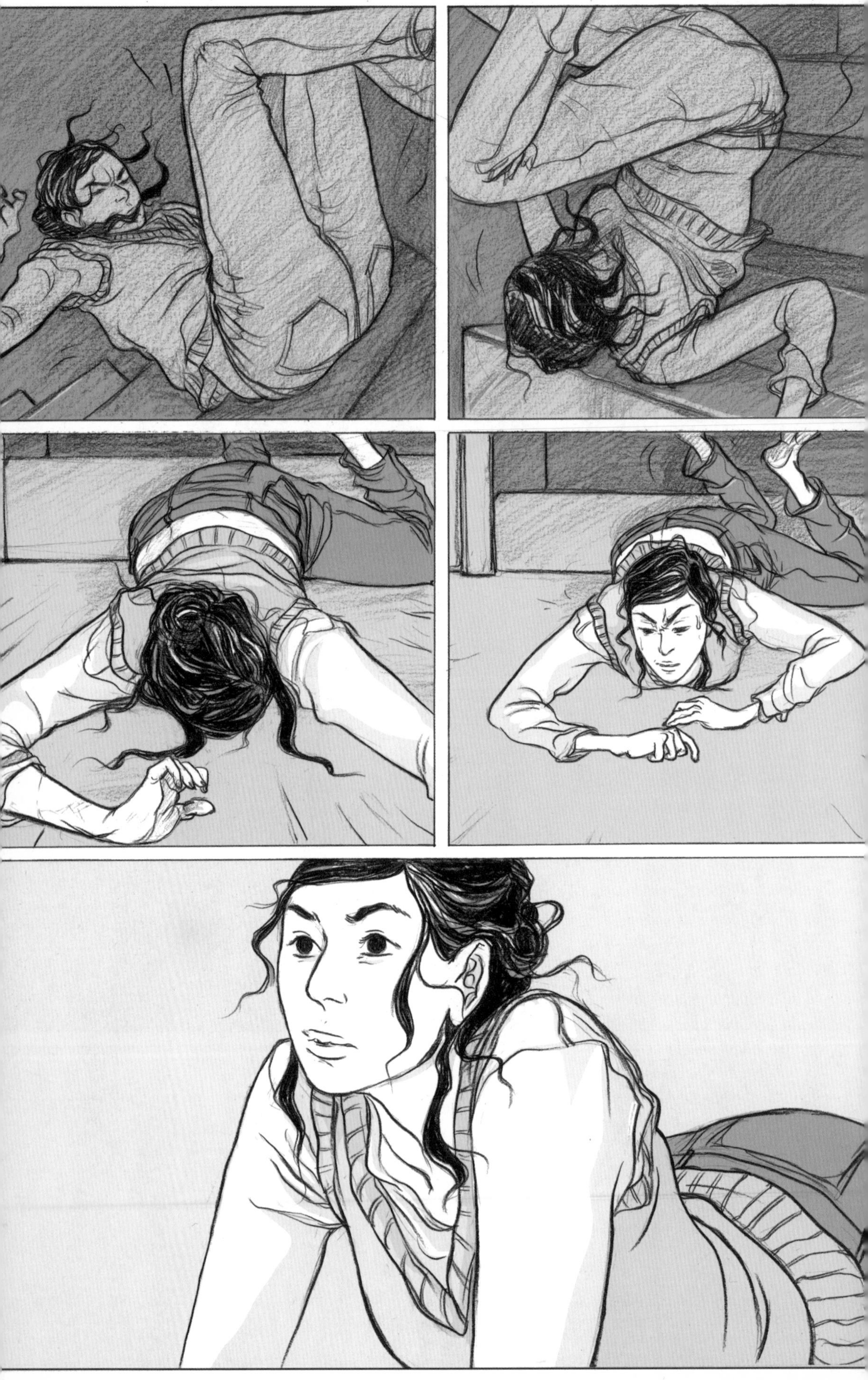

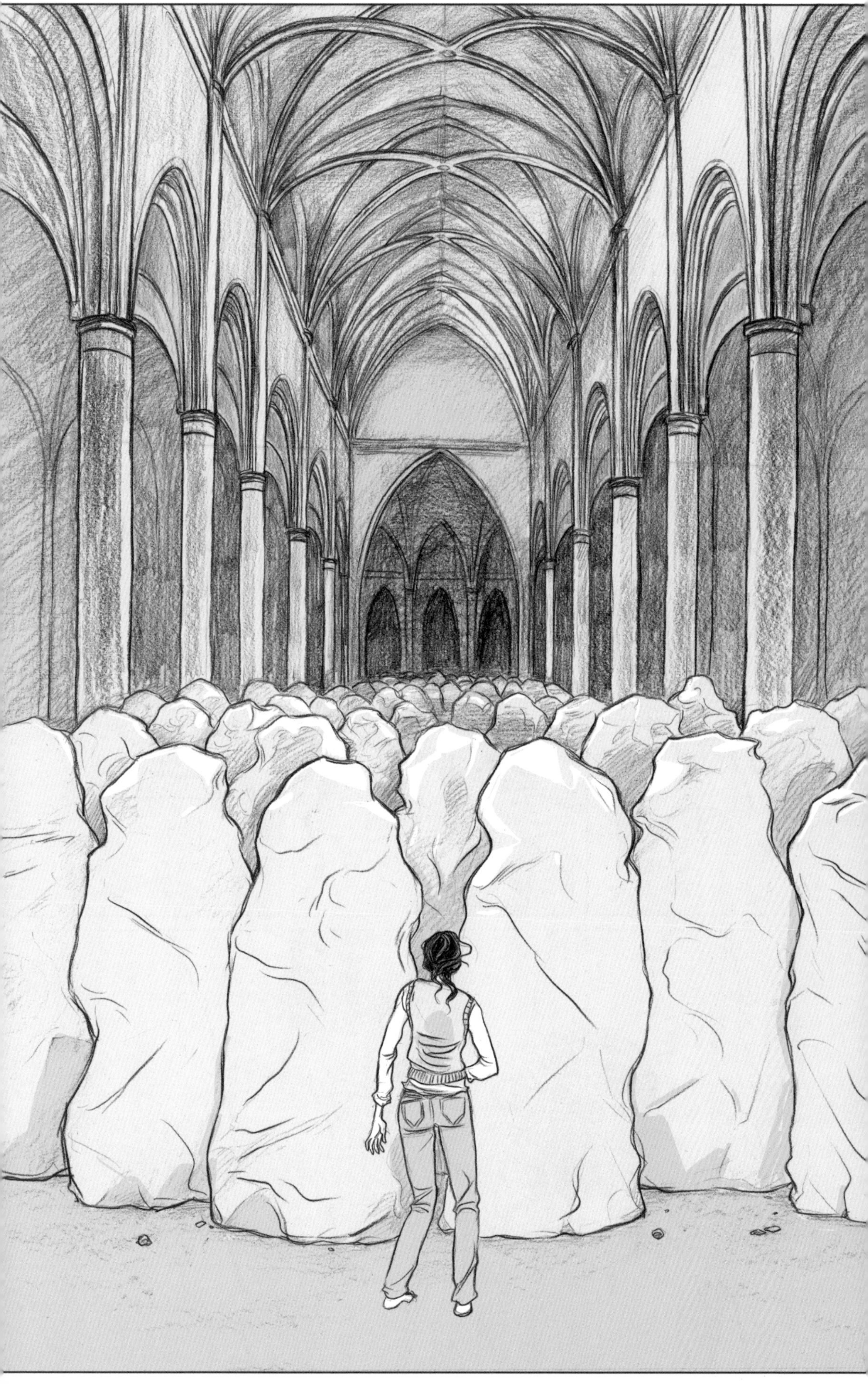

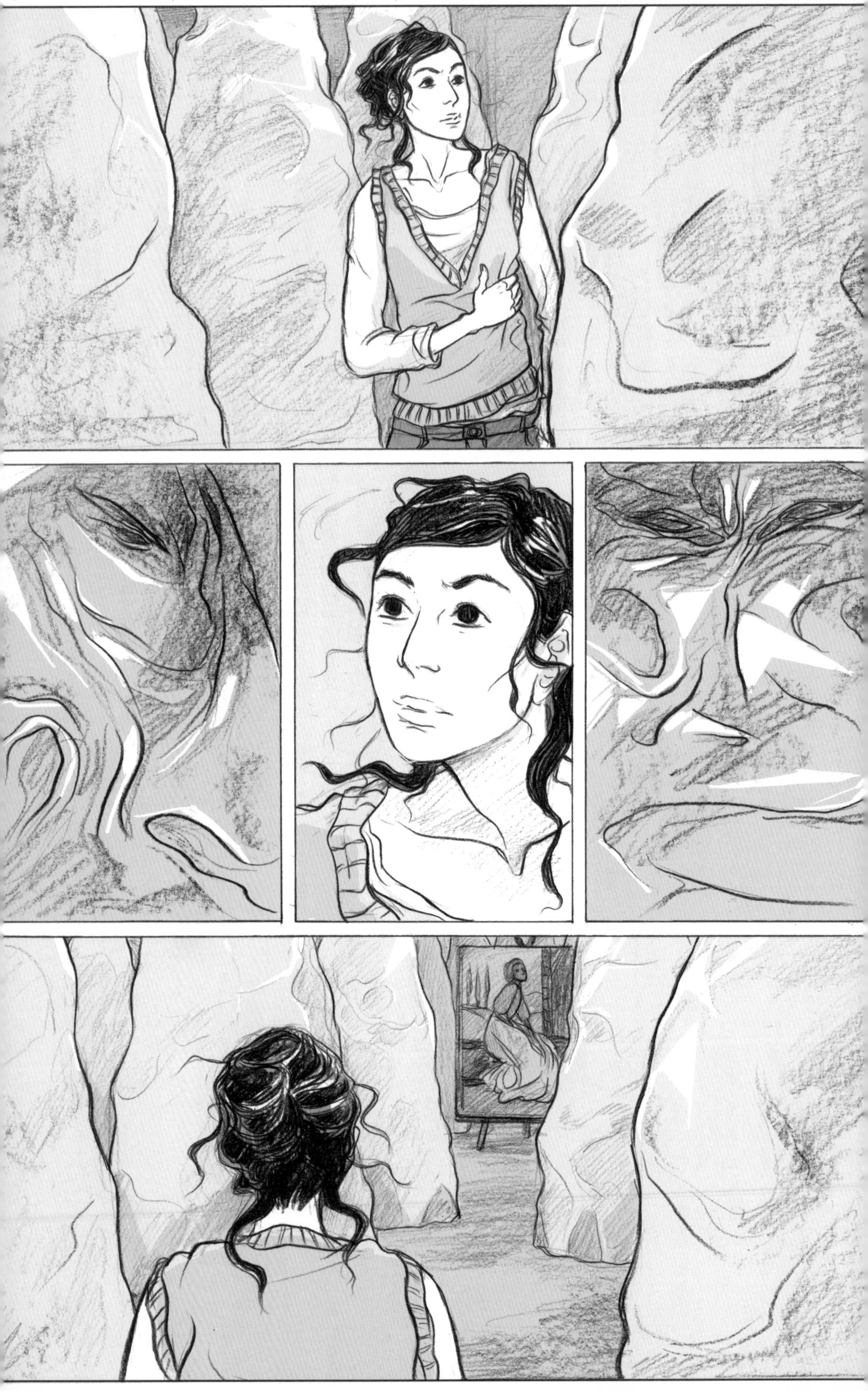

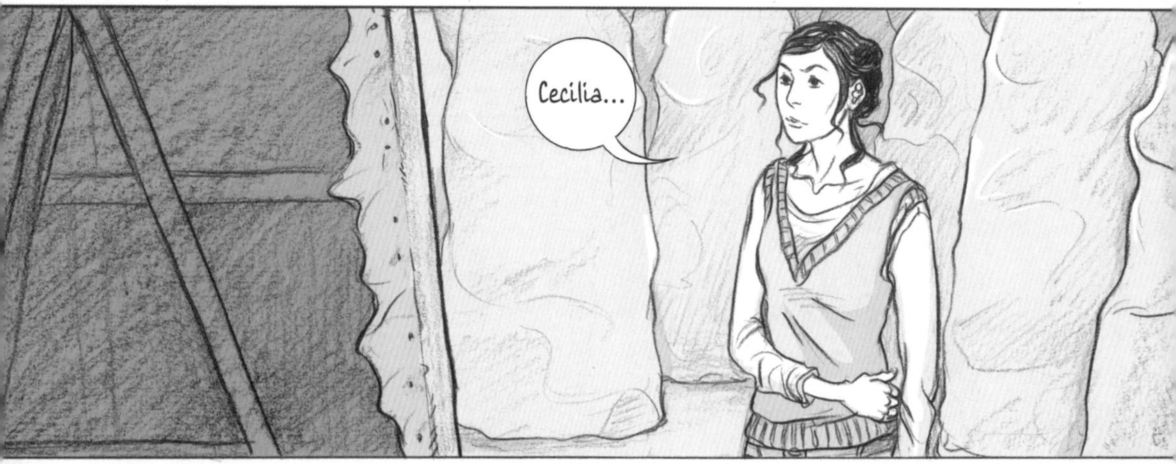
Cecilia...

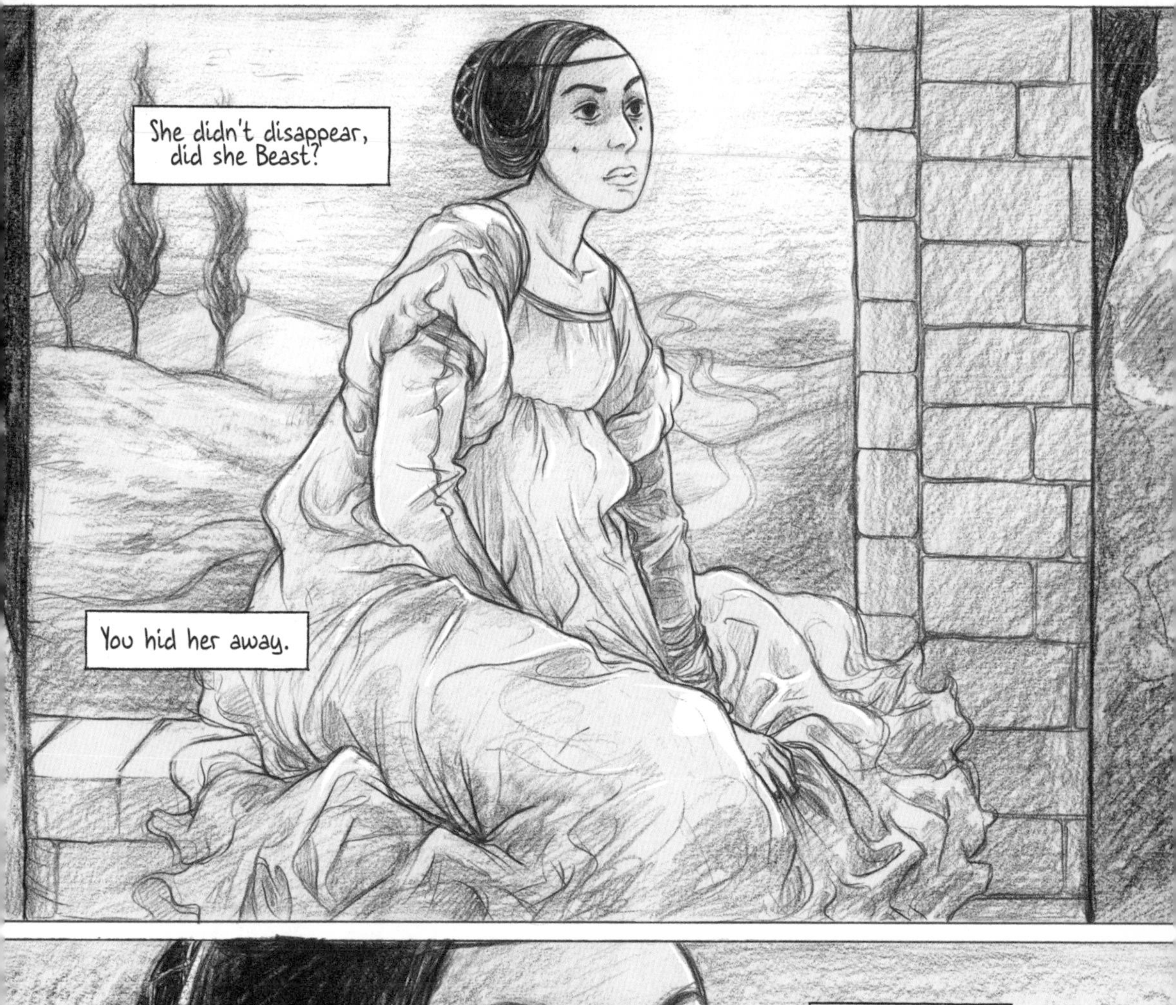
She didn't disappear, did she Beast?
You hid her away.

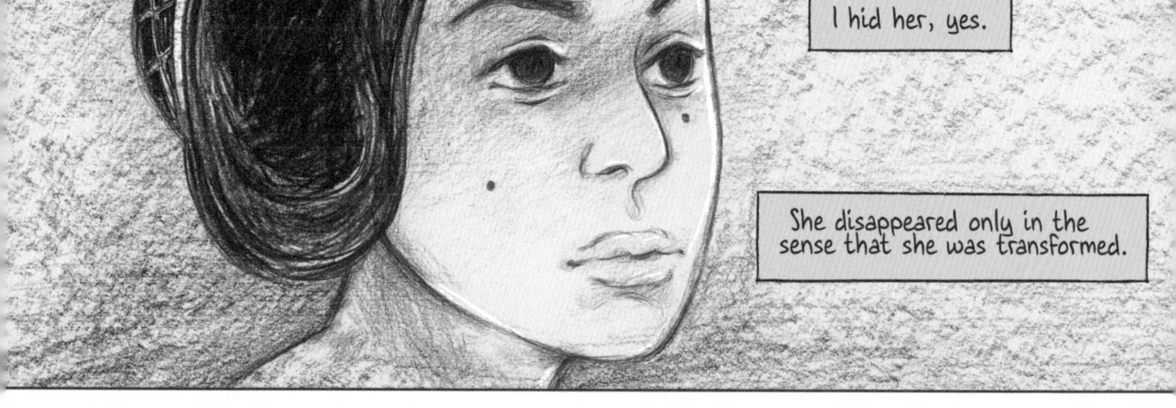
I hid her, yes.
She disappeared only in the sense that she was transformed.

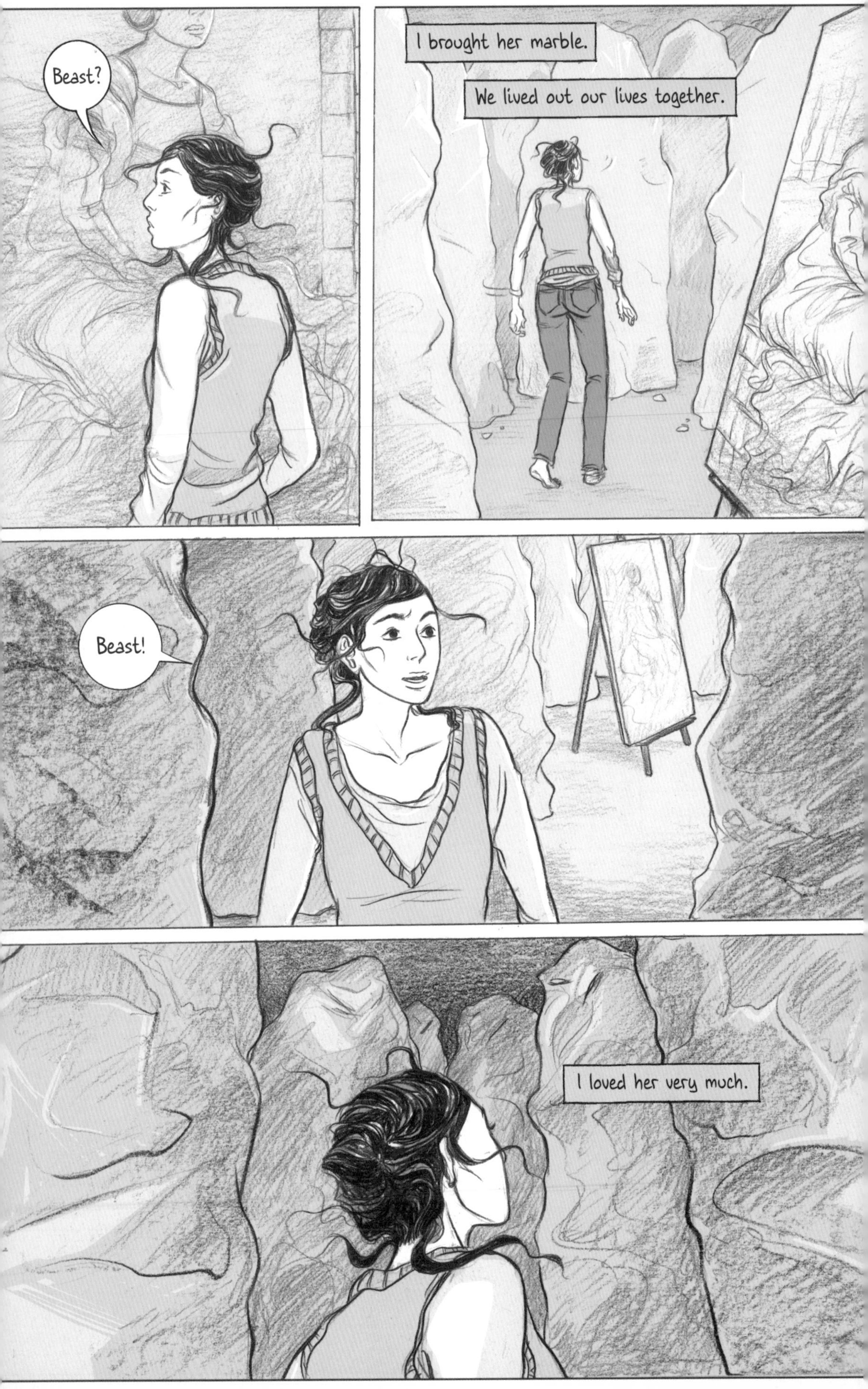
Beast?
I brought her marble.
We lived out our lives together.
Beast!
I loved her very much.

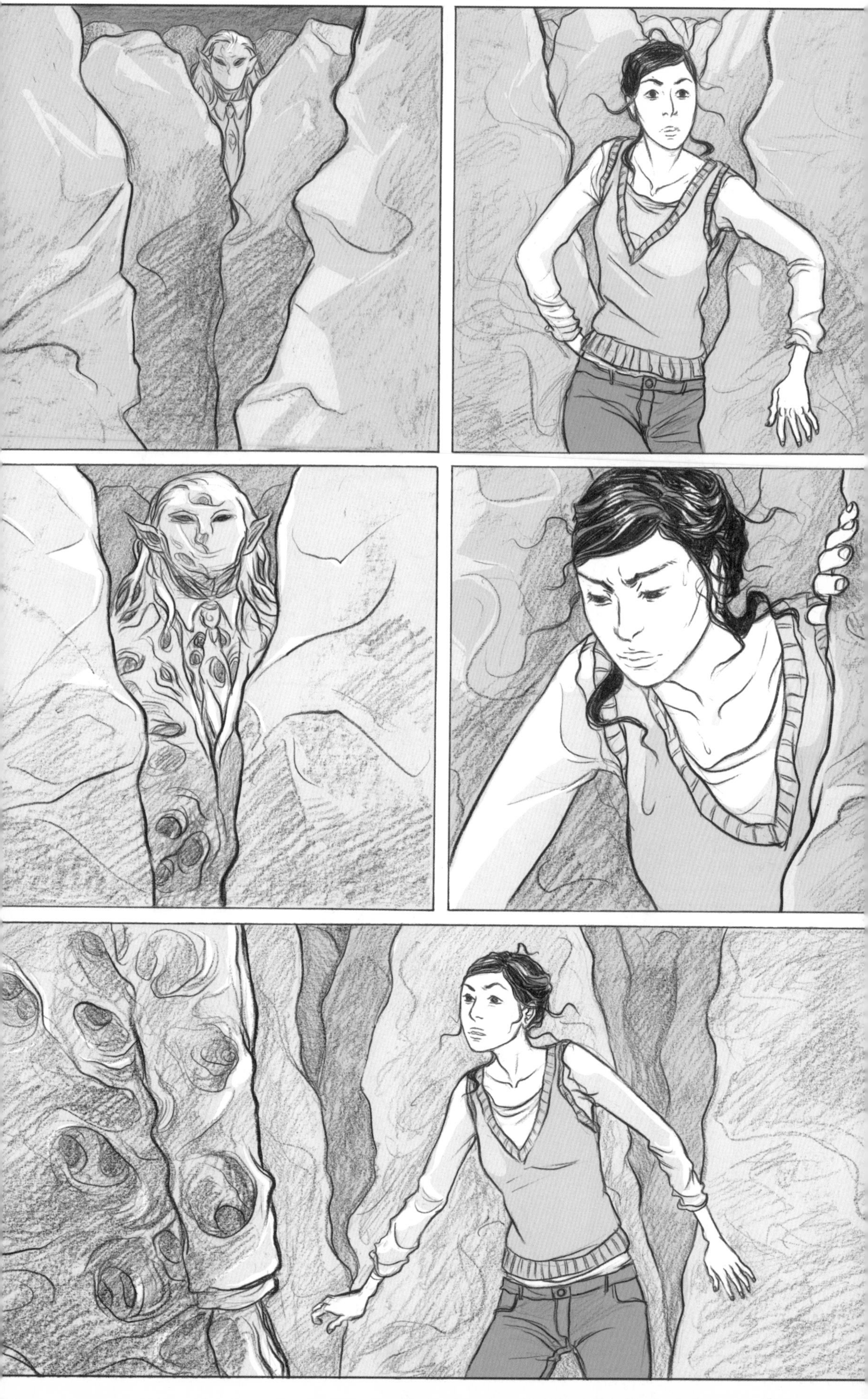

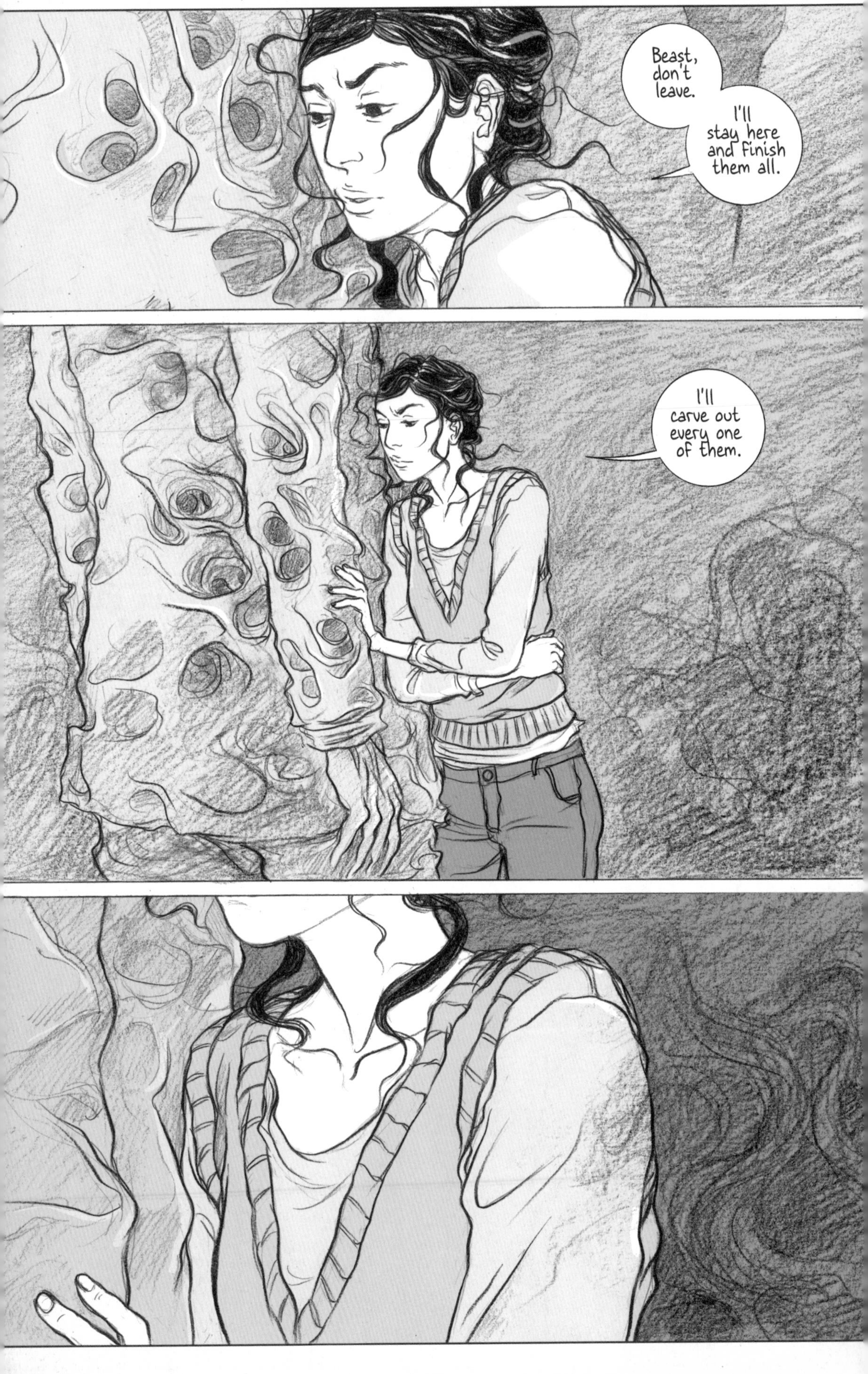
Beast, don't leave.
I'll stay here and finish them all.
I'll carve out every one of them.

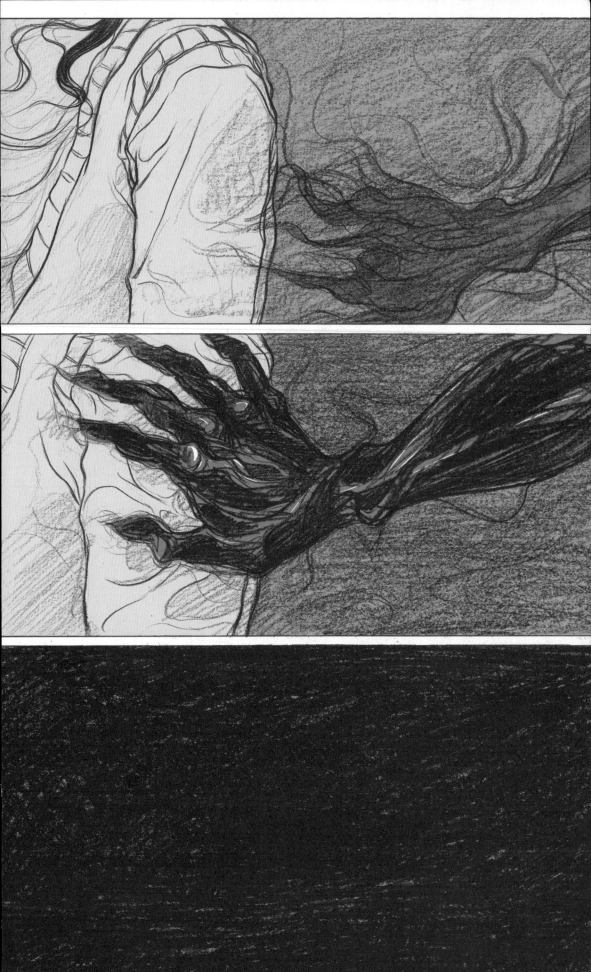

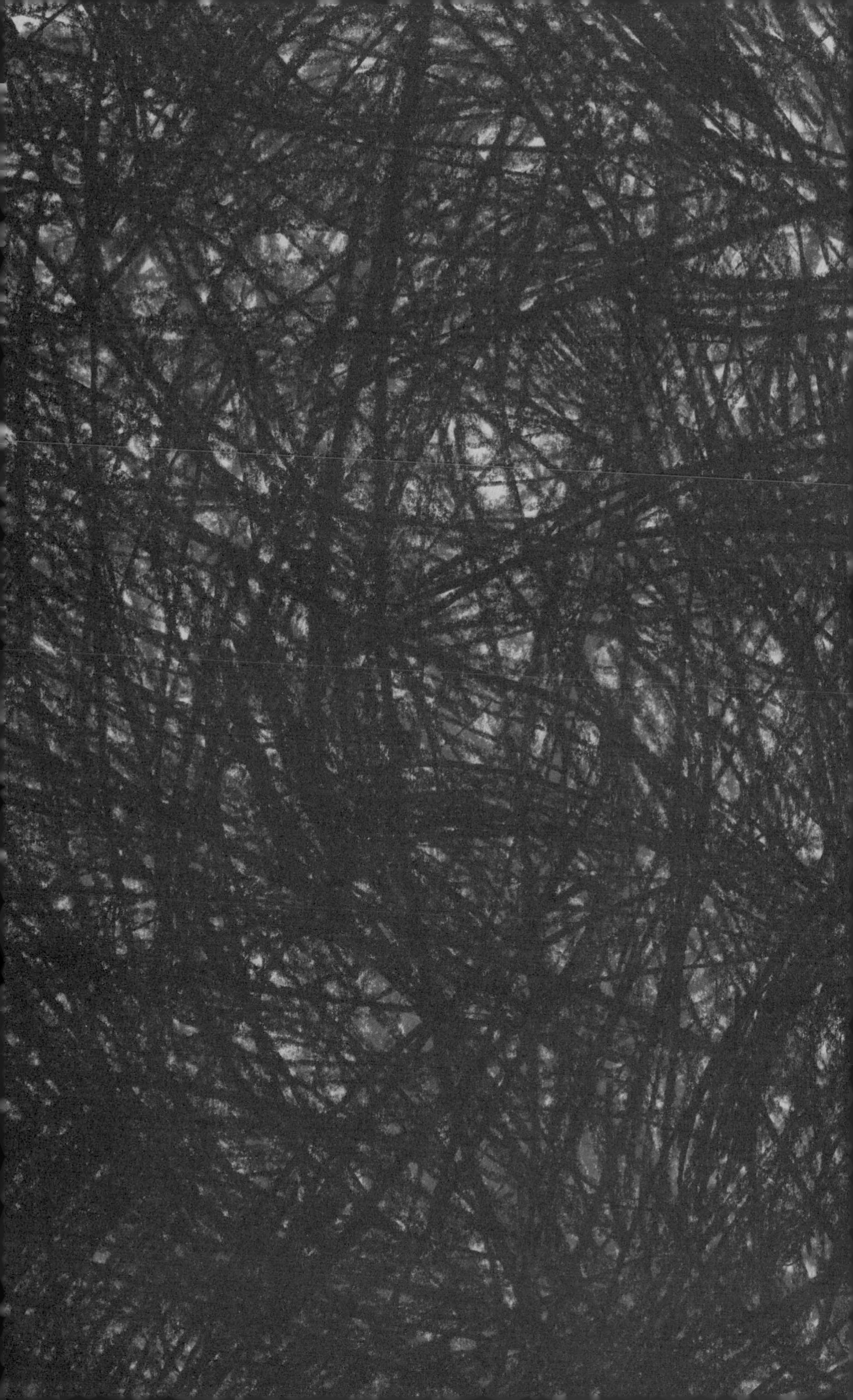

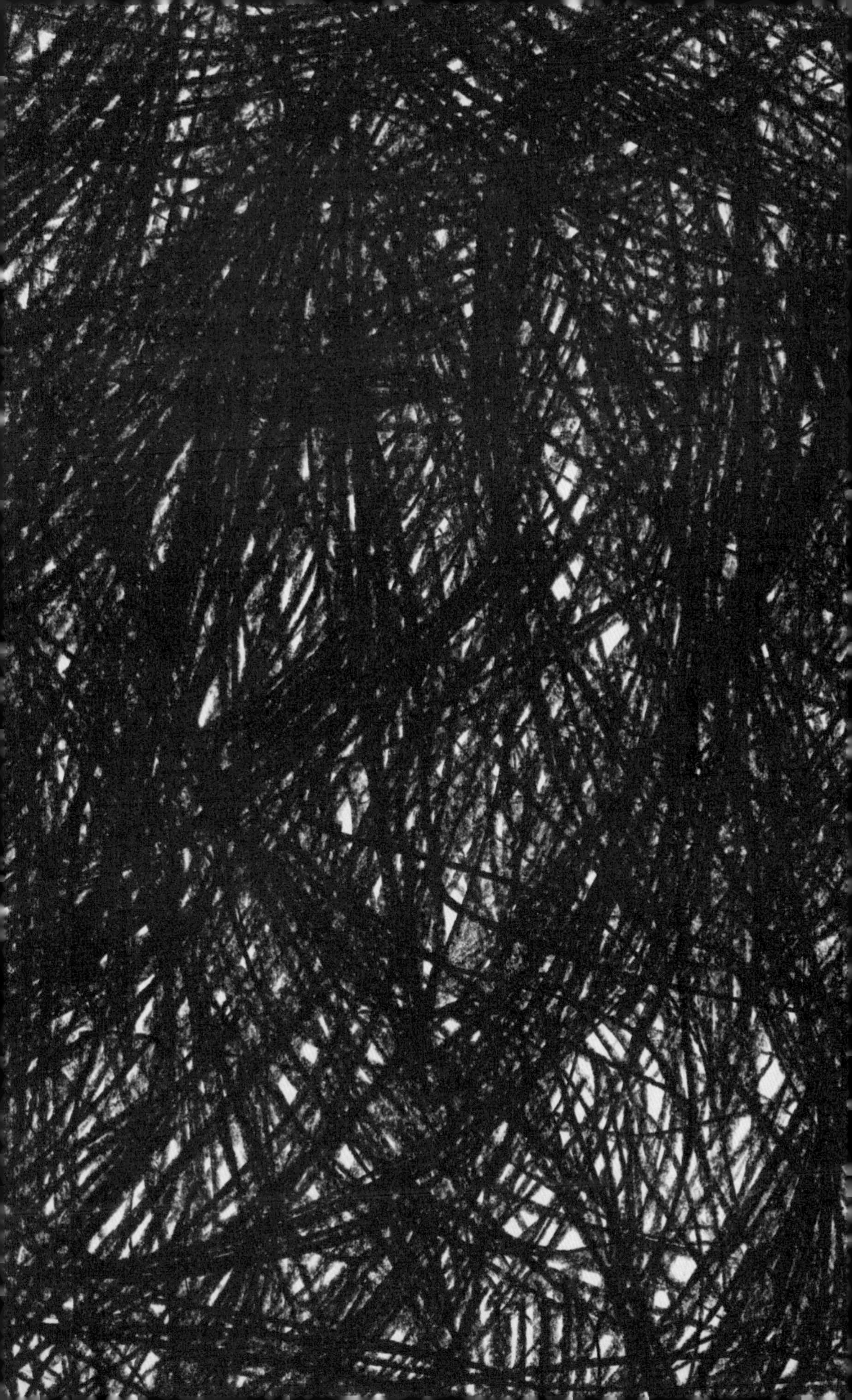

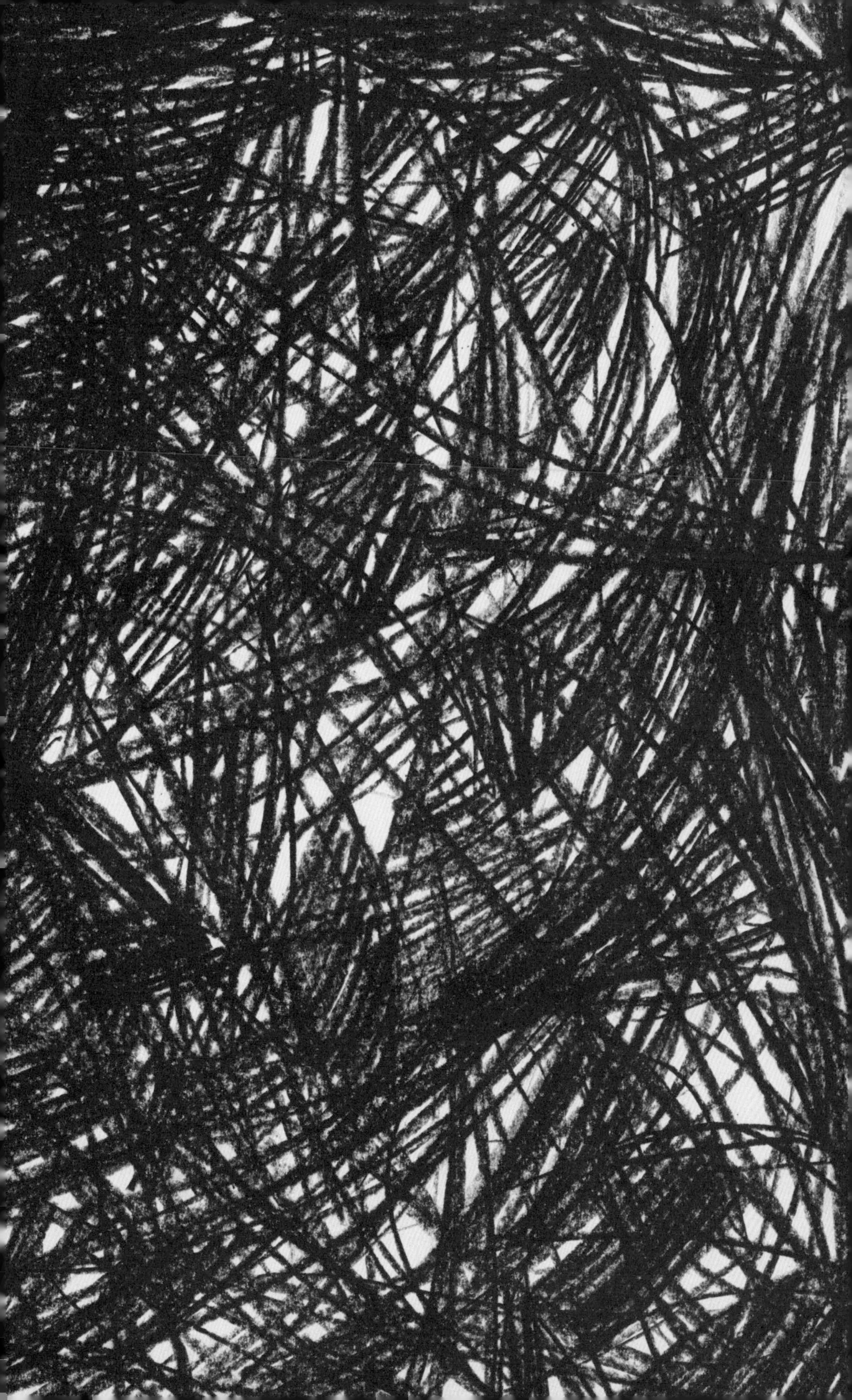

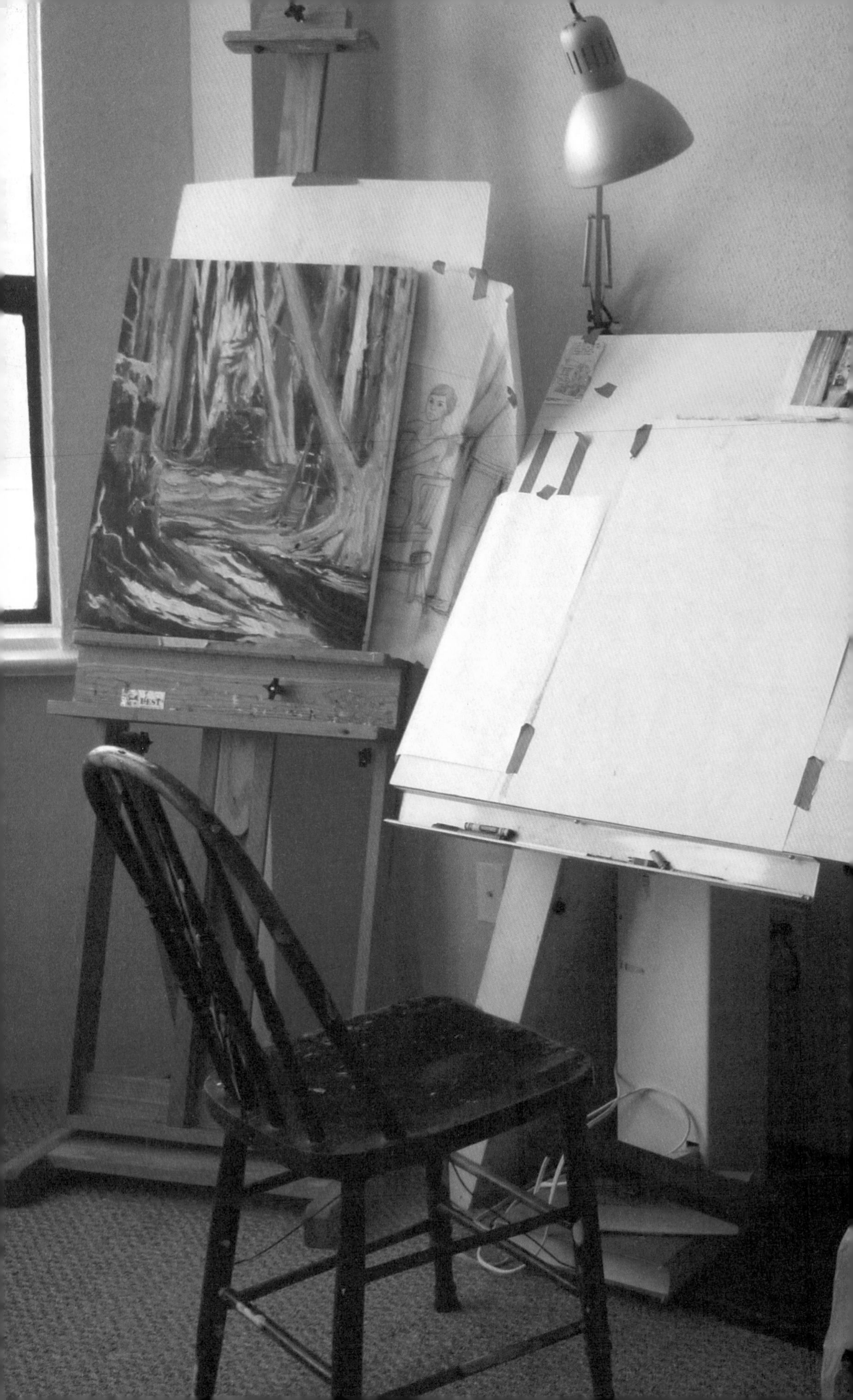

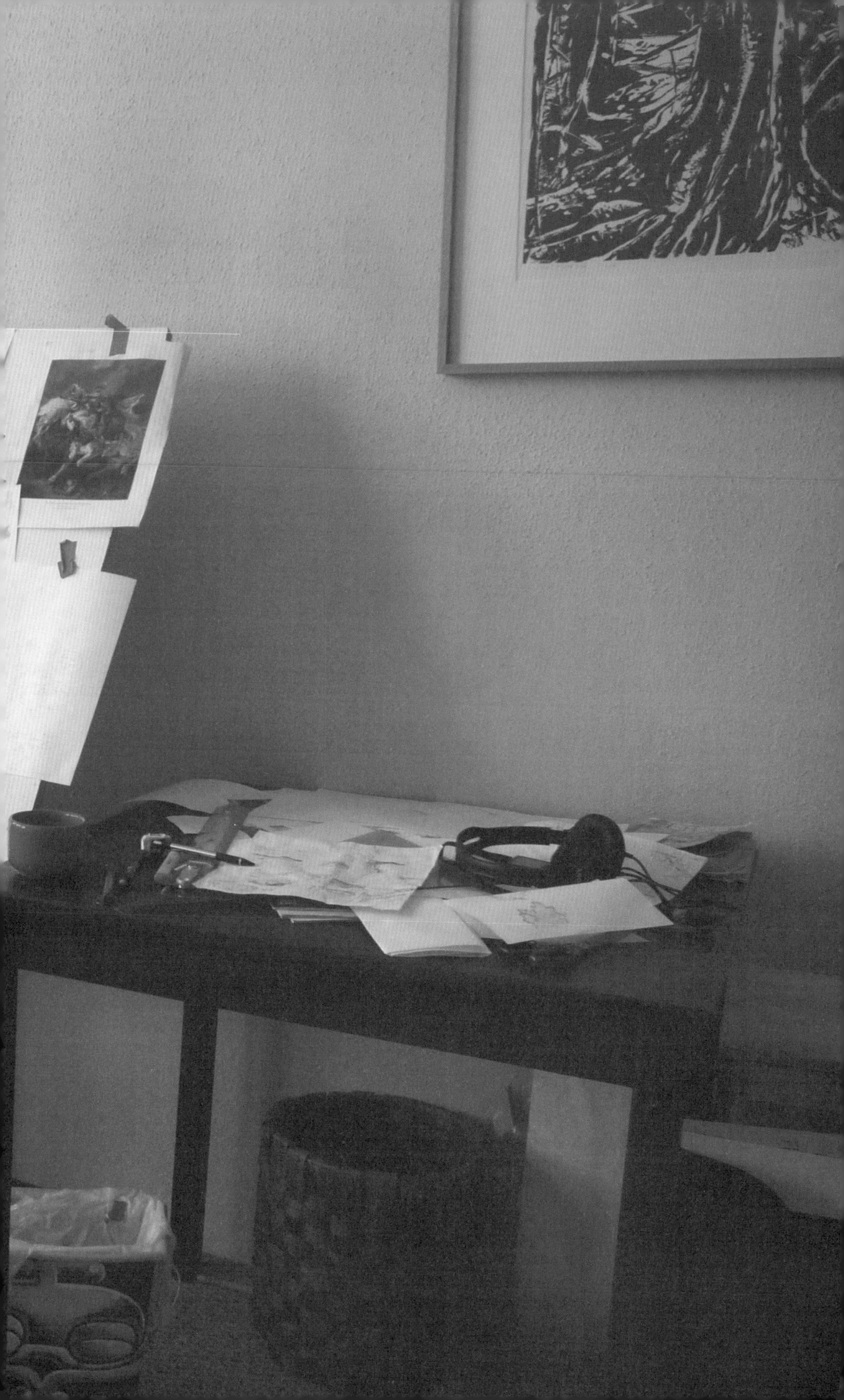

After-word

Beast started to take form in my head a week or two after I lost my old dog, Buddy. Don't ask me why we named him that. At 12 years old, I actually thought that it was a terribly original thing to name a dog. He was my buddy, right? It made such elegant sense. Fourteen incarnations of *Air Bud* later, I can't even think about it without smacking the palm of my hand to my forehead.

I couldn't afford to lose Buddy any more than any of us can afford to lose a person or creature who is dear in our life, but who nonetheless goes ahead and dies on us. In the weeks afterwards, everything looked a little different. A little skewed, and terribly Buddyless. My brain was rearranging itself around what, for me, was an enormous and unwelcome shift.

I thought often of women in my visual arts classes, boldy telling the professors (who were visibly not rolling their eyes) that for their end of term projects they were going to do paintings of their dogs, dearly-departed or otherwise. I felt for them. I didn't think (and I still don't think) that a close relationship between an animal and a person is such a bad basis for making art.

One night, I had a very vivid dream. I was adrift on a battered old barge with a handsome pea-coated sailor, and every so often in the oceanic twilight, we would watch as giant floating cages full of human bodies drifted past our vessel. But really, best of all, my dog was there with us - Buddy, our companion on the high seas, making what would otherwise be a rather grim and uneventful dream into a story I wanted to go back to again and again in my head.

And that was that. I decided I would make a comic about it. It would be told from the perspective of a sickly young French woman named Colette, travelling across the Pacific ocean during the Napoleonic Wars. Her ship would be beset, in a suspensful cages-full-of-bodies sort of way, by an emperor-hating Pirate Lord. And of course, near at all times would be Buddy, or in this case, "Bodi" (naturally I couldn't let my pre-teenage mistakes plague me forever).

I told my boss and my parents and my best friend all about it, and quit my job in anticipation of immediate success and financial security. I wrote several abortive scripts. I fretted over it for a while, and then decided that the whole thing was unsalvageable.

I won't tell you at full and winding length how my mess of pirate story evolved into *Beast* as it exists now. Colette stayed, needless to say, in a less physically sickly state. The sailor had to go, because whatever I was doing, it wasn't turning out to have the sort of romantic happy ending that I'd originally amused myself with. Buddy-as-Bodi made the jump successfully, inhabiting the background, as he did in my dream, to keep things from getting too grim. And somewhere in the empty space left by the first story, half in the old world and half in the new, was Beast.

I decided as soon as I'd thrown away my last awkward, crumpled in on itself attempt at a comic script, that I was too insecure and unpracticed to just heft up something out of nothing. I decided that I needed a framework, and since I'd just read Angela Carter's *The Bloody Chamber and Other Stories*, and because many of my favourite authors often re-wrote fairy tales, or threaded them in and out of their novels, I thought I might try something similar.

Beauty and the Beast has always been my favourite fairy tale. What generally made fairy tales less enjoyable for me, as a child, was the inevitable and meddling arrival of the Handsome Prince. Handsome Princes bored me to death, and I had this idea that as soon as one showed up and married the female protagonist, she would never do anything exciting ever again.

I loved the beast, though. He was different. Sad, and sort of helpless. It was him who needed rescuing. I should say, maybe, that *Beauty and the Beast* was my favourite fairy tale up until the point where the beast is transformed into the Handsome Prince, and turned out to be the one doing the rescuing after all, go figure, with his big house and his endless wealth. In my head, the beast always remained the same old, thoughtful monster. A fairy tale must have a transformation of some kind, but it doesn't necessarily have to be first and most obvious option.

Beast isn't a direct retelling of *Beauty and the Beast*, but that's where it began, as I picked up and sorted out the pieces from my first attempt at a story. I think that's why fairy tales beg to be endlessly retold. They are not complete in themselves. They offer us a beginning, and we complete them by telling them, even if we're only reading from a picture book. We let the princesses and the dragons and the enchantments represent whatever we need them to.

At that time in my life, that story became about making decisions, big scary decisions, about what I was going to do with myself. What I was going to have to change, in order to do it. What I was going to have to give up, and what I was going to have to face that was terrifying, and murky, and unsounded.

Now, as I write this, I'm on the verge of completing the last scene. Not the last scene of the story, but the last of the several scenes that I've decided, at one point or another, to add into the middle. The majority of *Beast* - the first 100 pages or so, including the ending - was finished by the beginning of 2007, and after a few months of holding my breath and waiting for something exciting to happen, I had to put those pages aside, get over my dissapointment, and trundle on with projects that would pay my rent and keep me fed.

I view those circumstances, now, with gratitude. If I'd sent *Beast* off in that form, I believe it would have been an incomplete book. Now, at least, I know it's the best sort of incomplete I can make it.

Beast is still the hardest thing I've ever worked on, even now, following two years of limbering up and getting more comfortable with drawing comics. I still sweat out every panel, with much frustrated erasing, and weeping, and sending my boyfriend out for muffins. I still haven't quite got a handle on drawing Colette's face.

I'm inclined to think it's a good sign that the work has kept me struggling. If I'd come back to it and found it easy - easy to finish and polish off, to understand and mimic - then I'd be worried. As it is, the story still has a live current. Even now, I could hunker in the middle of it, connecting the wires, forever.

There's an essay I sometimes re-read in order to brace myself for work, in which the poet Seamus Heaney writes that, "the successful achievement of a poem [can] be a stepping stone in your life." I love this analogy, though I often imagine the stepping stones as being rather slick, and jagged, and wobbly.

When I was first working on *Beast*, I told myself every day that I was allowed to make mistakes - endless mistakes, even. Partly, that's what allowed me to do it, not knowing for certain that I could. It kept me hopeful that I might be treading some new ground, even if only for myself, because there is no forward motion without risk. That was an easier attitude to assume when it was just me and the work, and I didn't have to think about publication, much less publication dates. But it's an attitude I try to repossess every time I sit down to draw. And I'm proud of those mistakes. I earned them, and they have lead me somewhere. They were the leap from one wobbly stepping stone to another.

I have dedicated this book to my parents, Mark and Leslie Churchland. When I was thirteen, they helped me photocopy my first comic book, so I could hand it out to my friends. Fourteen years later, things are not so very different.

There are a few more people I'd like to thank, as well:

My sister, who bakes me bread. There is no more endearing trait in a human being.

Eric Stephenson and Joe Keatinge, and the rest of the guys at Image Comics, for putting this book out. It rewards every risk I took making this, that there are people now willing to take a risk on me. Also Richard Starkings, for letting me put my stamp, for a moment, on his own series, and for turning my illegible handwriting into the elegant font with which I lettered this comic. And of course Justin Norman, the comics Godfather in my group of friends. I owe him several hundred breakfasts. And thanks, incidentally, to my compatriots in breakfast-owing, James Stokoe, and Marley Zarcone. Speaking of people who bake me things.

Thank you to Brandon Graham. I met him not long after I started working on Beast, and nothing has altered the course of it more. And thank you to Claire Gibson, whose opinion and help I have relied on so completely at every stage of the work, emotionally and editorially, that I cannot imagine it existing without her.

Now I have just made a fresh cup of dark tea, and my dog, Moss, is lying on the floor snoring. I have one last page to draw, but then that is its own kind of beginning.

Marian Churchland
12:25am, July 14, 2009

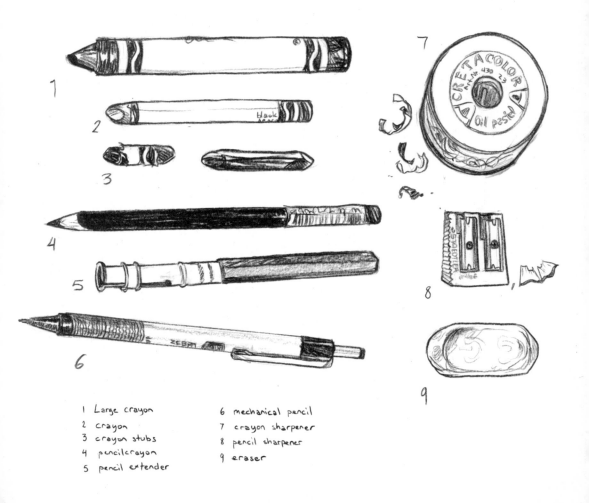

1 Large crayon
2 crayon
3 crayon stubs
4 pencilcrayon
5 pencil extender
6 mechanical pencil
7 crayon sharpener
8 pencil sharpener
9 eraser

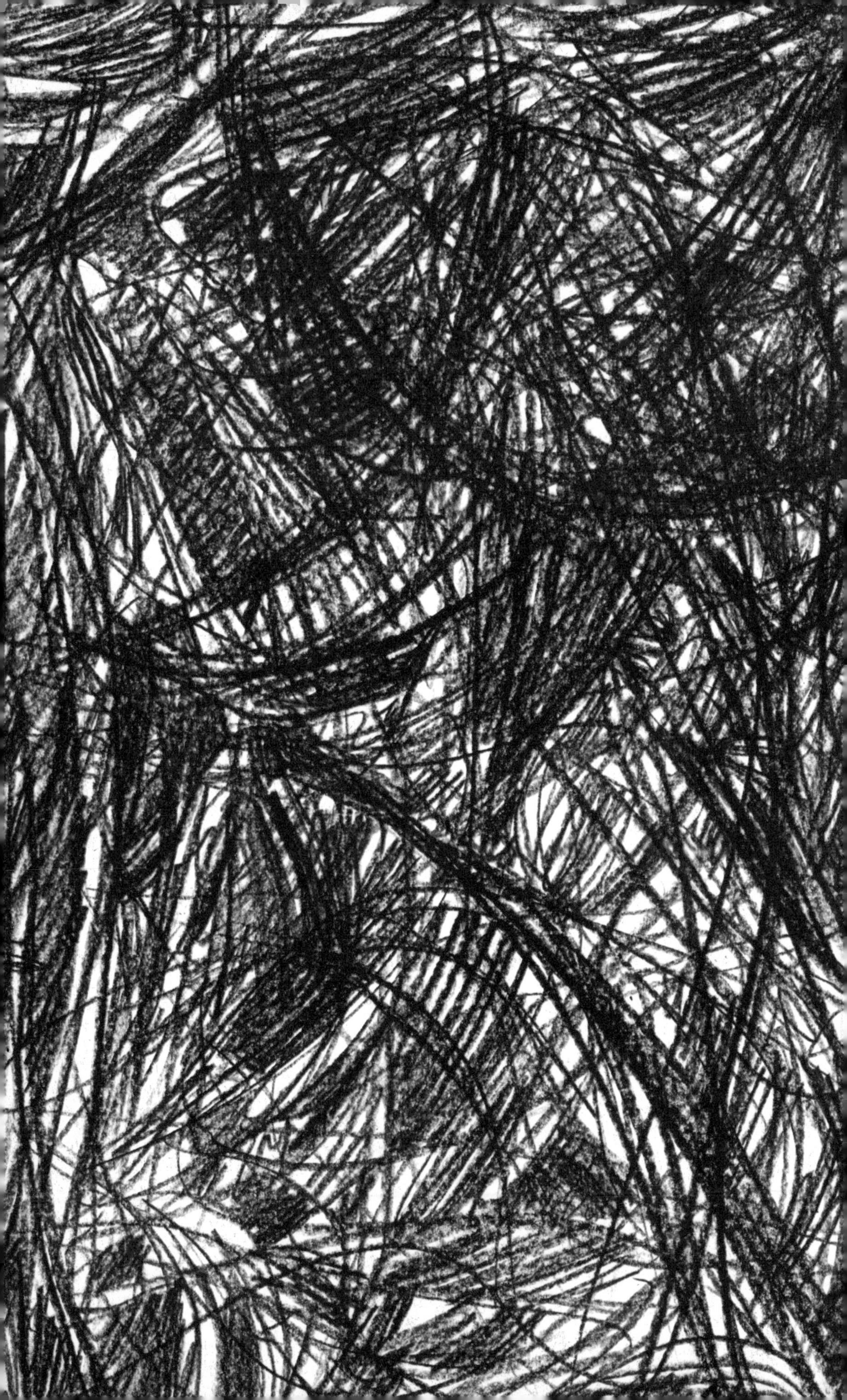